MEDIEVAL
IRELAND

An Archaeology

For my mother and in memory of my father

MEDIEVAL
IRELAND

An Archaeology

Tadhg O'Keeffe

TEMPUS

First published 2000
First paperback edition 2001

PUBLISHED IN THE UNITED KINGDOM BY:

Tempus Publishing Ltd
The Mill, Brimscombe Port
Stroud, Gloucestershire GL5 2QG
www.tempus-publishing.com

PUBLISHED IN THE UNITED STATES OF AMERICA BY:

Tempus Publishing Inc.
2A Cumberland Street
Charleston, SC 29401
www.arcadiapublishing.com

Tempus books are available in France and Germany
from the following addresses:

Tempus Publishing Group	Tempus Publishing Group
21 Avenue de la République	Gustav-Adolf-Straße 3
37300 Joué-lès-Tours	99084 Erfurt
FRANCE	GERMANY

British Library Cataloguing in Publication Data.
A catalogue record for this book is available from the British Library.

ISBN 0 7524 1926 9

Typesetting and origination by Tempus Publishing.
PRINTED AND BOUND IN GREAT BRITAIN.

Contents

Cover illustration: Fethard Castle, county Wexford

List of illustrations

Colour plates

Preface and acknowledgements

Archaeology makes very great demands on us. First, it demands *conviction* that we in the present can speak about the past from things — objects, buildings, landscapes — which we know to have had a life in the past but which we can only see and touch in the present. That is a far greater intellectual challenge than may at first appear to be the case: what distinguishes Archaeology — the upper case spelling is used deliberately — from mere antiquarianism is the belief that broken pot sherds and crumbling walls are not mere curios from 'olden times' but actual portals into our past. Secondly, Archaeology demands *rigour* in the methods by which we attempt to journey through those portals. An obvious example is the excavator who records strata and find-spots with great care lest some piece of information which is needed to make the journey goes unnoticed; less obvious but no less significant is the vigorous debate among archaeologists on the intellectual methods by which we try to reconstruct the past. Finally, and most importantly, Archaeology demands that we possess *imagination*. That word conjures up notions of fantasy, of unreality, and that is unfortunate: the past, whether we label it as prehistoric or medieval, only exists now in our imagination; we cannot revisit it, so we can only think about what it might have been like.

We already know quite a lot of the story of Ireland in the middle ages, and this is thanks to documentary sources. The men, and more rarely the women, who held power and whose decisions and actions provided the dynamic of history are not anonymous to us, nor is there a shroud of mystery over the multifarious institutions — monarchy, aristocracy, Church, legislature — to which they belonged. That information has reached us by its successful negotiation of two obstacles. The first was the culling of information by medieval scribes when they sat down to write: only information which was worth knowing or worth remembering was recorded, and so accessions of kings, proceedings of manorial courts, and statutes of parliaments, all found their way into the record, whereas the names and life-stories of most of the people of the middle ages are lost forever. The second obstacle is destruction. We possess comparatively little of what was written down in the middle ages. While the destruction of that record was sometimes extrinsic to the actual documentary material, as was the case in Dublin in 1922 when so much of Ireland's medieval record was lost in the burning of the Public Record Office, the loss or survival of historical material generally reflects the value of that material to those into whose hands it passes. Archaeologists, of course, ply their trade with a rather different raw material, but the story of the past as it is expressed in that raw material reaches the present by the same routes. The fashioning of an artefact or the construction of a building was as conscious an act in the middle ages as the making of a documentary record; each served a function, and each conformed to rules of style and grammar. And the archaeological record, like the documentary record, is also vulnerable to forces of destruction. That destruction can sometimes be accidental, but it is often out of neglect, and that is especially sad because it tells us that the past no longer has a value, and that the material of the past no longer holds memories.

This book is an attempt to wrest memories about Ireland's medieval past from the things and places which have managed to make it to the present, and to reconfigure those memories as a set of stories which unfold over the five centuries from AD 1100 to 1600, a chronological span which I describe here as *later* medieval. We are at an exciting time for the study of the archaeology of this period. While twenty years ago there were few regions in later medieval Europe which were better understood than Ulster, there were also few as poorly understood as the other regions of Ireland. When Terry Barry, in his ground-breaking book *The Archaeology of Medieval Ireland*, described this branch of archaeology as being 'in its infancy' in Ireland (1987, 1), he was describing very well its stage of development in southern Ireland. Much has changed since then. Excavations over the past decade and a half, particularly in the coastal towns, have yielded an extraordinary amount of new and diverse information, and quite a lot of it has been published. The archaeology of the later middle ages is now taught in most Irish universities, even including those that do not have formally-constituted departments of archaeology, and in recent years the numbers of postgraduate students pursuing research on later medieval topics have matched those pursuing research in Irish archaeology's traditional hunting ground, prehistory. Perhaps the most exciting development of all is the most recent: the development of a theoretical awareness among archaeologists interested in the medieval world. When I entered university as an undergraduate in the early 1980s it seemed that archaeological interpretations of the middle ages had no life outside the oxygen tent of history. We now recognise that archaeology is not about filling in those gaps in our understanding which are left by history, but about how people of the past behaved individually and collectively, consciously and unconsciously. It is about a world which existed without being written about but which still made a record of itself. Archaeology, above all else, is about us: we cannot see the past except through the filter of our own experiences in the world and our interpretations of the world.

I have tried to make this the sort of book which I would have liked having on my shelves as a student, although I do not intend it to be a text-book. My approach is to treat the evidence thematically rather than chronologically, and within that thematic framework I have tried to balance description and explanation, and detail and generalisation. In my professional life as a university teacher of archaeology I try to promote the sort of inter-disciplinary agenda which Tom McNeill signposted so successfully twenty years ago in his *Anglo-Norman Ulster*, and this book reflects that approach by its inclusion of matters which also have homes across artificial boundaries in the cognate disciplines of history, historical geography, architectural history, and art history.

I have sub-titled this book *An* Archaeology, not *The* Archaeology, for two reasons. First of all, it is not possible for any one person to be a true master of all the evidence which we have for later medieval Ireland, and to use the definite article would therefore be arrogant. Secondly, and perhaps more importantly, I am conscious that I have written an archaeological narrative which is fairly traditional in its treatment of the evidence, and I wish to signal by my use of the indefinite article that there are other types of book to be written about archaeology and later medieval Ireland, including ones which develop along more conceptual or theoretical lines than I have attempted here.

I have pleasure in acknowledging my colleagues in the Department of Archaeology, UCD, for providing the perfect climate for reflection on matters archaeological. Professor Barry Raftery, Head of the Department, has been especially generous in his encouragement and support, and I am most grateful for this. My thanks also to Peter Kemmis Betty for his enthusiasm for this book, to David Jennings for the distribution maps, to Niamh O Broin for her very fine drawings of artefacts, to Conor Brady and Niamh for the illustrations of sites which, as always, are models of clarity, and to Tony Roche and Eamon McEneaney of Dúchas and Waterford Corporation repectively for taking the trouble to find appropriate pictures for me. Margaret, my wife, cheerfully tolerates my absorption in matters medieval, and it is no exaggeration to say that this book would not have been written without her companionship. Well-acquainted herself with the world of medieval Ireland, I trust she will forgive me for incorporating many of her ideas and insights into my text.

The dedication of this book expresses another long overdue debt.

Introduction: Ireland in the later middle ages

The history of Ireland from the 1100s, the century of invasion, to the 1500s, the century of reformation, is well-known, and many recent publications (among them Lydon 1998) provide excellent, up-to-date summaries, but it can only be rehearsed here in very simple outline. Before looking at that history we can start with an explanation of the words which we use to describe the populations of later medieval Ireland.

Anglo-Normans, Gaelic-Irish, Anglo-Irish

No modern historians would use the word 'Norman' to describe those people whose invasion and colonisation of Ireland in the late 1100s so dominates our memory of our medieval past. First of all, those who invaded Ireland were not from Normandy, nor would they have identified particularly closely with Normandy. Most of them were people of Norman descent, but were born and reared in England and southern Wales; some among them were even Flemish. Secondly, Henry II, the king during whose long reign Ireland was invaded, was not Norman but Plantagenet. Given their origin in Normandy, and more immediately in England and Wales, the invaders and colonists of late twelfth- and thirteenth-century Ireland might best be described as 'Anglo-Normans'; other terms such as 'Anglo-French' and 'Cambro-Norman' have been used to describe them, and these too are acceptable, although neither has achieved the currency of 'Anglo-Norman'. The term 'Gaelic-Irish' is rather self-explanatory. It may even seem tautological, but it usefully distinguishes the Irish of indigenous pre-1169 ancestry from those whom we describe as 'Anglo-Irish': these were people born on the island of colonial families which had come to Ireland in the late twelfth and thirteenth centuries and who had adopted Gaelic-Irish ways of life in the later thirteenth and fourteenth centuries; it was these 'Anglo-Irish' people for whom the old adage that 'the Normans became more Irish than the Irish themselves' was coined.

All these labels, Anglo-Norman, Gaelic-Irish and Anglo-Irish, or at least the concepts of ethnicity and cultural identity which they express, are well-established in historical writing in Ireland, and they are used in this book because they allow us to fix our archaeological evidence, whether it is landscape, architecture or material culture, to the historical narrative. They do need, however, to be deployed cautiously and critically in archaeological explanation, and an examination of the analytical value of their use in the archaeology of later medieval Ireland would be a very useful exercise (O'Keeffe 2001a).

Ireland in the twelfth century

The arrival of Anglo-Normans in Ireland in 1169 as mercenaries in the employ of Diarmait Mac Murchada, the deposed king of Leinster, provides an obvious starting point for any account of the history of later medieval Ireland (**colour plate 1**), but the events of that year can only be understood by looking back through the twelfth century, and perhaps even as far back as the eleventh and tenth centuries. The arrival of these 'foreigners', as contemporary annalists described them, may have been unexpected but it was not unprecedented, as foreigners had been used as mercenaries in Ireland before 1169. Even the warfare which was generated by their arrival was not a new experience: since the tenth century there had been considerable military activity on the Irish landscape, all of it related to the struggles for political domination between the major provincial powers. We should also note that Ireland had experienced influence from the Norman world for up to a century before the soldiers and settlers started arriving, as we will see throughout this book: suffice it to give as an example here the pivotal role of the English Church in effecting and giving shape to the reform of the Irish Church in the early 1100s.

The Anglo-Normans succeeded in restoring Diarmait to his lands, and then set about making territorial claims for themselves. Slowly, the eastern parts of Ireland came under their military control (**1a, b**), and these were eventually settled by peasants from England and Wales. These processes of conquest and colonisation should be seen in the context of the migratory movements of both military aristocracies and peasant populations across Europe in the twelfth century. Among the many significant long-term consequences of the success of the Anglo-Normans in Ireland, two stand out in particular. The first is that it drew Henry II into Irish affairs; Henry was naturally concerned that his subjects were expanding their territories overseas without his acquiescence, and when he came to Ireland in the early 1170s it was to have the Anglo-Norman adventurers swear fealty to him, and to make *post facto* grants of the Irish lands to them. Ireland thereafter remained a problem from which subsequent medieval English kings never really extricated themselves. The second consequence was the derailing of any movement towards centralised power and theocratic kingship among the Gaelic-Irish; indeed, native kings, even in those lands which remained beyond the reach of Anglo-Norman settlers, were obliged to recognise the nominal overlordship of the Anglo-Normans and to pay homage and tribute to their king.

Colonial Ireland

The Anglo-Norman colony itself had comparatively little political or cultural cohesion. Rather, it was a number of colonies or colonial regions, each defined in political terms as an earldom or a lordship, and each with its own settlement dynamic and landscape identity. The boundaries between these colonial areas and the lands in Gaelic-Irish control shifted endlessly: in some parts of Ireland stable boundaries between the Gaelic-Irish and the colonists were sustained by peaceful relations, but elsewhere there were frontiers nourished by tension, and these were the frontiers which the colonists peppered with castles.

Anglo-Norman Ireland was at its most prosperous in the second half of the thirteenth century, and Gaelic-Irish lands which lay beyond the limits of royal authority were few (**1c**), but by the close of that century the frontiers had begun shifting to the severe

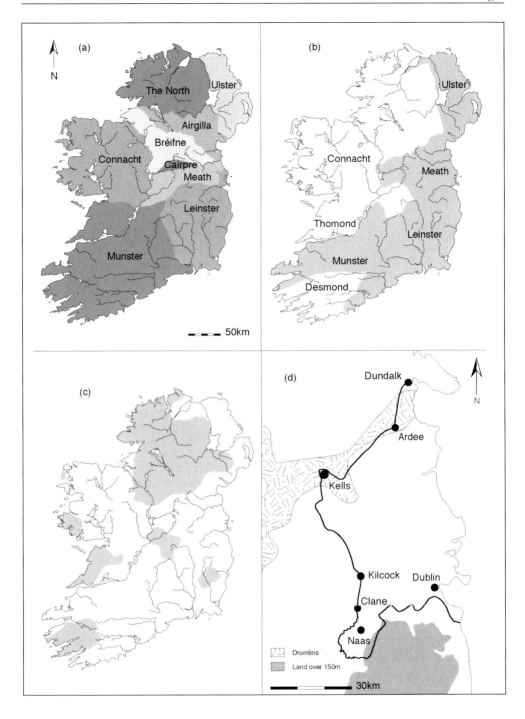

1(a) *Ireland's political geography on the eve of the Anglo-Norman invasion (after Byrne 1987)*
 (b) *The Anglo-Norman colony in Ireland c1210 (by F.J. Byrne, in Martin 1987)*
 (c) *Irish districts outside the limits of royal authority, c1300 (by K.W. Nicholls, in Lydon 1987)*
 (d) *The boundary of the English Pale as described in 1487-88 (after O'Keeffe 1991)*

disadvantage of the colonists, and the fourteenth century quickly became a period of crisis. Although militarised frontiers had successfully kept the populations apart in the 1200s, the 1300s saw Gaelic-Irish incursions into colonial land and the consequent destruction of colonial settlements. An even more powerful destructive force was cultural assimilation: interaction with the indigenous population had given the colonists a familiarity with Gaelic-Irish customs and language, as well as access to a reservoir of potential spouses, and by the middle of the fourteenth century many of the colonial families, such as the Butlers of the earldom of Ormond, and the fitzGeralds of the earldoms of Desmond and Kildare, had become 'gaelicised'; these are the 'Anglo-Irish' whom we mentioned above. By the end of the fifteenth century the only significant territory populated by loyal subjects of the crown was around Dublin, and this was known as the Pale (**1d**). In 1494 or 1495 an attempt was made, by act of parliament, to enclose this area within a great earthen rampart; both as a barrier to prevent cattle-thieving and a fitting metaphor for colonial decay, this rampart seems never to have been finished.

The Tudor reconquest and the end of the middle ages

Within half a century of the attempted enclosure of the Pale, the English crown, by astute political manoeuvring against the fitzGeralds of Kildare, the powerful Anglo-Irish family whose rebellion in 1534 ended in abject failure, had begun to restore its interest and the scale of its influence in Ireland. Henry VIII set about gaining control of the Church, and in the early 1540s the monasteries of Ireland were dissolved and their lands confiscated. Programmes of re-colonisation of Ireland were begun shortly afterwards: counties Laois and Offaly were planted with settlers from England and Wales in the 1550s, Munster was planted (unsuccessfully) from England in the 1580s, and Ulster was planted from England and Scotland at the start of the seventeenth century.

The date at which the middle ages might be regarded as having 'ended' is arbitrary. We can be sure than nobody in the sixteenth or seventeenth centuries felt that their world was changing from medieval to modern. What they would have been aware of, however, were political events and their wider social, cultural and economic implications, whether it was the failed rebellion of the fitzGeralds in 1534 or the arrival of Oliver Cromwell and the bloodshed which accompanied him around Ireland a century later. This book treats the medieval period as ending in 1600, not because that marks a halfway point between these two events but because the seventeenth century seems from what little archaeological work has been devoted to it to have a different personality from the sixteenth and earlier centuries: exotic ceramic imports and grand houses which are barely defensible are just two manifestations of the emergence of Renaissance culture in Ireland around 1600. The archaeology of that transformation and its aftermath in the late 1600s and 1700s is no less interesting than the archaeology of what came before it, but it is a lot more difficult to write about, and one must hope that researchers will soon and earnestly turn their attentions to it.

1 Earth-and-timber castles

Stone castles may provide the most eloquent expression of the success of the Anglo-Normans in replacing native kings at the upper levels of Ireland's medieval socio-political hierarchy, but it was largely by the construction of earth-and-timber fortresses that the colonists actually secured their foothold in Ireland. Only the earthworks of these fortresses survive above ground, and the great majority of these are identified today either as mottes or as ringworks (**colour plates 2, 3**). This classification has proved to be a useful analytical tool and our discussion here will be structured around it, but we need to be conscious that these earthworks are mere skeletons, defleshed by time of the timber architecture with which messages of power and domination, as well as of aesthetic sensibility and cultural affinity, were communicated.

It was with these earthworks, and particularly the mottes, that Ireland's rich tradition of castle-scholarship was inaugurated almost a century ago. For several years Thomas Westropp, a prolific writer on matters of antiquarian interest, and Goddard Orpen, a distinguished historian whose *Ireland Under the Normans* (1911-20) remains definitive, debated vigorously the origins and cultural contexts of Irish 'motes' (Westropp 1904; 1905; Orpen 1906; 1907a; 1907b). Westropp maintained that these monuments were invariably native, pre-colonial creations, but Orpen, with his command of the historical sources and his familiarity with contemporary research in England, was more persuasive in his advocacy of an Anglo-Norman context for them. In recent years some mottes — or at least motte-like settlement-earthworks — have been identified both in the landscape of pre-colonial Ireland (Graham 1993, 42-4) and in the parts of the island into which the colonists appear never to have ventured (McNeill 1997, 72-4), and this evidence, slight though it is, has enticed most scholars away from the dogmatism with which Orpen presented his case. The recent suggestion that some of the mounds and enclosures previously identified as Anglo-Norman earthworks were actually ritual monuments of later prehistoric date (Herity 1993) represents a further rehabilitation of some of Westropp's ideas. Nonetheless, Orpen was undoubtedly correct about the chronology, origins and functions of *most* of the sites which we regard as mottes, and it is with these sites that we must start.

2   The motte at Clonard, county Meath. This earth-and-timber castle was constructed very close to the site of a renowned early medieval monastery; the Anglo-Norman appropriation, by military means, of important ecclesiastical sites was symbolic as well as strategic

Anglo-Norman motte-and-bailey castles

The term *motte* derives from an actual medieval term, *mota* or *motta*, which was first used in the twelfth century to describe the earthwork component of a castle (*Colloque de Caen*, 18; Higham and Barker 1992, 361). The term was also used in medieval Ireland: the motte at Cloncurry, county Kildare, for example, was described as a *mota* in 1304 (*Red Book of Ormond*, 27-31), but most of the sites were merely described as castles in the middle ages. The mound at Clonard, county Meath (**2**), erected by Hugh de Lacy in 1182 (*Expugnatio Hibernica*, 195), could be described as a 'classic' Anglo-Norman motte: it has a circular ground plan, its sides are precipitous, and its summit is flat. At 11m in height its size comfortably exceeds the 3m which Müller-Wille (1966, 7) suggested was the minimum height acceptable in defining an earthen mound as a motte. Clonard has not been excavated, but we can surmise that its comparatively small summit was surmounted by a timber tower (a *bretasche* or *britagium*). The now-grassy slopes of the motte may, like those of other mottes (Pounds 1990, 18), have been revetted by planks or stone slabs to prevent soil wash and to make climbing even more difficult.

It has been suggested by Kieran O'Conor (1998, 18) that at least 476 mottes were erected in Ireland between the late 1100s and the early 1300s, but the number of extant sites is considerably smaller, and an estimate of around 350 (McNeill 1997, 63) is very reasonable. Indeed, given how difficult it is to destroy a monument as large as a motte it is unlikely that the original total was as high as 476. Regarding chronology, the great majority of mottes in Ireland are located in the lands which were under Anglo-Norman control by 1200 (**3**), and many of them can probably be dated, like Clonard, to the period 1170-1200. There is no evidence that any Anglo-Normans involved in Irish politics prior to 1169 were also involved in castle-building; this is in contrast to England where, in the 1050s, several mottes seem to have been constructed by Norman lords who had taken up residence with the blessing of Edward the Confessor (Pounds 1990, 6). Motte-construction certainly continued into the early decades of the thirteenth century in Ireland. The building in 1218 of a *mote et britagium* — a mound and timber tower — at Roscrea, county Tipperary, was recorded retrospectively in 1245, and while this is the last unequivocal record we have of the construction of one of these monuments, it does not necessarily represent the actual end-point of the tradition (Cunningham 1987, 124-5). By the time of the Anglo-Norman penetration into Connacht in the late 1230s the motte was no longer needed as a campaign castle, or at least was no longer considered suitable for the purpose, so that province has very few examples. The fashion for mottes had already been established in Anglo-Norman society in eastern Ireland, however, and there is no reason why mottes should no longer have been built as the settlement pattern in that region was filling-out during the thirteenth century. This may explain why parts of eastern Ireland have such a dense distribution of these monuments. We could speculate that mottes were still being built in eastern Ireland as late as the early 1300s, as has been suggested (O'Conor 1998, 18), although the fashion for mottes had, despite some exceptions (Gardelles 1972, 15), died out in much of Europe long before the fourteenth century.

Clonard was one of the largest estates created in the subinfeudation — the feudal subdivision of land among lords — of Meath, and its motte is one of the largest of the 84 mottes still extant in that lordship (Graham 1980a). The scale of mottes in Meath appears to be related to the social rank of those for whom they were constructed. Motte-ownership (or castle-ownership, to be more exact) appears to have filtered down the social hierarchy to the level of those lords who held small estates for considerably less than the service of a single knight, and not surprisingly these low-ranking lords possessed comparatively small mottes. Indeed, some of these small mottes have dimensions which, were it not for corroborating historical information on an Anglo-Norman presence, would suggest that they are actually prehistoric burial tumuli. Clonard is also one of 34 mottes in the lordship of Meath to be accompanied by a bailey, an embanked enclosure at the foot of the mound which we presume to have contained a range of structures (like halls and kitchens) essential to the successful functioning of the entire castle. Earthwork baileys are found with castles which, like Clonard, protected the most prosperous manors. But baileys were also constructed in the shadows of those mottes which were tucked in among the hills separating the rich agricultural land of Meath from the less fertile lands of the Gaelic-Irish; in those frontier locations the baileys presumably accommodated garrisons. Mottes of lesser lords in Meath tended not to have baileys, but while these mottes now appear as isolated monuments in the landscape, we should not forget that there may have been palisaded enclosures associated with them in the middle ages and that these are not detectable without geophysical prospecting and excavation.

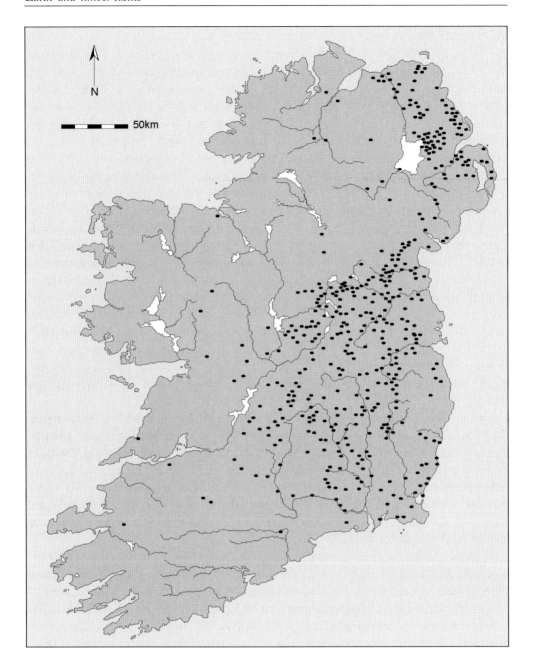

3   A distribution map of mottes in Ireland (after O'Conor 1998)

Regional patterns

We have used the lordship of Meath as a case study, and it is reasonable to ask how typical were its mottes in terms of morphology, distribution, and patterns of ownership. The only valid comparisons we can make are with the mottes of the earldom of Ulster and the lordship of Leinster (**figure 1b**); the royal demesne lands—the lands retained by the crown, in other words—were centred on the major ports, were quite small in area, and had low numbers of mottes, while most of Connacht and much of Munster simply did not have mottes built in them by the colonists, as we can see in **Figure 3**.

In modern counties Antrim and Down, the heartland of Anglo-Norman Ulster, 95 mottes have been identified, and 23% of these had baileys; most of these earthworks are unquestionably a product of Anglo-Norman control, but small numbers of mottes located in western county Down and on the fertile lands of central Antrim, both areas which apparently remained in Gaelic-Irish hands, have been attributed to native Irish lords (McNeill 1980, 102-3, 113-4). This attribution raises an interesting question of interpretation in historical archaeology, and one which we will have cause to return to again (p 77): there is no reason to deny the medieval Gaelic-Irish either the capacity or the motivation to build their own mottes, as we shall see, but in the absence of a documentary record of an Anglo-Norman presence in an area, and especially one which was bounded by colonial lands (as was central Antrim), might we not interpret the mottes as hard evidence that Anglo-Normans were actually present? Leaving aside this matter though, we do observe that mottes in Ulster are as variable in scale as those in Meath, suggesting that here too motte-ownership was not restricted to the upper echelons of artistocratic society. However, Ulster mottes generally are lower in height and have much broader summits than those in Meath. Remains of rectangular halls were revealed in the excavations of three mottes in county Down, Clough (Waterman 1954), Lismahon (Waterman 1959) and Rathmullen (Lynn 1981-2), and we may surmise that these and other Ulster mottes were deliberately made low and broad so that they could accommodate such structures. Why the Anglo-Normans of Ulster wanted their halls on the summits of mottes when Anglo-Normans elsewhere in Ireland seem to have been content with having their halls at ground level is something we will never know.

There are in excess of 150 mottes in the lordship of Leinster, the largest single land-block in colonial Ireland, but they are much less densely distributed than in Meath and Ulster. Ownership of these monuments did not permeate as deeply the many levels of aristocratic society as had happened further north (McNeill 1990a). There are low, flat mottes in Leinster which compare very well with those in Ulster (as at Castlegrace, county Carlow, for example), but the centres of the great manors were marked by very substantial, steep-sided mottes (as at Clonmore, also in county Carlow) comparable with those in Meath.

The evidence of excavation

Few mottes in Ireland have seen scientific excavation, and it is unfortunate, given what we know of regional differentiation, that almost all the sites which have been investigated are in Ulster. One exception is the motte at Lurgankeel, county Louth, excavated in the 1960s but never published. On the summit of this was found a tower and an encircling palisade

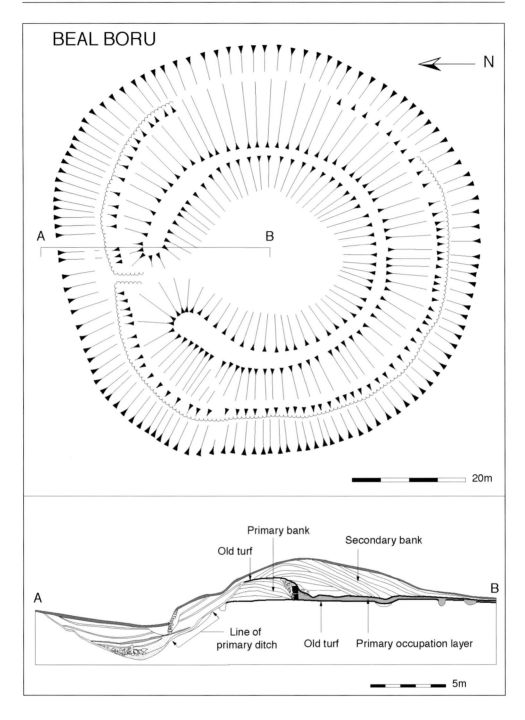

4   *A plan and cross-section of Beal Boru, county Clare (after O'Kelly 1962): a ringwork castle or an unfinished motte?*

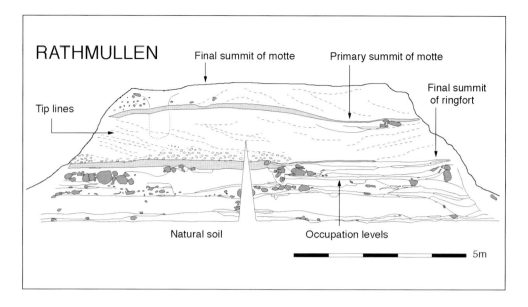

5   A cross-section of the mound at Rathmullen, county Down (after Lynn 1981-2), showing the monument's transformation from a raised-platform ringfort with multiple layers of occupation to a motte

(Barry 1987, 42). The other exception is Beal Boru, county Clare (**4**). This site began life as a ringfort, a Gaelic-Irish settlement earthwork of early medieval date, and its destruction — 'Toirdealbach Ua Conchobhair burned and demolished Boromha' — is recorded in 1116. The site was re-edified by the Anglo-Normans around 1200, and the present earthwork is essentially of that date. The excavator identified Beal Boru as the castle which, according to an annalistic reference of 1207, 'the English of Meath and Leinster' attempted to build 'near the Borowe', and he suggested that the present earthwork represents an unfinished motte (O'Kelly 1962). The late Dermot Twohig suggested that Beal Boru may be a ringwork (Twohig 1978), a type of Anglo-Norman earthwork-castle which we will discuss presently (pp29-33), but one aspect of the archaeology of the site is certainly consistent with the excavator's interpretation of it as an unfinished motte: the lack of evidence for a palisade on the top of the bank.

Three of the excavated mottes in county Down, Rathmullen and Lismahon, which have already been mentioned, and Castleskreen (Dickinson and Waterman 1959; 1960), and one motte in county Antrim, Dunsilly (McNeill 1991), were constructed, like Beal Boru, on native Irish ringforts. The ringforts at Castleskreen and Dunsilly were typical in their morphology: like thousands of other ringforts in Ireland, each was apparently penannular (almost a closed circle) in plan with an inner bank and outer ditch. But the earlier forts at Rathmullen (**5**) and Lismahon were more mound-like, and the Anglo-Normans simply topped them up to convert them into mottes.

Why were earlier settlement earthworks reused by the Anglo-Normans? There are two probable reasons. First of all, the value of extant earthworks as convenient, ready-made, foundations for very large earthworks would have been recognised, and it is unlikely that a lord would have directed his men to construct a motte on virgin soil when an existing earthwork could be appropriated. Secondly, native earthworks may have been colonised by new castles for symbolic gain. The mound-like ringfort at Rathmullen, for example, was still occupied when John de Courcy invaded Ulster in 1177. If its elevated interior in the early twelfth century reflected the political power of its indigenous owners, its elevation still further by the Anglo-Normans must have signalled very effectively the arrival of the new political authority. By the same token the fortress of Telach Caíl, now Delvin, county Westmeath, was almost certainly sealed beneath the motte of Gilbert de Nugent's castle in the late 1100s (Flanagan 1993). It is likely that the remains of other important pre-Anglo-Norman royal residences remain to be found beneath Anglo-Norman mottes.

Gaelic-Irish earth-and-timber fortifications

The matter of Gaelic-Irish fortications brings us to two difficult issues: the native adoption of the motte, and the chronology of ringforts. The latter cannot be regarded as fortified sites, and discussion of them would therefore appear to be more appropriate to Chapter 3, but it is contended here that the later history of the ringfort phenomenon cannot be separated from the process of native encastellation, and so we turn to it now.

The chronology of ringforts

Ireland has more than 45,000 ringforts according to the most recent account (Stout 1997, 53). These embanked and ditched enclosures of penannular plan, usually between 30m and 40m in diameter, generally contained houses and other structures, and archaeological evidence consistently points to the early middle ages, and specifically to the period between AD700 and 1000, as their era of construction.

The *a priori* case for attributing some ringforts to the later middle ages, particularly in those parts of Ireland outside of Anglo-Norman control, is based on the absence of any other settlement form of appropriate date in those landscapes. In other words, if the Gaelic-Irish did not live in ringforts, where *did* they live? The question is a reasonable one, but the answer continues to disappoint: we do not know. Historical or archaeological evidence for the late construction (as distinct from occupation or re-occupation) of ringforts is meagre (Lynn 1975a, b). The relative density of ringforts in areas which remained Gaelic-Irish in the later middle ages has been used to argue that these people were still using ringforts at quite a late date (Barrett and Graham 1975), but even that evidence is circumstantial. Some high-status, defended residences of the Gaelic-Irish in the thirteenth and fourteenth centuries are described as *longphoirt* in contemporary sources (O'Conor 1998, 84-5), but there is little hard evidence about the form which these took, and we cannot assume them to be ringfort-like. The enclosing of properties with earthen ramparts is historically attested to in the sixteenth century (*Ormond Deeds* 1547-84, no.11; 1584-1603, nos 31, 32), but again we do not know how well these ramparts compared with those of ringforts; simple expediency rather than any affinity with the ringfort concept may explain these enclosures.

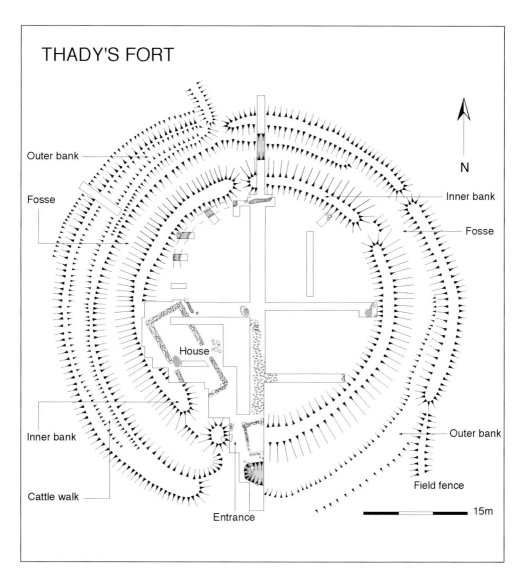

THADY'S FORT

Outer bank

Fosse

Inner bank

Fosse

House

Inner bank

Outer bank

Cattle walk

Field fence

Entrance

15m

N

6　*A plan of Thady's Fort, Shannon Airport, county Clare (after Rynne 1963), showing the house of c1600 in its interior*

There is a record of the building of a 'circular fort and princely palace of earth' at Clonroad, near Ennis in county Clare, in the early 1240s (*Caithréim Thoirdelbhaigh* II, 2), and this seems to be a good example of the construction of a ringfort in the later middle ages. However, the very fact that the form of the monument was even described suggests that similar monuments were not being constructed at that time and that the Clonroad monument might instead be regarded as a conscious use by a Gaelic-Irish lord of an archaic mode of enclosure and construction; indeed we may even speculate that it was a reflection of the renewed interest in Gaelic traditions, among them inauguration rites and art styles, which is especially well-attested from the fourteenth century (Simms 1987, 15-17). A date in the later middle ages has also been argued, using the evidence of archaeology rather than history, for the cashel (stone-walled ringfort) at the centre of the hillfort at Rathgall, county Wicklow (Long 1997, 238-42), but one wonders if here too a Gaelic-Irish lord had consciously returned to an ancient, pre-colonial tradition for the design of his residence.

A relatively short distance from Clonroad is 'Thady's Fort', a ringfort for which a late date has been suggested (Rynne 1963). The excavator argued that it was contemporary with the house of *c*1600 which was found inside it (**6**); it is an interpretation which has its supporters (O'Conor 1998, 91) and detractors (Edwards 1990, 19). Among the less contentious examples of the later medieval reoccupation of early-medieval sites in Ireland are the promontory fort of Dooneendermotmore, county Cork, where a new perimeter wall and a house were erected towards the end of the middle ages (O'Kelly 1952), the stone fort of Cahermacnaughten, county Clare, which had a tower erected above its original entrance in the fifteenth century, and the cashel at the centre of the bivallate, late Bronze Age or Iron Age hillfort of Caherdrinny, county Cork, which contains a fragmentary fifteenth-century tower-house and a collection of small house-sites of probable late medieval or post-medieval date. There is also very good documentation in annalistic sources for the late occupation of crannógs (O'Sullivan 1998) and such finds as late medieval native pottery provide corroboration, but there is no evidence for the large-scale construction of these artificial islands in our period.

It must be conceded that most of the excavations of ringforts have taken place in the eastern half of Ireland in areas in which the Anglo-Normans would not have encouraged ringfort-building; indeed, Giraldus Cambrensis remarked of Ireland that 'you will find here many ditches, very high and round and often in groups of three, one outside of the other, as well as walled forts which are still standing, although *now empty and abandoned*' (*Topographica Hibernica*, 103; *italics mine*). It is possible that excavation will eventually reveal the ringfort to have survived into the later middle ages in western Ireland, but we cannot suspend discussion of this issue until a statistically significant number of western ringforts has been excavated, nor can we indulge in writing an archaeology based on what we anticipate will eventually be found; we must deal with the facts as we see them, and at this point in time our evidence suggests that the ringfort was a settlement phenomenon of the second half of the first millennium AD. Why, then, did it not enjoy a longer life?

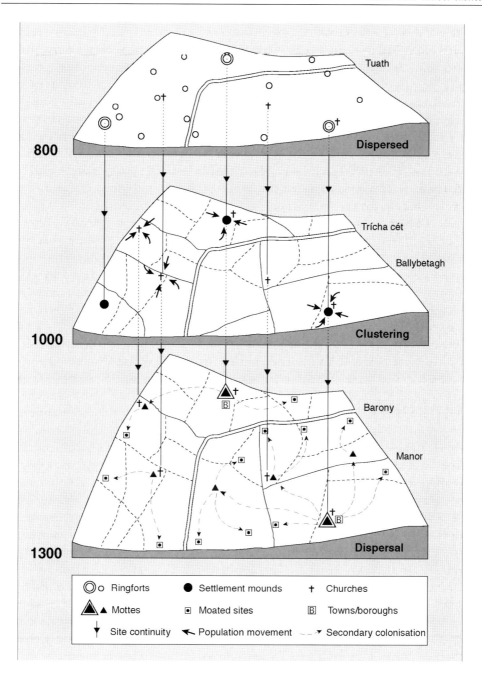

7   *A model of continuity and change in the Irish countryside, AD 800–1300 (after O'Keeffe 1996a). This graphic illustrates how the pre-colonial territorial organisation and macro-scale pattern of settlement of Ireland was largely retained by the Anglo-Normans after 1200. Indeed the most significant changes in the settlement and landscape history of medieval Ireland may have occured between c800 and c1000, and not after the invasion of 1169. In many parts of colonial Ireland the only evidence for rural settlement among the colonists is provided by moated sites, most of which are probably of late thirteenth-century date (see pp 73–80)*

Feudalism in Gaelic Ireland

The rate of ringfort construction across the island must have accelerated and decelerated at different moments and in different places during that half-millennium. Demographics presumably played a role, as fluctuating population numbers would have created or negated the need for new forts within extended family groups, but demography alone does not explain the apparent abandonment of existing ringforts in the period around the turn of the millennium, nor the very low numbers of newly-built ringforts in the early centuries of the second millennium AD. Instead, this remarkable change in settlement history is almost certainly related to the rise of feudalism in Ireland between the tenth and twelfth centuries (Doherty 1998, 312-29).

Viking activity in the late 700s and 800s contributed in large measure to radical changes in Irish society in the tenth century, particularly in the nature and role of kingship (Ó Corráin 1972, 29-32; 1978), and in concepts of warfare (Lynn 1975a, 33). Increasing levels of military activity, and the restructuring of social obligations needed to support them, are apparent in some of the terms — *óglachas*, 'the service of a warrior', and *biataigheacht*, 'a food-providing relationship', for example (Simms 1987, 101) — which came into circulation at this time. The transformation which we witness here in the lives of many of the early medieval Irish is a shift from clientship, the earlier form of social organisation (Patterson 1994), to the system of labour services which we regard as diagnostic of feudalism. These changes also manifested themselves in the organisation and use of the landscape. The land was subdivided for the purpose of taxation into a hierarchy of spatial units, the *trícha cét* and the smaller *baile*, and that new territorial configuration not only survived the arrival of the Anglo-Normans but it provided the spatial underpinnings of their manors, and it is even fossilised today in the modern townlands (**7**; Duffy 1981; McErlean 1983; Patterson 1994, 92-3). We can best understand the abandonment of the ringfort if we envisage actual population relocation taking place within this new territorial framework and under lordship control.

Two questions now emerge. Where did the feudal lords of tenth-, eleventh- and twelfth-century Ireland reside? Whither was this relocation? Before we even consider the evidence which may answer these questions, we can look for direction to Anglo-Saxon England, where the *hundred* and the *vill* (Lewis, Mitchell-Fox and Dyer 1997, 52-3) provide parallels for the *trícha cét* and the *baile*. Between the ninth and eleventh centuries there emerged, probably also under lordship control, both the English village (Roberts 1987, 72) and its associated open-fields (Hall 1988). Late Anglo-Saxon lordship is certainly manifest in *burhs*, defensible manor houses, of which Goltho in Lincolnshire is the best known (Williams 1992). It is also manifest in the great increase in new churches with secular patrons in the eleventh century, particularly in villages. Drawing on this evidence, we could hypothesise that in tenth- and eleventh-century Ireland the pattern of dispersed settlement in ringforts began to be replaced by a pattern of nucleation, that the pastoral needs of the people were satisfied in churches in those nucleations, and that power emanated from defended royal (or aristocratic) residences. Discussion of settlement nucleation and of churches in pre-Anglo-Norman Ireland belongs in the later chapters of this book, but the matter of fortification does concern us here, and we turn to it now.

In the early twelfth century the terms *caistél* or *caislén* were used in Gaelic-Irish sources to describe a small number of fortresses, mainly in Connacht (Graham 1988a; Flanagan 1996 O'Keeffe 1998a); the use of these terms has been taken as a good indication of the feudalisation of pre-colonial Irish society (Ó Corráin 1978). Other words for fortresses which were in use from the tenth century were *longphort, daingen, dúnad* and *dún* (Doherty 1998, 324-6). Modern translation of these terms is difficult, and in any case the contexts in which they were used suggests that meanings changed from one situation to the next; for example, the first of these, *longphort*, literally meant a port for ships, and the manner of its pre-colonial use suggests it was initially a coastal or naval encampment of Irish or Norse armies, but by the thirteenth and fourteenth centuries its meaning was no longer so confined (O'Conor 1998, 84-7). The terms seem also to have been interchangable, as witness the description of the fortress at Athlone, county Westmeath, as both *caislél* and *daingen*. Nonetheless, all of these terms indicate a new horizon of fortifications at a crucial time in Irish history, and therein lies part of their significance.

Caistél Dúin Leódha and Dún Echdach

What did these pre-colonial 'castles' look like? Unfortunately, we have very little information about the documented sites. Excavation has revealed traces of possible pre-colonial fortifications at Limerick and at Dunamase, county Laois (McNeill 1997, 12-13), but assessment of the evidence must await the excavation reports. A third possible site is at Downpatrick, county Down. Known variously as *Ráthceltchair, Dúndáleathglais,* and 'English Mount', this is one of the sites over which Orpen and Westropp wrangled in the early 1900s. Here, a large mound stands off-centre in a massive enclosure; the monument has been identified as a pre-colonial royal fortress with a later, unfinished motte inside it (McNeill 1997, 12), as an enclosure castle of the 'ringwork' type (Barry 1987, Fig.14), and as an example of a ritual monument of Celtic Iron Age date (Herity 1993).

More intriguing still are *Caistél Dúin Leódha* at Ballinasloe, county Galway, and *Dún Echdach*, now Duneight, county Down. The first of these, which combines both *caistél* and *dún* in its name, is known to have been in existence in 1124 (O'Keeffe 1998a). It is now destroyed but we have Molyneux's tantalising early eighteenth-century description of it as 'a Danesmount, with a large trench round it: 'tis almost so flat one might almost take it for a fort'. 'Danesmount' was Molyneux's term for a high, motte-like mound, and the description of the top of the mound being flat supports the identification of this as a motte-like earthwork (Nicholls 1982, 389). Indeed, there is no reason why we should not simply describe it as a pre-colonial Gaelic-Irish motte. Moreover, the evidence of this description of *Caistél Dúin Leódha* suggests to us that other documented fortresses of the same date in Ireland may have been motte-like. The great, flat-topped mound at Dunmore, county Galway, for example, might be identified therefore as the 'Dún Mór' (the Great Fort) which was demolished in 1133 having probably functioned as a feudal fortress (Graham 1988a, 115).

Those settlement mounds in the Irish landscape which are described as 'raised' and 'platform' ringforts (Edwards 1990, 14) may also be relevant here: some excavated ringforts in county Down — Ballynarry (Davison 1962), Rathmullen, Gransha (Lynn 1985), Big Glebe (Hamlin and Lynn [eds] 1988, 41-4) and Deer Park Farms (Hamlin and Lynn 1988, 44-7) — had motte-like profiles and were occupied quite late in the time-span

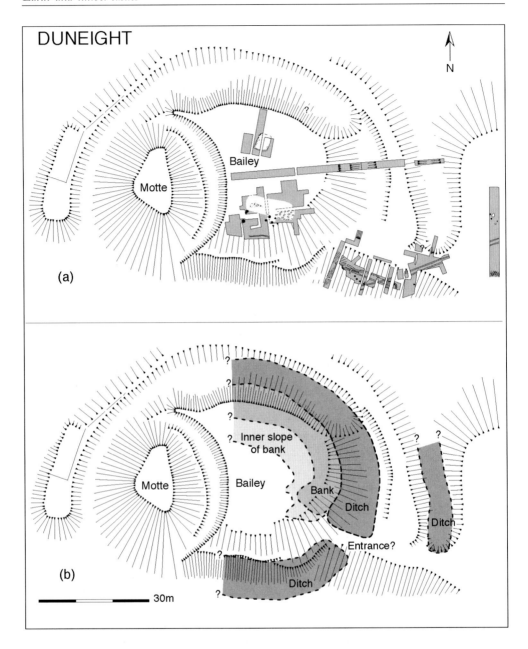

8 Duneight [Dún Echdach], county Down (after Waterman 1963): (a) a plan of the motte-and-bailey earthwork and the excavation; (b) possible lines of the pre-1011 banks and ditches as suggested by the excavations

of ringforts. The elevation of the occupation levels at all these sites would have made their defence easier and would have allowed those within a better view of what lay outside. The symbolism of elevation was probably also important, and it is not inconceivable that the owners of these sites had their interiors raised significantly so as to differentiate them from the conventional or standard ringforts of the pre-feudal age. None of these 'raised' or 'platform' ringforts is historically documented and we know nothing of their functions, either administrative or military, so we might be slow to describe them as mottes. But their chronology and morphology, combined with what we know generally of society and politics at the time of their construction, suggest that 'motte' is not an inappropriate appellation for them; we do need to remember, after all, that motte-building began in Europe not in the eleventh or twelfth century but in the tenth (du Bouard 1967), and that mottes were not exclusively built by the Normans.

The second site, Duneight, is more perplexing. Excavations inside and across the ramparts of the small bailey of a motte-and-bailey earthwork (Waterman 1963) revealed that it originated in pre-colonial times as an enclosure defined by an outer ditch and a reinforced inner bank, both very substantial (**8**). The plan of the enclosure was not established. However, it clearly was entered from the south-east, which is the normal direction from which ringforts were entered, but the sheer scale of its enclosing bank and ditch, combined with their very sharp curvature, indicate that this was not a conventional ringfort.

Duneight is *Dún Echdach*, and it was here that the annalists recorded the burning of a *dún* and the 'breaking' of a *baile* in 1011. The first of these words, *dún*, can be translated as 'fort'. When it appears in medieval contexts, the word *baile* seems normally to refer to a place rather than to any specific form of settlement; it first emerged in the age of pre-colonial feudalism as a descriptive noun for parcels of land which were subdivided for taxation assessment, and the close relationship between its usage and the evolution of Ireland's townland system is reflected in the *Baile-* (or, when rendered in English, *Bally-*) prefix of many Irish townland names. But in some contexts *baile* clearly signified settlement, and usually nucleated settlement, as we will see in Chapter 5. That is probably the best interpretation of its use at Duneight. Thus, we can interpret the events at *Dún Echdach* in 1011 as the burning of a fort and the breaking of settlement.

There is no doubt that Duneight saw occupation by the Anglo-Normans, but the morphology of the earthwork investigated by Dudley Waterman might owe very little to them. The bailey was originally a creation of the pre-colonial era. The motte was not excavated, and its stratigraphical relationship with the bailey was not established, so the possibility remains that it too was part of that pre-Anglo-Norman monument. The suggestion, then, that the early eleventh-century *dún* and *baile* of *Dún Echdach* were actually the 'motte' and 'bailey' of Duneight (Doherty 1998, 327) deserves serious consideration.

Anglo-Norman ringworks

Most of the mottes that we identify in Ireland are in areas which we know to have been under colonial control, and the great majority of them are unquestionably of Anglo-Norman origin. But their distribution is puzzling. The map (**3**) is almost a freeze-frame graphic of colonial diffusion up to 1200, but we know that the Anglo-Normans spread further west into Connacht. Why, then, are mottes not a feature of western colonial landscapes?

The preferred answer among many archaeologists today is that earth-and-timber castles were indeed built in western Ireland but that the earthen substructures of these castles were not mottes but 'ringworks'. Comprised of a slightly-raised circular or near-circular area enclosed by a substantial inner bank and outer ditch, the ringwork, or 'ringwork castle' as it is sometimes styled, is understood to have been an alternative to the motte in England and Wales (King and Alcock 1969).

Examples of the ringwork class of monument were identified in Ireland by Derek Renn three decades ago (Renn 1968), but the late Dermot Twohig is generally credited with introducing the idea that these monuments exist in Ireland, and for suggesting that they might be found in areas where mottes are absent (Twohig 1978; Nicholls 1982, 390-1). This idea was given wide circulation in the 1980s with the publication of lists and maps of forty-five 'possible' examples (Barry 1983; 1987). By 1992 the number of 'probable' and 'possible' ringworks had risen by one estimation (O'Conor 1992) to sixty-three, and the number has risen since then with newly-suggested identifications listed in the county inventories of the Archaeological Survey of Ireland (O'Donovan 1995; Moore 1996; Grogan and Kilfeather 1997; O'Brien and Sweetman 1997).

While there is clearly a consensus among many archaeologists that ringworks exist in considerable numbers in Ireland, it is not a view which is universally accepted (McNeill 1990b, 262-3; 1997, 63; O'Keeffe 1990a; 1995a; 1998a). The divergence in opinion concerns not so much the interpretation of individual monuments but the method by which archaeologists classify earthworks and retrieve their cultural context.

Whereas 'motte', 'castle' and a number of other terms which we have already discussed had historical meaning, even if that meaning shifted from one context to another, the term 'ringwork' has no medieval meaning: it is a modern archaeological creation which gives prominence, without the sanction of history, to a particular morphological element of an earthen monument-type, namely its ring-plan. This method of monument-classification is well-established in archaeology, and a critique of its value is not really needed here, but in the context of Irish archaeology the identification of the ringwork as a type of Anglo-Norman fortification is very problematic indeed. The problem is the difficulty in distinguishing on the basis of field-morphology between Anglo-Norman ringworks and Gaelic-Irish ringforts.

That there is such a difficulty is widely-acknowledged, even among those archaeologists who argue in favour of the existence of ringworks in Ireland: 'it is hardly surprising that these ringworks have not been noticed, since their surface morphology would have been *virtually indistinguishable* from the indigenous ringforts' (Barry 1987, 45; *italics mine*). There is, in fact, *no* exclusively field-morphological distinction to be made between ringforts and ringworks. They are the same things, and the reason we use different words is to convey what we today perceive to be differences of function, culture, and context. An earthen enclosure of ring-plan which is known to have been built by the native Irish in the early middle ages, for example, will always be identified as a ringfort, but an earthwork with identical morphology which is known to have been built by the Anglo-Normans will be

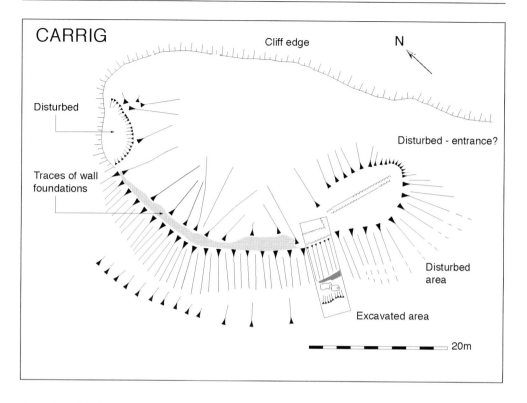

9   Plan of the late twelfth-century enclosure castle of Carrig, county Wexford (after Bennett 1984-5)

identified as a ringwork. Given that we have 'ringfort' and 'ringwork' to communicate different cultural meanings, how then do we classify a monument which conforms to their shared morphological definition when the contextual information about that monument is either ambiguous or non-existent? And how do we deal with the possibility that early medieval earthwork enclosures could have been reused by the Anglo-Normans with little significant alteration to their morphology?

These are questions which are central to the archaeologist's method and philosophy. But if we do not wish to subject the idea of the ringwork — or, indeed, the idea of the ringfort — to this type of scrutiny, we can still chisel away at the integrity of the ringwork idea by use of simple statistics. Archaeological excavation consistently reveals penannular settlement earthworks in Ireland to be early medieval ringforts, so there is a strong statistical likelihood that any earthwork of that nature in Ireland will turn out on excavation to be pre-1169 rather than post-1169 in date, and Gaelic-Irish rather than Anglo-Norman in origin. It is therefore incumbent on those writers who support the idea that ringwork castles were built in Ireland to provide firm evidence to support their attribution of certain ringfort-like earthworks to the Anglo-Normans. In some instances this is possible. Excavation at the earthwork at Carrig castle, county Wexford (**9**), for example, revealed it to be an Anglo-Norman enclosure, and the description of it as a ringwork (Bennett 1984-5) is reasonable, particularly in view of the historical information pertaining to its Anglo-Norman origin. Pollardstown, county Kildare (Fanning 1973-74), is less convincing, but its identification as a ringwork (Barry 1983) should be regarded as not improbable. A great ditch around the *donjon* (great tower) at Trim, county Meath, has been identified as the remains of an earth-and-timber castle erected by Hugh de Lacy shortly after he established Trim as his capital, and Terry Barry has made a strong case for regarding it as a ringwork (1983); recent excavations by Alan Hayden seem to confirm the identification. Tom McNeill, who is less enthusiastic about the ringwork model than most Irish scholars, also makes a strong case for regarding the smaller of two promontory forts at Baginbun, county Wexford, as another Anglo-Norman earthwork enclosure (1997, 62), and this too might be described as a ringwork. In the case of the majority of the alleged ringworks, however, the criteria on which the identifications are based are not made explicit, and this makes them difficult to assess. Few of the ringwork identifications published by the Archaeological Survey of Ireland in its county inventories are argued closely, so inevitably one has the impression that the earthworks in question are regarded as ringworks because they appear to be military and because they are located at places at which there was (or may have been) an Anglo-Norman presence. This may be an unfair judgement, but it is, in the absence of a proper explanation for the identifications, an inevitable judgement. There is strong case for thinking that a number of the identifications are simply incorrect, and these have been discussed in print (O'Keeffe 1990a; 1998a). Suffice it to say here that some of the putative ringworks have morphological characteristics which indicate they may be unfinished mottes (Farranfad, county Down, and Beal Boru, as we discussed above), prehistoric ritual earthworks (Dungar, county Offaly), standard ringforts (Rathangan, county Kildare), ringforts which were simply re-occupied late in the middle ages (Rahinnane, county Kerry, and Raheen, county Limerick), or, finally, the fosses dug around Anglo-Norman stone castles simply to add extra protection (Adare, county Limerick, Ferns, county Wexford, and Rindown, county Roscommon).

This discussion of the ringwork idea may appear somewhat one-sided, and the opposition to the idea may seem a little too vigorous. It is a discussion intended to provoke a response because the matter at stake is very important. The suggestion that Ireland has ringwork castles in significant numbers impacts directly on our understanding of the patterns and processes of Anglo-Norman colonisation in Ireland: as the rate of identification of new ringwork sites continues, we are being drawn inexorably towards the conclusion that the Anglo-Norman colony in Ireland was more heavily fortified and more densely settled than was believed to be the case only a quarter of a century ago, but if the identifications are not correct — and there is good reason to suspect that quite a few are not — we are being led towards a false conclusion. Future research may diffuse this writer's scepticism and may prove 'ringwork-hunting', to paraphrase Tom McNeill (1997, 60), to have been a valuable exercise, but at this moment there is little empirical evidence to support the idea that ringworks are a significant element in the archaeological record of colonial Ireland.

Let us return, finally, to the problem which has nourished the search for ringworks: the absence of mottes in parts of Ireland in which we know there to have been an Anglo-Norman presence. This absence should surprise us only if we regard the colony as homogenous both politically and culturally, but also in its perception of danger. But the Anglo-Norman colony was not like this; rather, it was a mosaic of lordships and earldoms, each sufficiently liberated from centralised authority to develop its own settlement dynamic. The complex relationships between colonists and natives allow us to believe that the immediate protection which an earth-and-timber castle offered was not needed everywhere, and indeed some parts of Ireland must have been peaceful enough for the building of stone castles or stone halls to have begun *ab initio* without an earlier motte-phase. It is true that some parts of Ireland had a heavy density of mottes (Meath and Ulster), some parts had a lower density (Leinster), and Connacht and Munster (apart from south Tipperary) had very few mottes, but it is also true that the political autonomy of these areas, combined with the specific relationships between colonists and hosts, can explain this regional variability.

2 Stone castles and defensible houses

Nothing dominates our perceptions of the middle ages more than the stone castle. Its life-story appears inextricably linked with the history of the medieval world itself: its emergence parallels the emergence of feudalism, and its full maturity reflects both the power of medieval aristocracy and the fundamental insecurities of life in an age of militarism and territorial aggrandizement. Only when the medieval period ends does the castle seem to become redundant.

Medieval Ireland was a heavily encastellated land, and perhaps the most so in Europe (**10**; Lydon 1967). Harold Leask estimated that 3,000 castles (including earth-and-timber castles and late semi-fortified houses) were built in Ireland between the late 1100s and the 1600s (Leask 1951, 153), and Terry Barry has estimated that 7,000 tower-houses, later medieval castles of a particular type, were built between the late 1400s and the 1600s (Barry 1996, 140). These figures are difficult to corroborate, but the magnitude of Barry's estimated figure finds support in mid-seventeenth-century sources, particularly the Civil Survey (Simington [ed] 1931-61), which contains a record of a considerably greater number of castles than the Ordnance Survey recorded in the mid-nineteenth century: in the eastern part of county Kildare, for example, the Ordnance Survey maps have less than a dozen castles marked on them but the appropriate sections of the Civil Survey indicate well in excess of a hundred castles. None of this means that later medieval Ireland was an exceptionally dangerous place — nor, for that matter, an exceptionally safe place — to live. Castle-ownership filtered far lower down the strata of medieval society than popular imagination allows.

The study of the medieval castle in Ireland has been well-served by several syntheses. The best-known of these, if only because for half a century it was the only book of any substance on the topic, is by Harold Leask. This was first published in 1941 and was last revised in 1951. One of the key works in the historiography of medieval Ireland, Leask's book has bequeathed to us a particular model of castle development in Ireland: earth-and-timber castles in the early colonial period (1170-1220), followed by stone castles of increasing architectural sophistication later in the colonial period (1220-1310), followed by a hiatus in building-activity, first as war and famine grip the country, and then as the country adjusts to their aftermath (1310-1430), followed by a re-emergence of the castle, albeit transformed into the tower-house (1430-1650), and followed, finally, by the semi-fortified house of the later sixteenth and seventeenth centuries. Leask's work is certainly not impervious to criticism, either for its methodology or it conclusions, but judged by

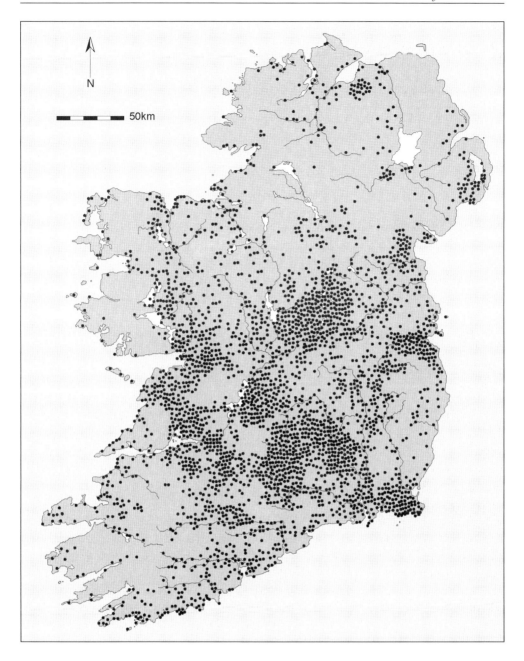

10   *A distribution map of stone castles — the majority of them later medieval tower-houses — in Ireland (after Stout and Stout 1997)*

the standards of mid-twentieth-century castle-scholarship in general it is a work of high standard which has served Irish scholars extremely well. Tom McNeill's recent synthesis (1997) includes many of the same castles as Leask but, whereas Leask divorced the castles from the circumstances of their creation, McNeill explores fully their place within contemporary polity and society, skilfully integrating this with the complexities of type and function. His book thus represents a very welcome and very significant step-forward from Leask's book. Paul Kerrigan, in his study of later castles (1995), has also emphasised the context in which the buildings functioned, and his concern for the military attributes of the castles of the late sixteenth century and later is commensurate with the sort of historical information which is preserved about them.

Anglo-Norman stone castles

Almost all the extant Anglo-Norman stone buildings of a non-ecclesiastical nature in Ireland appear to have been equipped for defending or were parts of larger complexes which were so equipped; from the narrow perspective of militarism, then, they qualify as castles. Their owners were either kings or land-holding aristocrats. In some cases, such as Trim, county Meath, the stone structures replaced the earth-and-timber castles with which the colonists first secured their foothold on new lands, while other castles, such as Carrickfergus, county Antrim, were built *ab initio* in stone.

Ireland is quite an interesting laboratory for castle-studies because its occupation by the Anglo-Normans in the late 1100s and early 1200s coincides with a phase of intense experimentation with formal plan-types across Europe. Few places offered as many opportunities as Ireland for new architecture to be built without the encumberment of older structures; when one visits Chepstow in Wales, for example, one is conscious of the endless marrying of new architectural ideas to older structures, but nowhere in Ireland do we see that sort of accretion.

Very few of the wealthiest Irish castles of the twelfth and thirteenth centuries rival the wealthiest contemporary English or Continental castles, in either scale or sophistication. The explanation for this is a combination of several factors. First, Ireland was a small and underpopulated arena, and large and complex fortresses such as those found elsewhere in Europe were not needed, or were perceived not to be needed. Secondly, the resources for building on a massive scale were not available during the early stages of colonisation when castles needed to be built, and few of the Anglo-Norman adventurers had rich estates back home in England or Wales from which they could siphon resources. Finally, the labour required for building castles may not have been available, or it was simply inadequate. Castles were almost certainly built by forced labour, and even when labour was plentiful the progress of building was slow (Pounds 1990, 18). In England the availability of Anglo-Saxon labour and know-how imparted English characteristics to many early Norman castles (Renn 1994) and cathedrals (Grodecki 1958); the same cannot be said of Anglo-Norman buildings in Ireland.

Of Ireland's extant baronial castles only Trim can be regarded as being of the same architectural rank as the finest castles elsewhere. This judgement is based not so much on its scale — it is the most extensive castle in Ireland by some distance — but on the

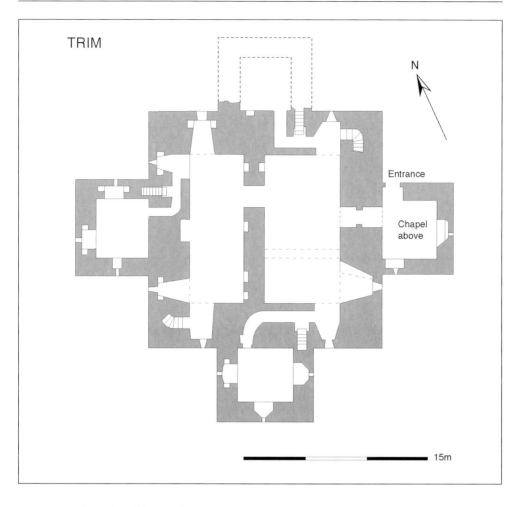

11   An outline plan of late twelfth-century Trim donjon at first-floor level (after Leask 1951)

sophistication of the design of its *donjon* or 'great tower' (**11**), and its possession of an early example of a curtain wall protected by round towers (**37**). The *donjon*, now known from dendrochronological studies to have been started in the 1170s (Condit 1996), is certainly the most unusual — one might even say exotic — of Irish *donjons*. It was once characterised as an anachronistic building because its plan, with its twenty different wall-faces and twelve corners, seemed to contravene certain principles of defence (Leask 1951). However, its Greek Cross plan suggests that the tower's patron, Hugh de Lacy, was more concerned with complex Christian symbolism and display than with defensibility; that Christian symbolism extended to the presence of a chapel directly above the entrance to provide spiritual rather than military protection for those entering the tower. Also, the labyrinthine access-ways through the tower may be interpreted not as a defensive device intended to confuse enemy intruders but as a conscious marriage of architectural planning and the complex social order of the castle's household.

Some of the royal castles in Anglo-Norman Ireland are also buildings of international interest. The early thirteenth-century royal castles at Dublin and Limerick are very unusual among Anglo-Norman castles of that date in Ireland and Britain in having near-symmetrical courtyard plans, cylindrical flanking towers and gate-towers, but no *donjons*. The best parallels for their overall plans and for some of their particular features are to be found in France (Knight 1987, 78-79; McNeill 1998, 53-54; O'Keeffe 1998a, 200, n81). The later royal castle at Roscommon, built around 1280 (**colour plate 4**), has a more symmetrical plan than either Dublin or Limerick and should be regarded, typologically and functionally, in the same context as the great Edwardian castles of north Wales; the documentation of the building-activity at Roscommon suggests that it may have been constructed a little earlier than Conway, Harlech and Beaumaris, so it is not inconceivable that it represents the earliest use in an Edwardian context of the type of courtyard plan for which the series is famous (O'Keeffe 1998a, 200).

Large courtyard castles with symmetrical ground plans were not restricted to royal castles. Ballymote, county Sligo, for example, was built at the same time as Roscommon. Indeed, it would not look out of place in Wales. Stylistic ideas were clearly moving between north-western Ireland and Wales in the late 1200s and early 1300s, as witness two other baronial castles in Ireland, Ballintubber, county Roscommon, and Greencastle, county Donegal: these have polygonal corner towers comparable with those used in north Wales at Caernarvon and Denbigh, while the entire plan of Greencastle was clearly emulative of that at Caernarvon (McNeill 1997, Fig. 59). Ballintubber covers a very extensive area, and its corner towers are so far apart than they could hardly have provided adequate fire along the wall. These three baronial castles of Ballymote, Ballintubber and Greencastle may have been sophisticated machines for the defence of households and the prosecution of military authority but, as at Trim, symbolism was clearly very important also in their designs; it is symbolism which probably explains their importation of architectural forms — circular or polygonal corner turrets — from contemporary royal buildings.

Halls and Great Towers

A number of the earliest stone castles of the Anglo-Normans in Ireland appear to have 'great towers' or *donjons*, essentially 'chamber towers' in which the private chambers of the lord and his household were arranged vertically through three or four storeys; these *donjons* used to be called keeps, but that term is not so popular in modern literature on castles. 'Great halls' were located elsewhere in castle complexes, and both their size and their physical separation from the chamber towers suggests that these halls were not places where households normally dined and were entertained but were reserved for public banquets and for the administration of public affairs. In contrast to the chamber towers, the great halls were frequently contained within comparatively low, rectangular structures; when these structures were single-storeyed the halls occupied the entire area, but when the structures were two-storeyed the halls occupied the upper floors.

The *donjon* at Trim stands in the centre of the castle's enclosure; there was a separate great hall along the curtain wall overlooking the river Boyne. The nearly-square *donjon* at Carrickfergus was erected shortly after John de Courcy established himself in Ulster in 1177 (McNeill 1981). It is a far more conventional building than the Trim *donjon*, and it would not look out of place alongside the *donjons* at places like Scarborough in Yorkshire, buildings which are sometimes described in the literature in England as 'tower keeps'. The great hall at Carrickfergus no longer survives above ground, but its windows are preserved in the curtain wall adjacent to the *donjon*. At Adare, county Limerick, is a smaller *donjon* of square plan. It is located within an inner enclosure, and in the outer enclosure are two halls, a small one dating from *c*1200, and a larger, more complex hall dating, according to McNeill's reading of its fabric (1997, 23), from later in the thirteenth century.

Several Irish *donjons* of rectangular plan have cylindrical drum-towers at their corners. The earliest of these may be Carlow Castle, erected at the start of the thirteenth century (**12**). The unfinished *donjon* at Terryglass, county Tipperary, which is a little less symmetrical in plan, could be of a similar date. Lea Castle, county Laois, may date from the middle of the thirteenth century. Ferns, county Wexford, has been identified as the fourth example of the class (Leask 1951), but McNeill makes a convincing case for regarding it not as a *donjon* but as a sophisticated type of enclosure castle with a small light-well acting as the courtyard (McNeill 1997, 124). The type of *donjon* represented by Carlow, Terryglass and Lea has been described as an indigenous creation (Leask 1951; McNeill 1997) but there are good formal parallels in western France (O'Keeffe 1990b), and given that this is an area with which Ireland had close contacts in the middle ages as we will see in chapters 5 and 6, these parallels should be regarded as significant. Late medieval (fifteenth century) examples of the type are found at Dunmoe, county Meath, Delvin, county Westmeath, and Enniscorthy, county Wexford.

Ireland also has a small number of impressive cylindrical *donjons* (**colour plate 5**). The best known of these is at Nenagh, county Tipperary. This was built in the late 1100s and early 1200s. Some decades later, probably in the 1220s, it was elevated to a fourth storey. A new gate-building, complete with a great hall above the passage, was erected around the same time. Dundrum, county Down, has another cylindrical *donjon*, which can be identified as the *magna turris* mentioned in 1211-12 (McNeill 1980, 7). It is known that a great hall was also built at Dundrum, but nothing remains of it.

By contrast, the dominant buildings at Greencastle, county Down, and Athenry, county Galway, were once regarded as 'keeps' (Leask 1937) but are now identified as halls, and the private chambers of both castles were not in separate *donjons* but were positioned along the curtain walls and in the flanking towers (McNeill 1997, Fig. 48).

Other thirteenth-century castles, especially in western Ireland (Holland 1996), also have as their focal buildings rectangular towers with halls at first-floor level, but the comparatively small size of some of these halls, combined with a lack of evidence for private chambers elsewhere within many of the fortresses in question, suggests that these were simply private spaces for the use of lords and households rather than great public chambers. Indeed, the term which is now used to describe some of these buildings, 'hall houses' (McNeill 1997; Sweetman 1998), is an acknowledgement of their essentially domestic nature. Among the many fine examples are Moylough and Cargin, both in county Galway. The term 'hall-house' does not really convey just how impressive are some of these buildings. For example, the large rectangular buildings — described as 'keeps' at the time of their first publication — at the early thirteenth-century castles of Ballyderown, county Cork (O'Keeffe 1984), and Grenan, county Kilkenny (Waterman 1968), had substantial,

12   *The great tower of Carlow Castle, built in the early 1200s, had a rectangular block and four corner towers. The design, which is found at a small number of Irish castles of the thirteenth century, may be of western French origin*

well-lit halls at their first-floor levels, and the presence of a small mural oratory at Grenan, the better preserved of the two buildings, suggests that its hall was essentially a private space; indeed, the small oratory was directly above the entrance, and we can interpret this — as we did the chapel in the *donjon* at Trim — as an arrangement intended to provide spiritual protection to those entering below (Coughlan *forthcoming*). It would probably be wrong, of course, to think that none of these halls was ever used for public events. Functions were not fixed forever in the architecture of the medieval secular world, and this is very apparent in the ambiguous and interchangeable use of words like *turris* ('tower'), *domus* ('house'), *camera* ('chamber'), and *sala/aula* ('hall') in medieval documentary contexts (Barthélemy 1988). One can easily imagine furniture being moved and timber partitions being wheeled into place when the need arose, at least in large halls like Ballyderown. Indeed, there is a stump of a cross-wall in Grenan which suggests that one end of the hall was partitioned at least partially from the remainder of the hall.

Ballymoon Castle

One of the most remarkable of all Anglo-Norman buildings in Ireland is Ballymoon Castle, county Carlow (**colour plate 6**; Leask 1944; McNeill 1997; O'Keeffe 2001b). It appears to have been built at the end of the thirteenth century or the start of the following century, but nothing is known of its history. A local tradition that the castle was left unfinished seems to be correct because the manner in which almost all the walls terminate at the same horizontal level is inconsistent with destruction in war or deliberate dismantling by post-medieval stone-robbers (**13**). Ballymoon must have already cost an enormous amount of money when it was abandoned.

Ballymoon was intended to be a suite of rooms around a central, almost-square, courtyard; the boundary walls of the courtyard may never have been built to their full height, and most (if not all) of the rooms were left unroofed. A large first-floor hall was planned along its north wall and a second hall, also at first-floor level, was planned along its west wall. The first of these halls was to have been a very grand room indeed: a double fireplace was built to warm the dais end, and large windows with plunging sills were set high in the side walls beneath the timber roof to cast light on those assembled in the hall. The second hall would not have been as large, but the *in situ* remains of moulded window stones suggests it would have been no less impressive a sight. Smaller rooms around the courtyard, several of them with their own garderobes (toilets) and fireplaces, were intended to provide lodgings. The location of the private chamber of the castle's 'owner' — we are not quite sure who he was or what we should call him — is not certain, but it was probably at one or other end of the larger hall.

No attempt was made to give Ballymoon a sophisticated system of defence and this, given its remote location in hilly land under constant threat from the Gaelic-Irish, is surprising. There are no cylindrical towers to provide lines of fire along its walls, and the square towers which it possesses are not only placed asymmetrically and at irregular intervals but are primarily garderobe towers. There are cross-shaped loops penetrating the outer walls (**14**), but they too are irregularly disposed to constitute a formal system of defence, and some of them are inside the projecting towers beside the garderobes. The gateway was simply a passage through the suite of rooms, even if it was protected by some

13   *Ballymoon Castle, county Carlow. Visible in this photograph are the foundations of the inner wall, and (on the left-hand side) the remains of one of the great hall windows. The condition of the outer wall is consistent with the view, held in local tradition, that the castle was never finished. The low tree-covered earthwork in the distance is a moated site, possibly contemporary with the castle*

14   Ballymoon Castle, county Carlow, looking southwards along the site of the unfinished east range; the rooms along the east and south sides of the castle were provided with cross-loops

form of machicolation or fore-building. Despite all this, Ballymoon would have been quite a well-protected building because its outer wall was clearly intended to rise to a very considerable height.

The patron of this extraordinary building must have been a man with considerable resources. The fact that Ballymoon had not been a place of any significance before the castle was started suggests that it was ear-marked to be important and that the castle was going to be at its core. It is tempting to attribute the castle's abandonment in an unfinished state to the well-documented antagonistic activities of the Gaelic-Irish in the Carlow region, but the explanation may be a little less exciting: perhaps the scale and elaboration proposed for the building were over-ambitious and the project had to be abandoned for reasons of finance, or perhaps the project was shelved with the death of the castle's patron. Is it possible that the castle was being built by, or was intended for, Roger Bigod, the earl of Norfolk, who held the Liberty of Carlow (in which Ballymoon is located) for over thirty-five years until his death in 1306?

Gaelic-Irish stone castles in the thirteenth century

The building of earth-and-timber fortresses by the Gaelic-Irish in the twelfth century is historically-documented, as we saw in the previous chapter. However, we know very little about the Gaelic-Irish construction and use of castles between the end of the twelfth century and the middle of the fourteenth century, whether those castles were of earth-and-timber or of stone.

The process of castle-building by the indigenous Gaelic-Irish population of eastern Ireland was largely derailed by the arrival of the Anglo-Normans. It seems likely that the process of castle-building continued uninterrupted in the non-colonial parts of western Ireland, but we have not yet identified more than a small number of castles which are its product, and even some of those which have been identified as Gaelic-Irish may actually be of colonial origin. The stone castle at Connor, county Antrim, illustrates the problem. Located at the centre of its territory, it may have been the residence of the king of Ui Tuitre in the middle of the thirteenth century (McNeill 1997, 158-60), but its form — a polygonal enclosure — has good colonial parallels (McNeill 1997, Fig. 100). While it may be a Gaelic-Irish copy of a locally-popular colonial type, perhaps we should consider two other possibilities: first, that it was simply reoccupied by the Gaelic-Irish having been built by colonists in an aborted attempt to control Ui Tuitre, and secondly, that it was built with labour and know-how hired from the colony by the local Gaelic-Irish king. Another problematic site is Castle Kirke, county Galway: it has been identified as one of two castles erected by the sons of Ruaidhri Ua Conchobair in the 1230s (McNeill 1997, 161-3), but a case has also been made for it being a colonial castle (Perros 1997, 2), and its architecture — a two-storeyed block with corner pilasters and an upper hall — certainly has parallels in that context (Lynn 1986, 102-3; O'Keeffe 1998a, 194).

The fourteenth century: termination or transformation?

The fourteenth century was regarded by Harold Leask as a period in which comparatively few castles were erected in Ireland. There is certainly a dearth of historical references to new castles in this period, and historical sources do convey the impression that famine, plague and endemic war together stretched to breaking-point the resources of the colonists, Ireland's established castle-builders. Leask presented his material in such a manner that for many generations of students of Irish castles the differences in scale and architectural conception between, on the one hand, the great royal and baronial fortresses of the late 1200s and early 1300s, and, on the other, the small but elegant tower-houses of the 1400s and later, were not inconsistent with a century-long hiatus.

The model of hiatus in the fourteenth century is no longer so firmly held, principally on the grounds that there are more historically-documented acts of castle-construction between 1200 and 1300 than Leask recognised (Barry 1993). But the very act of searching for castles with which to challenge the model privileges unnecessarily the model itself. After all, the idea of a fourteenth-century hiatus between the colonial halls or enclosure-castles and the later tower-houses presupposes that we can date accurately the majority of the tower-houses to the fifteenth and sixteenth centuries. Our dating is not accurate, however: comparatively few tower-houses have historical dates, and, as Tom McNeill has correctly pointed out (1997, 173-4), there are no certain criteria by which we can distinguish work of 1350-1450 from that of 1450-1550. In any case, the offer of subsidies by central government to prospective builders of tower-houses in the Pale in the early fifteenth century cannot be interpreted, as Leask had argued (1951, 76-7; *see* pp50-1 below), as the beginning of tower-house construction on the island. Moreover, there is no reason why the fourteenth century period should have seen a slump in the construction

15   *The sixteenth-century hall and tower of Coolhull Castle, county Wexford (Photograph: Dúchas, The Heritage Service, reproduced with permission)*

of new castles. Periods of unrest were sometimes periods of prolific building-activity, and nowhere is there better evidence of this than in England during the civil war of the early twelfth century when many new castles and churches were erected; given that fourteenth-century Ireland saw the building of many new churches (McNeill 1986), it seems inherently likely that new castles — a more urgent need — were also built.

Mention may be made here of one interesting group of castles in south county Wexford which illustrates very well why the fourteenth century should be seen as a period of continuity, not discontinuity. Coolhull (**15**) is the castle by which this group is generally known (Jordan 1991, 36-7). Here a long hall lit by fine twin-light windows has a high chamber tower at one end. This splendid building may date from the sixteenth century. Other examples of the same type and date have been identified in this county (O'Callaghan 1980-1). One castle in the group, Rathumney, connects these post-1400 structures with the hall-houses of the thirteenth century. What remains at Rathumney is a long building which had a stone partition separating the chamber from the hall, and that chamber probably rose over the roof of the hall as in the other Coolhull-type castles, but Rathumney's details, such as they survive, suggest it is a hall-house dating from the end of the thirteenth century.

Tower-houses

The tower-house is the dominant type of late medieval castle in Ireland but we must be careful not to forget that it was but one building in the typical castle complex of the late middle ages. Many tower-houses had associated bawns which were enclosed by stone walls or, less frequently it seems, by quick-set, palisades, or earthen banks.

In 1591 Ludolf von Münchhausen, a German travelling in Ireland, described the houses of noblemen as follows:

> Their houses are usually built in the form of a tower surrounded by a wall. Yet they do not live in those but keep them as a fortress. Nearby they keep a house, badly built unlike our farm-houses, where they light a fire in the middle. Right at the top is seated the man of the house with his wife, around them the servants according to their rank (Ó Riain-Raedel 1998, 230).

If the house — would 'hall' be a better word? — was the place for eating, the tower was clearly the private space into which the household retreated at the end of the day. It is not inconceivable that von Münchhausen was brought into the tower that night and that he simply made no record of it. Richard Stanihurst, writing about the same time, noted that castles in Ireland had towers in which the household could sleep safely and 'big and spacious palaces of white clay and mud' in which the household feasted (Lennon 1981, 146).

There are extant sites which we might identify as the type of castle in which von Münchhausen was welcomed as a guest. At Carrigogunnell, county Limerick, for example, there was a house or a hall in the bawn a short walk away from the tower. Elsewhere in Ireland, as at Shrah, county Offaly, and Athclare, county Louth, for example, the tower had a house or hall attached to it. The finest examples of separated halls and chambers are probably in the castles of Newcastle West and Askeaton, two great fortresses of the earls of Desmond which are located in county Limerick (McNeill 1997, Figs 106, 109); each of the halls was actually built in the thirteenth century but refurbished in the 1400s.

Far more common, however, are castles in which these various activities — eating, sleeping, entertaining guests — were simply contained within the one building, and that building was usually a tower. Luke Gernon described one for us in *c*1620:

> We are come to the castle already. The castles are built very strongly, and with narrow stairs, for security. The hall is the uppermost room, let us go up, you shall not come down again until tomorrow. The lady of the house meets you with her train. Salutations past, you shall be presented with all the drinks in the house, first the ordinary beer, then *aqua vitae* [whisky], then old ale, the lady tastes it, you must not refuse it. The fire is prepared in the middle of the hall, where you may sollace yourself until supper time, you shall not want sack or tobacco. By this time the table is spread and plentifully furnished with a variety of meats, but ill-cooked and without sauce. When you come to your chamber do not expect canopies and curtains (Leask 1946, 91-2).

Designs

Irish tower-houses display very considerable architectural diversity, but some degree of generalisation is possible. The ground plan is usually square or slightly rectangular, the stairs rise to the left of the main doorway and then ascend in a clockwise direction from the main door to the parapet, each of the rooms is reached by a door off the stairs, and there is barrel-vaulting over one or two of the rooms. The larger windows tend to be towards the top, and they are often mullioned. Windows lower in the towers are smaller and narrower, and their design sometimes indicates that they were used for firearms. The parapets, if they survive, may have crenellations and machicolations; chimneys and gables may be flush with these or concealed behind them. Larger tower-houses, particularly in southern and midland Ireland, can have a series of smaller rooms opening off the main stairs, sometimes at the same floor level as the main rooms but sometimes also at split levels. In those same tower-houses it is not uncommon for the spiral stairs to terminate at the upper room and for other stairs to ascend to roof-level in another corner of the building. Fireplaces are generally set into the walls, and it is generally into the long side walls rather than the short end walls. Gernon's observation that the fire was in the centre of the hall finds support at only a few castles: at Clara, county Kilkenny, for example, a tower-house at which many of the above features are present, the upper hall must have had a central hearth and a louvre in the roof because there is no fireplace in the side walls (**16**). Tower-houses today have their stone-work exposed, but in the middle ages they, like the Anglo-Norman castles before them, would have had a skin of harling which protected the stone-work from water-penetration. That harling also gave castles a white colour. Hence we have references in medieval contexts to 'white castles of stone' (*Caithréim Thoirdelbhaigh* ii, 2) and 'white-gleaming castles' (Leerssen 1996, 177).

Some late medieval lords possessed quite massive tower-houses. Barryscourt Castle, county Cork, has a substantial tower-house of fifteenth-century date (**colour plate 7**) comprising a rectangular block with large rectangular towers at two corners and a small turret at a third corner; there is a very fine private chapel in one of the towers (O'Keeffe 1997). One of the finest of all tower-houses is at Bunratty, county Clare. The principal residence of the O'Briens of Thomond in the fifteenth and sixteenth centuries, this is a great four-storey block flanked by square corner turrets of varying sizes; arches span the distance between the two north turrets and the two south turrets. There was no shortage of accommodation for the household and guests, and there were even private chapels in two of the turrets; there were also fourteen garderobes. Movement through Bunratty is via a bewildering network of stairs and passages. Bunratty, like Ballymoon of two centuries earlier, is a complex and sophisticated expression of Medieval social organisation and identity.

Tower-houses often reveal their builders to have had an aesthetic consciousness. Few towers lack elegance as they rise from gentle batters to crenellated parapets, and the crenellations themselves are sometimes rather like plumage as they rise spike-like to much greater height than is needed. Virtually all towers possess at least some moulded stonework on their interior and exterior walls. Doors and windows facing the outside world invariably have dressed surrounds; sometimes they are further embellished with symmetrical motifs picked out on the surface of the stone. The window types — among them ogees and cusped-ogees, single and in pairs — can generally be paralleled in

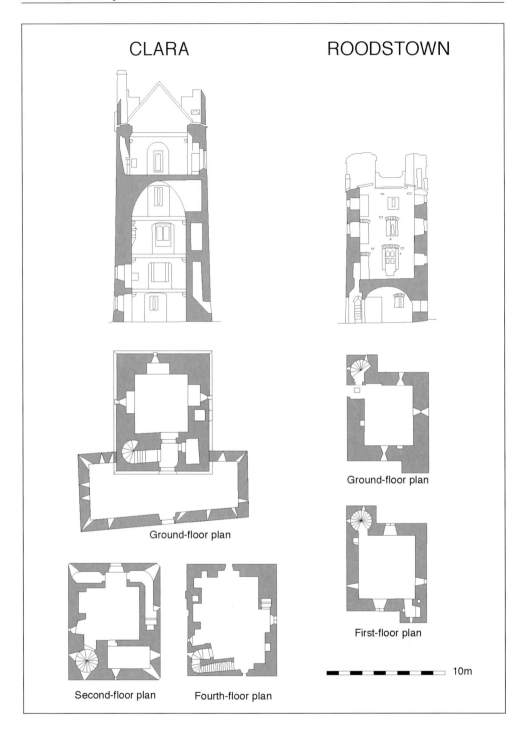

16   Cross-sections and floor plans of two fifteenth-century tower-houses. Left: Clara Castle, county Kilkenny, a typical tower-house of the Ormond earldom in Kilkenny and southern Tipperary. Right: Roodstown Castle, county Louth, a typical tower-house of the English Pale (after O'Keeffe 1997)

contemporary churches; an especially good example of this is at Lackeen Castle, county Tipperary, where the twin-light window with a quatrefoil which lights the upper hall can be paralleled very closely in the west façade of the nearby Augustinian friary at Lorrha. Windows and doorways sometimes carry actual carvings in relief of various motifs: for example, at the small fifteenth-century urban tower-house in Carlingford, county Louth, which is known as the Mint, there are interlace designs which seem to be straight out of the repertoire of early-medieval Irish art. Sheela-na-gigs, caricature-like carvings in relief of small, naked female figures, usually in explicit poses, are also found on tower-houses, usually half-way up the wall or at one of the corners; these symbols may have been intended to ward off evil. The most remarkable display of sculpture on the exterior wall of a castle is unquestionably at Lynch's Castle, an urban tower-house in Galway city (Johnson 1998). In an extraordinary demonstration of the sculptor's craft, plaques and armorials of Lynch and Fitzgerald families, and a plaque bearing the royal arms of Henry VII, share space on its walls with rows of vine leaves and fabulous gargoyles. Ornamental sculpture was not confined, however, to the exteriors of tower-houses: the arches of the window embrasures in the upper hall of Ballynacarriga Castle, county Cork, for example, have vine leaves and simple interlace as well such religious symbols as the Instruments of the Passion and the Crucifixion. Similar religious iconography embellishes the windows in the hall of Granny Castle, county Kilkenny.

Regional traditions of tower-house architecture

What is most remarkable about the tower-house is that it was popular among all of late medieval Ireland's populations, whether they were Gaelic-Irish or of colonial extraction. Its distribution, however, is not even across the island: the heaviest concentrations are in the southern half of Ireland, from Wexford through Kilkenny, Cork and Tipperary, to Limerick, Clare and Galway, and there are concentrations in coastal regions, particularly along the south and east coasts; central Ulster and the north midlands have low numbers of examples (Ó Danachair 1977-79). Within this uneven spread are very many local and regional traditions of architectural forms. Along the river valleys of north Cork, for example, are towers with curving corners (among them are Castlecooke on the river Araglin, Cloghleigh on the river Funcheon [**colour plate 8**], and Cregg and Lohort on the river Blackwater), and in the Ards area of south-east Down, for example, are some towers (Kilclief, Jordan's, Audley's) with two turrets projecting to the front of a square block with a great arched machicolation spanning the distance between them.

One of the most striking regional traditions can be identified in the lands of the English Pale, that part of Ireland which remained loyal to the Crown in the fifteenth and sixteenth centuries (O'Keeffe 1991). Not all the towers here are of the same plan or superstructure, but there is consistency within a narrow spectrum of forms. Most are simple three- or four-storey blocks with vaulted lower storeys, and many have between one and four projecting angle turrets of square or circular plan; where there are two turrets they are normally arranged in diagonally-opposed corners (**16**). Multiple turrets are a particular feature of tower-houses of the north end of the Pale (counties Meath and Louth). Tower-houses belonging to the clergy and attached to Pale churches (**17**), and those located along the streets of Pale towns, also display these characteristics.

17 *Newcastle Lyons church, county Dublin, probably dating from c1400. Its well-preserved western tower — which was primarily a residence rather than a bell-house — has many parallels in the English Pale*

One of the most elaborate of the Pale tower-houses is Dunsoghley, county Dublin, built in the fifteenth century. It is a four-storeyed rectangular block with rectangular turrets of varying size at its four corners. Dunsoghley's central block has a vaulted lower storey, as is normal in the Pale; the only vaults in the corner towers are simple corbel vaults at roof level. The upper room of the central block has its original timber roof. Parallels in the Pale for the plan-type represented at Dunsoghley include Castletown (Dundalk), county Louth, Killeen, county Meath, and Kilsallaghan, county Dublin.

Harold Leask attached great national significance to the tower-houses of the Pale, arguing that the offers of £10 subsidies made by the government in 1429 to landowners willing to build small towers to specified dimensions marks the beginning of the Irish tower-house sequence (1951, 76-77). However, the appropriate parliamentary act was not worded in such a way that we can interpret it as a call to create a new architectural idiom. On the contrary, it seems more likely that the authors of the act had in mind a type of building already existing on which the new subsidised towers could be modelled. In any case, this was not the first time that subsidies were offered to prospective castle-builders (Barry 1995, 224).

The provision of grants for the Pale tower-houses was the first of two governmental strategies for the defence of the region, the second and later strategy being the erection — or at least the proposed erection — of the earthwork in 1494-5 (O'Keeffe 1991). The grants for the castles were not taken from the royal purse but were generated by levies imposed on the inhabitants of the Pale counties. The grants remained available into the second half of the fifteenth century, but they were probably no longer on offer once the parliament of 1494-5 decided on an earthwork and entrusted the county administrations with its construction.

Examples of '£10 castles', as Leask styled them, are difficult to identify with confidence. Some tower-houses, such as Donore, county Meath, seem to conform to the measurements laid down in the 1429 act, but none of the buildings for which a grant is actually recorded still survives. The fact that we cannot readily identify subsidised tower-houses is clearly significant. A sum of £10 would not have made the difference between building and not building, and landowners already intent on having tower-houses probably felt that £10 was an insufficient inducement to abandon their preferred tower-house designs.

Tower-houses allowed the privileged inhabitants of the Pale, and indeed of other parts of Ireland, to sleep safely at night. However, we cannot possibly measure the impact of the tower-houses on the patterns of Gaelic-Irish raiding in the Pale. If the towers did provide adequate protection for the Pale it was simply by dint of their numbers, and not because they were intervisible or were located along the routes by which the Gaelic-Irish traditionally raided English land. It is interesting in this regard that the guidelines for those builders of tower-houses who wished to avail of the grants make no reference whatsoever to the siting or specific location of the towers.

Origins of the Irish tower-house

The search for the formal origins of Irish tower-houses is somewhat handicapped by the intractable problems of fourteenth-century archaeology. We simply do not know, even in very broad outline, the trajectory of castle-development in that period. It is likely that tower-houses were being built in the fourteenth century (Cairns 1987; O'Keeffe 1987; Barry 1993), but this is simply a readjustment of the chronology, not a resolution to the problem of origins.

We can dismiss, first of all, the case for importation of the tower-house idea from outside Ireland. The case for Continental influence is especially weak. Small tower-form castles proliferate in late medieval France, Ireland's closest Continental neighbour, but they bear no close resemblance, either in design or in detail, to the Irish towers. Scottish and Northumbrian tower-houses provide some points of comparison with Irish towers, and many of them seem to be earlier than the earliest Irish towers, but the formal and conceptual parallels between the series are not strong enough to sustain the idea that the tower-house idea crossed into Ireland from northern Britain; in any case, the greatest concentration of tower-houses in Ireland (Munster and south Leinster) is very distant from the sea-crossing between Ulster and Britain. The only Irish buildings to display strong Scottish characteristics are the fortified houses of early seventeenth-century Scottish planters in Ulster (Jope 1951).

By contrast, the case for the Irish tower-house being the product of indigenous architectural development with no significant external input is very strong. We can dismiss any suggestion that the first tower-houses in Ireland were built by the Gaelic-Irish; it is

18 The circular tower-house of Balief Castle, county Kilkenny; this is of sixteenth-century date

unlikely that they could have created tower-house forms not having had much experience previously in building halls or chamber towers of stone. The old colonial families, however, were accustomed to the type of sophisticated architectural environment which a tower-house provided, and so the origin of the Irish tower-house is to be sought in their company.

The *donjons* of the thirteenth century are certainly part of the tower-house pedigree; indeed, they were still in use when the fashion for tower-houses began. There are very obvious differences in size and detail between the two types of building, but we are compelled to see a connection because both contained private rooms, and those rooms were graded from bottom to top. The indebtedness of the tower-house to the Anglo-Norman *donjon* is perhaps most apparent in the circular tower-houses which are scattered in small numbers across north Cork, Tipperary, Waterford, and Kilkenny (**18**): it is no coincidence that Anglo-Norman *donjons* of circular plan are concentrated in south Tipperary (Ardfinnan, Kiltinan), east Cork (Inchiquin), and Waterford (Dungarvan,

Mocollop). The rectangular hall or hall-house was, as we noted above, the preferred form of castle residence in later thirteenth-century Ireland, and it may also therefore have been an influential form in the evolution of tower-houses, despite its comparatively low height. The presence of small and large rooms at each storey in many southern Irish tower-houses (see, for example, the fourth-floor in Clara Castle: **16**) may even reflect the manner in which long halls were partitioned into large and small units.

Thus far we have only considered the *formal* origins of tower-houses. Far more central to our understanding of later medieval Ireland than tracking the movement and development of architectural forms and motifs is the origin of the *idea* of the tower-house as an arena in which social and domestic rituals are played-out. This is a matter which has not received much attention in the literature, but it would repay close consideration. Suffice it to speculate here that the emergence of the tower-house represents a seismic shift in how the lordly class of the later middle ages viewed itself: first, the vertical and hierarchical arrangement of spaces within the towers may have a homologous relationship with the social order of the later medieval world, and secondly, the multiplicity of such towers, often within sight of each other, suggests that later medieval lords felt an affiliation with each other, and that the power enjoyed by any one lord was somewhat reinforced by the visual reminders on the landscape that other lords held similar power by similiar means.

Sixteenth- and seventeenth-century tower-houses

The tower-house continued in vogue into the seventeenth century. One of the finest examples, Derryhivenny, county Galway, has an inscription informing us that it was built in 1643, while Maurice Craig has drawn attention to an even later example (dated 1683) at Castle Ffrench, also in county Galway (1982, 109). A precise chronology of the architectural forms and details of tower-houses of sixteenth- and early seventeenth-century date is not possible, but some of the features which indicate such a date include gables and high chimneys which are flush with the outer walls, mullioned and transomed windows which are sometimes arranged symmetrically, and an absence of internal stone vaults. The tradition of the tower-house was probably in abeyance from the first or second decade of the 1600s, and, with very few exceptions, it certainly did not survive long into the second half of the seventeenth century.

Although we are accustomed to looking at them, such features as exposed gables and chimneys, and large windows, are actually quite incongruous in tower-houses. It seems best to interpret them as importations from a genre of domestic architecture — the great aristocratic house — rather than as features which slowly developed as part of the tower-house tradition. The importation may have had a symbolic motivation. At Grange, county Kildare, for example, a typical tower-house of the Pale tradition was capped with curvilinear battlements of no practical value, and the parapet had some elegant chimney stacks through which there were no flues (**19**). It is true that mullioned and transomed windows served a real purpose in allowing in more light, but they also changed the interaction between the worlds inside and outside the castle. On the one hand, the occupants of castles could enjoy a complete view of the outside world by gazing through large, glazed windows; those outside the castles, on the other hand, had an even more

19   *Grange Castle, county Kildare, with its battery of high — and mainly fake — chimney stacks
(Photograph: Dúchas, The Heritage Service, reproduced with permission)*

tantalising hint of the luxuries inside than was the case when castle windows were narrow and only dim light emanated from them.

Most tower-houses of the 1500s and early 1600s were equipped for defence with firearms, although the presence of gun-loops cannot be taken as an indicator of a late date: the earliest recorded use of firearms in Ireland is in 1487, and cannon is first mentioned as being used in the following year (Kerrigan 1995, 19, 21), but the earliest record of a gun in Ireland is in the middle of the fourteenth century (de hÓir 1984). We can see the impact of the advent and widespread availability of gunpowder on the designs of some tower-houses. At Burt, county Donegal, for example, diagonally-opposed flanking turrets were built for the purpose of providing artillery fire along all the walls, while the tower at Mashanaglass, county Cork, had small triangular gun-room projections at two of its corners. The circular or square flanking towers (complete with small apertures through their walls) which mark the corners of bawn-walls around many tower-houses reflect the use of guns in the protection of residential properties.

From the middle of the sixteenth century a new type of fortification arrived in Ireland: the so-called 'star-shaped' fort. Many examples of these survive, and quite a few are very well documented (Kerrigan 1995). The best-known examples, if not also the finest, are James Fort and Charles Fort in Kinsale, county Cork, built around 1605 and 1680 respectively to defend the entrance to the town. Ramparts with spike-like projections to carry heavy guns were also built around towns. Star-shaped forts cannot really be regarded in the same context as the castles which we have been discussing. First of all, the design of these forts was a new introduction from overseas; the design had originally been generated in Italy or France late in the fifteenth century, and from there it spread northwards to England, Germany and the Low Countries, and eventually to Ireland. Secondly, and more imporantly, most star-shaped fortifications appear fundamentally to have been places of aggressive defence populated by professional soldiers.

Defensible houses at the end of the middle ages

Defensible houses — residences capable of being defended but not intended to be fortress-like in appearance — appeared in Ireland towards the end of the 1500s. The house at Carrick-on-Suir, county Tipperary, tacked onto the front of an earlier castle in 1585, is the finest of all (**20**), although it is rather atypical among the surviving examples in having a low and elongated façade which conceals a splendid first-floor hall. There has been no national survey of defensible houses of the late 1500s and early 1600s, but dozens may survive, and it is apparent that they conform to a restricted range of specific designs. One design is that represented by the houses at Kanturk, county Cork, and Portumna and Burncourt, both in county Tipperary. Built around 1610, 1620 and 1640 respectively, these have central blocks of rectangular plan and projecting corner towers of square plan. Portumna, the finest of the group, has a central block so wide that it needed a longitudinal spine-wall for stability and flooring. Another very similar design is represented by Rathfarnham, county Dublin, and Raphoe, county Donegal, built in the 1580s and 1630s respectively, but here the corner turrets are splayed in the manner of bastions on a star-shaped fort. A third comparable design is represented by two Cork houses, Mountlong

20   Ormond Castle, Carrick-on-Suir, county Tipperary, is Ireland's only intact Elizabethan mansion. The towers in the background survive from an earlier castle

and Monkstown, both dating from the 1630s, and with one related Galway house, Glinsk, probably of the same date. In these buildings the central block is only one bay in width so the exterior views are dominated by the corner towers. In addition to these four-towered houses, there are early seventeenth-century houses with three projecting towers (Coppinger's Court, county Cork), with cross-shaped plans (Ightermurragh, county Cork), and with T-shaped plans (Ballincar, county Sligo).

These defensible houses did not *develop* out of tower-houses, as has been suggested (Kerrigan 1995, 65; O'Conor 1998, 25). Rather, they represent Ireland's belated *rapprochement* with the Renaissance, and in doing so they articulate a significant change in the self-perception of Ireland's gentry as the middle ages gave way to the modern period.

Epilogue

Andrew Saunders' much-quoted definition of a castle as 'a fortified residence which might combine administrative and judicial functions, but in which military considerations were paramount' (1977, 2) seems, at first glance, to be entirely reasonable. It expresses well our expectation that castles are places of physical strength and lordly power, while it also indicates the latitude which we allow ourselves in attaching the word 'castle' to different types of structure. Most syntheses on medieval castles spring from such a definition. But whose definition is this? Did inhabitants of the medieval world make judgements about the defensive capacities of buildings before deciding to call them castles? Orderic Vitalis observed that the late Anglo-Saxon landscape had few of the fortresses (*munitiones*) which the Normans called *castella*, and a century later Giraldus Cambrensis remarked that the Irish cared little for *castella* (O'Keeffe 1998a, 187). But did these men define 'castle' as we do? We cannot answer these questions, and that is precisely the point: the medieval world has not told us in unambiguous terms exactly how we should interpret the word 'castle'.

Castle-studies in Ireland, as elsewhere, have suffered for more than a century from a sort of military determinism. When 'complexity of defences' is offered as a defining feature of 'true castles' (O'Conor 1998, 76) and some structures excluded from consideration on that account, it is without the authority of the people of the middle ages who used them. The desire of medieval builders and their patrons to create impregnable barriers in stone, and to reconcile that need with the need for habitable dwelling-space, has long been viewed as the dynamic of the medieval castle's architectural evolution. This is the model which modern English scholarship has inherited from JH Round (1902) via RA Brown (1976), and Irish scholarship from Harold Leask; the reputation of the late thirteenth-century Edwardian castles of north Wales as the apogee of medieval castle architecture clearly rests on this premise. The problem with this way of thinking is that it effectively reduces the patrons and users of castles to passive participants in the process of architectural development. The truth, as always, is far more complex. Castles, like churches, were actually physical expressions of complex medieval ideas about the world.

3 Country life: landscape, settlement, farming

The bond which rural people in modern Ireland have with land and with place is as much emotional as practical, and the slow rate of change in rural habitats acts towards its reinforcement. Rural communities share a sense of neighbourhood which has less to do with the proximity of one household to another than is the situation in urban environments but is based instead on direct or ancestral blood relationships. Those bonds which exist among rural people, and between them and their landscape, are very deeply embedded, and they reflect ancient — pre-feudal, at any rate — social orders which were based not on the concept of tenure but on kinship and familial proprietorship of land.

Anglo-Norman manors

The feudalisation of Gaelic-Irish society at the end of the first millennium AD involved, as we noted earlier (p26), the creation of new divisions of land of which the modern townland is the descendant. The actual boundaries of these land units, however, must have reflected very closely the rural geography of Ireland in the immediate pre-feudal period; it is difficult to see how a new system of territorial organisation could have been created so effectively unless constructed on the foundations of existing territories. By the same token, the land units of the Anglo-Normans — the cantreds and manors — were themselves coterminous with the territories of pre-colonial Ireland, and they even preserve the native Irish toponymy (**21**).

The pattern of manor formation by the Anglo-Normans in Ireland is well-established: large fiefs created during the early stages of conquest and colonisation were sub-divided by their lords into smaller holdings, but with the lords retaining their demesne land, and those smaller holdings were, in their turn, subdivided into still smaller holdings, again with these lesser lords retaining demesne land. The larger manors were generally held in return for military service, but lesser lords held their small tenements at an annual rent and with suit owed at the manor court.

The concept of manor was quite a complex one. Manors were units of land with fixed boundaries, but they were also self-regulating vehicles of social and economic

21   *The Anglo-Norman manor of Oughterard, county Kildare, preserves a pre-colonial place-name, and probably also the boundaries of an earlier estate. This photograph shows an abandoned ancient roadway and a small, ruined, tower-house (see Fig. 23)*

organisation, presided over by lords but populated by an assortment of graded tenants. The demesne portions of the manorial land were farmed by the lords. The remaining portions of land were let to the tenants. Some tenants held land by burgage tenure, for which they paid a rent; these we will meet in Chapter 4. The remainder of the tenants were *paysans*, peasants. The term 'peasant' suggests greater social homogeneity among rural dwellers than was the case, and modern parlance has robbed the word of honourable connotations. Some of these peasants were 'free tenants' who held their land in perpetuity, either by military service or by payment of a money rent.

Free tenants of Gaelic extraction were certainly not unknown on the manors (see, for example, Nicholls 1982), but the majority of such tenants came from England or Wales. We know very little of how they came to be in Ireland. They may have been compelled to make the journey to Ireland, and resettlement here would not necessarily have been a bleak prospect for them: Ireland was less densely populated that their homeland, and labour services on its manors may have been less exacting than was customary on the larger island. The chronology of their immigration is also unknown to us. A vision of a 'caravan of settlers ... arriving in the castle bailey on the morrow of the imposition of military domination' (Davies 1990, 43) may be justified in certain parts of the colony, but we should note that the Anglo-Norman estate of Kilsheelin, located in the richly fertile valley of the river Suir, was still predominantly Gaelic-Irish in the middle of the thirteenth century (Hennessy 1996, 121, 123). The likelihood is that different parts of the colony attracted settlers at different periods and with different levels of success. This process depended considerably on the energy of the lords themselves: some manorial lords may have involved themselves only peripherally in the detail of manorial organisation beyond their own demesne boundaries (Dyer 1985, 27-8), while others must have adopted a more hands-on approach to the matter of attracting settlers.

At the lowest end of the spectrum of inhabitants on the manors were the betaghs (*betagii*), tenants who were not free but who could be sold or given away with their holdings at the whim of their lords; however, in some cases (Empey 1982-3, 340-1), betaghs may have enjoyed a better deal than English cottiers (the equivalents on the Irish manors of the villeins on English manors). The betagh was not a new creation of the colonial period but had been a feature of pre-Norman Ireland (MacNiocaill 1966), and the draconian conditions in which they generally subsisted on the Anglo-Norman manors may have been what they had been accustomed to on pre-Norman estates. On the Anglo-Norman manors they often held their land *en bloc*, and the place-name Ballybetagh — the place/settlement of the food-providers — may signpost this.

We know the details of manorial organisation from the extents — fiscal surveys — of manors. Most of these documents date from the late thirteenth and fourteenth centuries, but this does not negate their value for reconstructing manorial organisation in the formative years of the colony: these surveys were intended to catalogue all forms of income issuing to the lord, and given that the rents and services by which the tenants of the manors held their lands had been fixed at the time of the conquest it matters little for the purpose of reconstructing the social geography of the manors that the earliest records of income usually date from the end of the colonial era (Empey 1982-3).

One manor among the many for which extents survive is the large episcopal manor of Cloyne, county Cork (**22**), an extent of which survives from the early fourteenth century (MacCotter and Nicholls [eds] 1996, 3-21). The detail of this extent is sufficient for us to understand its social and territorial structures. The colonial population here was divided into free tenants — their specific rank is not recorded — holding parcels of lands, sometimes in return for military service to the bishop, and cottiers who serviced the bishop's demesne land; gavillers, free tenants who were above the cottiers in social rank, are not recorded at Cloyne although they are recorded on other manors in Ireland. The free tenants held lands as large as six or eight ploughlands (up to a thousand acres), but there is no apparent correlation between the size of their parcels and the military services which they owed to the bishop; indeed, holdings of up to four ploughlands were simply held by rent and suit of court. The possessions of the cottiers — a cottage, sometimes with an acre attached — were very meagre, and their onerous tasks included tending the gaol, meadow and park. Cottiers also served on the bishop's 376-acre demesne at the small coastal fishing settlement of Ballycotton, and here their duty was to provide the bishop with fish, but they were at least guaranteed that the bishop would take no more fish than he needed. Other demesne lands attached to Cloyne had small numbers of English settlers of unspecified tenurial status, each with a messuage (the property on which the house was built) and a parcel of land of between two and twenty acres. Betaghs also lived on the Cloyne manor; some of them are recorded as farming 70 acres of their lord's demesne at Ballycotton, while others, referred to as *hibernici* (Irish), were located somewhere on the

22   Cloyne cathedral and Round Tower, county Cork; details of the manors or estates of the bishops of Cloyne are preserved in the Pipe Roll of Cloyne

ploughlands of one of the principal tenants. If the betaghs expected the bishop to be an especially caring lord they were sorely disappointed: he reserved the right to move them to wherever he wanted them to be, and to take possession of and sell their goods, and he obliged them to provide him with turf, to cart and stack his hay and corn, and to give him beasts or, if they had no beasts, their best garments.

Open fields, closed fields

Many factors conditioned agricultural yields on the manors. Manorial lords and their tenants had no control over climate, as they discovered to their detriment in the early fourteenth century when repeated wet seasons wreaked havoc on the crops. But for much of the thirteenth century the manors were successful machines for agricultural production. The rural population was probably quite low and surplus food was produced almost from the beginning of the colonial era. Indeed, as early as 1220 that surplus was being used to pay off debts (Lydon 1987a, 157). The capacity of manorial lords and their tenants to produce far more food than was required by themselves or their urban markets encouraged the crown to regard Ireland as a food factory for its overseas armies in the late thirteenth century (O'Keeffe 1998b).

How was manorial land farmed? The classic system of organisation of agricultural land in the twelfth and thirteenth centuries in England was the open-field system, and it has been argued that this was in operation on the Anglo-Norman manors in Ireland (Otway-

61

Ruthven 1951). In this system the farmland was generally divided into two or three sectors, each containing large fields, and within these sectors there was a rotation of arable crops. The land in one of the sectors was left as fallow; this was grazed, and its manuring made it good for arable use when it was needed again; meadow, low-lying, damp grassland, was regularly mown for hay for winter feed (**23**). Wheat (or less frequently rye) would generally be sown in winter on the land newly-released from fallow, and oats (or less frequently barley) would be sown in spring as the second cycle of crops (Down 1987, 463-77). Individual farmers often held their land in strips which were scattered across the fields in each of these sectors; the advantage of this system was that it ensured a fairly equitable distribution of good and bad land. The strips were not partitioned by permanent fences but were arranged in groups or furlongs which were cultivated as a unit, and it was these furlongs which then made up the fields.

There has long been a view that before and after 1169 the Gaelic-Irish only farmed infields and outfields (Mills 1891a; Leister 1976, 24), except when pressed into labour on crop-rotation systems by new colonial lords. It is true that there is no certain evidence for arable strips arranged within open-field furlongs prior to the Anglo-Norman arrival, but there is no reason why an open-field system should not have existed. Although we cannot properly assess its landscape significance, it is interesting that the heavy plough was used in Ireland in the tenth century (Brady 1993, 37). Furthermore, a text of that date or earlier indicates that the laying side-by-side of 'arable ridges' was, in one instance at least, an expression of 'mutual assistance and friendliness' between two dynasties (Charles-Edwards 1993, 419); this suggests a pattern of arable strips with ownership alternating from one strip to another, and that pattern would not be dissimilar to that which we have just described in the context of open-field farming. Nevertheless, when open-field farming is attested to historically or archaeologically it is on Anglo-Norman manors, and therefore we can only address it, as we do here, as an Anglo-Norman phenomenon.

The principal implement for breaking the ground in advance of sowing was, of course, the plough, but harrows, which were rectangular frames with downward-projecting 'teeth', were sometimes needed where the soil was particularly unyielding, not least in the immediate aftermath of scrub-clearance. Ploughs needed traction, and oxen were clearly the favoured beasts for this, at least on the demesnes. The manorial extents indicate that horses were also used, sometimes as an alternative to the heavier animals but sometimes alongside the oxen in the same plough teams. Oxen may have been slower, but they could be relied on to turn heavier soil more effectively (particularly in newly-created parcels of cultivation), they cost less to feed, and they did not need to be shod. Plough teams were not standardised, but teams of eight oxen appear to have been quite common. The Pipe Roll of John from 1212, which is our earliest record of agricultural practices in the colonial regions of Ireland, documents eight-oxen teams on a number of manors in Meath (Davies and Quinn [eds] 1941). At Ballyconnor, county Wexford (Barry 1977, 96-7; Colfer 1996) it is recorded in 1282-84 that two oxen had been stolen, leaving a stock of thirty-six, and that eight of them — clearly the demesne plough team — were to be kept inside a palisaded and moated enclosure.

The invention of the heavy plough or *carruca* (from which *carrucate* or ploughland is derived) had revolutionised arable farming across western Europe by the start of the

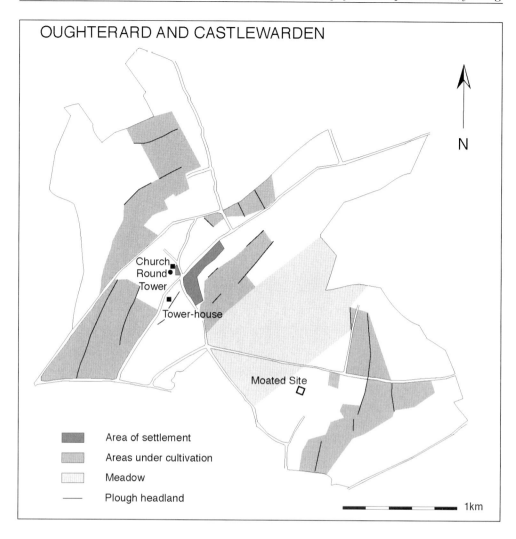

23   A reconstruction map of settlement and agriculture at the Anglo-Norman manors of Oughterard (to the north) and Castlewarden (to the south), county Kildare (after Hall, Hennessy and O'Keeffe 1985). The headlands formed by the turning of medieval ploughs provide the only landscape clues to the parcels of arable; those parts of this map which are not shaded presumably were also cultivated, but there is no evidence of this on the ground. Low-lying, marshy land between the two manors may well have been meadow in the middle ages; that land is now crossed by field drains, but these may not be of medieval date

second millennium AD. Some of its individual elements such as coulters and shares had long been features of ploughs, but it was the addition of the mouldboard for lifting and turning the soil which increased its efficiency so dramatically, and the further addition of iron-bound wheels facilitated both the movement of the entire apparatus and the maintenance of a consistent ploughing depth (Langdon 1988, 88-90; Brunner 1995, 25-6)

These fairly sophisticated ploughs appear to have been in use on the Irish manors — there is a reference to the purchase of axle-beams for the farms of Christ Church Cathedral, Dublin (Mills [ed] 1891b, 29-30) — and they would have allowed peasants to draw from the land the same rich bounty as in England.

Ploughing was an episodic activity in the middle ages, and its yield, although it did not need to be consumed immediately, had a short shelf-life. However, medieval ploughing had a long-term impact on the landscape, and nowhere is this better evidenced than in lowland England, particularly in the midlands (Lewis, Mitchell-Fox and Dyer 1997), and before proceeding to the Irish evidence we should consider briefly that evidence in England. Medieval peasants have bequeathed to the modern English landscape vast sheets of ridge-and-furrow corrugations arranged in long sinuous strips, often curving as a reversed 'S'. These English landscapes are now known to have originated in later Anglo-Saxon times, possibly in the ninth century, and their emergence is inextricably entwined with that of the village. The continued development of corrugated arable landscapes in Anglo-Norman times is powerful evidence of continuity in both the cultural identity and farming practice of the rural population of England across the historical divide of 1066, and the sheer scale of the ridges in many parts of England testifies to as many as seven or eight centuries of ploughing the same furrows.

The plough teams on these strips moved backwards and forwards along the length of the furlong, lifting and turning the plough at the end of each run. Ploughing stopped short of the furlong boundaries to give the team room for these manoeuvres, leaving bands of uncultivated ground at both ends of the furlongs. Small quantities of soil which had been dragged along the furrows in front of the plough or had stuck to its mouldboard slowly accumulated in these areas, and over time they formed substantial banks or 'headlands' at the ends of the furlongs. The reversed 'S' curves of so many strips are not easily explained, but they may be the result of the heavy and unwieldy oxen being made approach the furlong boundaries at an angle other than at 90° to allow easy turning.

Ridge-and-furrow is present in Ireland, but it is not as common as it is in lowland England, nor is it as accentuated, possibly because its life-span was considerably shorter. Flat ploughing — cutting one season's furrow through the previous season's ridge — may have been preferred in Ireland. At the adjacent manors of Oughterard and Castlewarden, county Kildare, the survival of headlands but not of any traces of ridges (**colour plate 9**) suggests that here flat ploughing was indeed preferred (Hall, Hennessy and O'Keeffe 1985). Notwithstanding this, Ireland's soils are not particularly well-suited to flat ploughing: heavy soils benefit from the drainage which is provided by deep, permanent furrows between ridges.

Ironically, our best means of tracing medieval open-fields in Ireland is by examination of the patterns of enclosure both on the ground and, more valuably, as they were recorded on eighteenth- and nineteenth-century estate maps and on mid-nineteenth century Ordnance Survey maps.

Two types of enclosed field of interest to us here are recorded on post-medieval cartographic sources for the manorialised lands of south-east Ireland, and both can be seen on the early eighteenth-century map of lands around Gowran, county Kilkenny (**24**). First, there are long, narrow fields which curve as they stretch across the paper landscapes, and

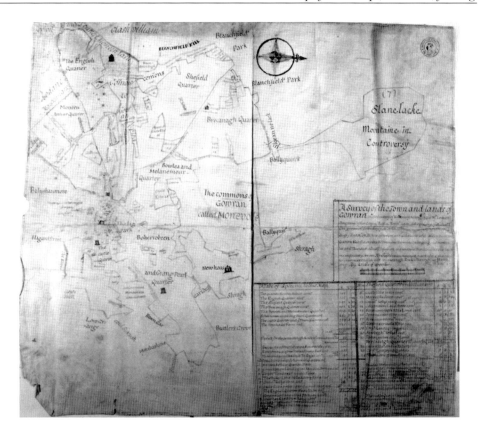

24   *An early eighteenth-century map of the Anglo-Norman borough of Gowran, county Kilkenny (NLI 21 F 55), showing the partial and piecemeal enclosure of strips and parcels of fields around the settlement (Photograph: National Library of Ireland, reproduced with permission)*

these represent very clearly the enclosure of several ridges of arable in the former open fields. The second type is comprised of larger fields which maintain the orientation and sometimes also the curvature of the smaller strips, and these represent the enclosure of entire furlongs or of parts of furlongs. Multiple strips amalgamated under the ownership of one individual by commercial purchase or by agreement among the farmers, may explain these fields. These large fields may, in many cases, simply preserve parcels of land which had never been subdivided into arable strips to be farmed by different men, although this may not be the case in Gowran where the land does appear to have been held as strips.

The chronology of the enclosure of manorial land is uncertain. It cannot be assumed that the process only began in post-medieval times, if only because estate maps such as that for Gowran, or Newcastle Lyons, county Dublin (Edwards, Hamond and Simms 1983), show that individual strips and bundles of strips had already been enclosed by the early eighteenth century. Nor can it be assumed either that the transformation of the landscape from 'open' to 'closed' was a single event, however long it took. The field patterns which were recorded at Gowran, for example, compare very well with the patterns which have been identified in English contexts as characteristic of the piecemeal enclosure of land in the late middle ages (Johnson 1996, 50-55). It is very likely that the enclosure of arable strips also started in the late middle ages in Ireland. Parcels of enclosed land are recorded from the fourteenth century: in the Dublin region, for example, demesne land which had been cultivated was not returning much money to its lord, the archbishop, and so it was converted to pasture, leased out, and enclosed (Otway-Ruthven 1964-8, 35-6).

Land which was enclosed may not actually have had any particular economic advantage over land which was not enclosed: it has been argued, for example, that land-enclosure in England between the sixteenth and eighteenth centuries did not increase agricultural yields or improve the productivity of labour (Allen 1992, 17). But once land was enclosed its status as private property was secure and there was no likelihood of it being reopened. Thus the collectivism of open-field farming was imperilled by the enclosure by an enterprising farmer of any portion of land within an open-field system. The well-documented absenteeism of many manorial lords during the 1300s, combined with the penchant among many lords for leasing their demesne lands from the start of the fourteenth century because it was cheaper than direct farming (Down 1987), may have loosened the seigneurial grip necessary to keep the fields open. One idea which might be explored in future research is that the enclosure of the landscape and the emergence of the tower-house were simultaneous and related phenomena in the late 1300s and the 1400s.

Milling

Cereal grain needed to be processed before it could be consumed. In dry weather that grain was harvested and separated, and then brought to the mill; in wet weather the thrashed grain needed to be dried before it could be milled. Corn-drying kilns were features of both town and country: a number of examples were found at the rears of street-fronting properties in Waterford (Hurley and Sheehan 1997, 276-7), while a very fine example of late thirteenth or early fourteenth-century date was found at Kilferagh, county Kilkenny (Hurley 1987), inside a moated site and in association with a barn, house and yard (**25**). Other examples were excavated at Ballynarahan, county Tipperary (Gowen 1988, 158-62) and Lough Gur (Cleary 1983, 67-8).

Milling could be a small-scale, domestic operation, as witness the fragments of rotary querns on many excavated urban and rural sites. The later medieval rotary querns are largely indistinguishable from those of early medieval date; however, one type of rotary quern — the pot quern, in which the lower stone has a lip or rim into which the upper stone sits — appears to be a new creation of the post-1169 period, and its distribution is largely confined to south-east Ireland (Caulfield 1969, 61).

Feudal custom dictated that grain had to be brought to the lords' mills. These mills were mechanised; they needed to be, particularly when a large population needed to be fed or when grain was intended for export. Mills powered by water were very common on both secular manors and monastic estates, and in the vicinity urban centres. Fast-flowing rivers or their tributaries provided ample water-power, but mill-races were sometimes necessary to direct the water towards the wheel and to provide a greater concentration of water. A

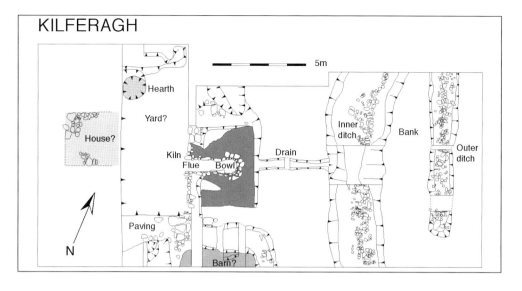

25   Kilferagh, county Kilkenny, corn-drying kiln (after Hurley 1987)

very fine mill-race survives at Athassel, an Augustinian priory in county Tipperary. Mill wheels were either horizontal or vertical, and in the case of the latter the rushing water could drive the wheel from below or could be directed to fall on the paddles from above. The wheels were connected to gears inside the mill buildings and these rotated the grinding stones. Mills are extremely well-documented historically (*see* Lydon 1981, for example), but the paucity of archaeological evidence is very disappointing. A later medieval mill-house of stone, a race, and a pond, were investigated at Ballyine, county Limerick (Walsh 1965; Rynne 1998, 82-3). Horizontal watermills of the mid-twelfth century and the early thirteenth century are known at Clonlonan, county Westmeath, and Corconnon, county Wexford respectively (Rynne 1998, 77). Remains of a vertical undershot grain mill were recently recovered at Patrick Street in Dublin (Rynne 1997). This was built in the thirteenth century but almost entirely rebuilt in the fourteenth century.

Windmills are first recorded in Europe in the late eleventh and late twelfth centuries in Normandy and England respectively, spreading elsewhere in Europe during the thirteenth century (Cipolla 1993, 143). The first reference to a windmill in Ireland is in 1281 (Rynne 1998, 79), but they were presumably built earlier than this. The earliest western European mills were of the timber post-mill type: the entire structure was erected on a massive, pivoting, timber post set into a mound, and the miller could simply swing the superstructure around so that the sails could catch wind from any direction. This limited the size of the grinding aparatus inside the mill, and consequently it limited productivity. No example of a post-mill has been investigated in Ireland, but a number of possible mounds have been identified (Moore 1987; Rynne 1998, 81). A windmill mound has been identified at Rindown, county Roscommon, albeit with a post-medieval cylindrical windmill on its summit (Claffey 1980). The other type of windmill, the tower-mill in which the structure and machinery stay stationary but the sails can be turned, had developed by the fourteenth century and was considerably more powerful than the post-mill but also than the watermill (Cipolla 1993, 144).

The processed grain was for consumption in bread, stews and pottages, but another outlet for it was alcohol. Ale, which was brewed professionally or in the home, was consumed in both aristocratic and peasant households; it seems that in the case of the former a gallon of ale per person could be consumed per day (Dyer 1983; 1989). In addition to the merriment which doubtless accompanied the drinking of ale, there were benefits of health — ale is rich in calories and vitamins — and of social bonding. As vessels for drinking are quite rare in the archaeological record, it is possible that a single vessel was passed around for communal drinking; Ludolf von Munchhausen, the German visitor whom we discussed in Chapter 2, noted that a single cup was passed around the household which he visited in county Tipperary in 1591 (Ó Riain Raedel 1998).

Protein diets

While the organisation of the field systems was for the purpose of optimising arable produce, manorial farming in the thirteenth century was mixed. The principal source of protein was animal meat, and butchered animal bones from urban as well as rural sites give an impression of how that part of the dietary balance was achieved. Although the rearing of animals was generally a rural pursuit, townspeople were important consumers; where there is good evidence from urban sites it suggests that meat was prepared, cooked and consumed in the backyards and houses of individual properties.

We might expect cattle to predominate in the medieval diet given our own modern tastes, and in some cases cattle bones are indeed in the majority, as, for example, at the urban site of Charlotte's Quay in Limerick (Lynch 1984, 322-25), the monastic site of Clontuskert priory (Fanning 1976, 169), and the rural manor-house site of Jerpointchurch, county Kilkenny (Foley 1989, 123). In well-stratified levels in North Main Street in Cork cattle dominated by more than 2:1 over other species (McCarthy 1997, 154-8). The fact that slaughtering seems to have taken place between the fourth and seventh year implies that such by-products of mature animals as milk, hides and horns were as important as meat. In addition to their valuable meat and hides, castrated males (oxen) and even cows in early pregnancy could be used for traction.

Transhumance settlements, or booleys, are attested in parts of Ireland and some clearly date from the closing centuries of the period under review here, as at Glenmakeeran and Goodland in county Antrim (**26**); the first recorded use of the term booley in Ireland seems to be in 1596 when Sir Edmund Spenser noted that the Gaelic-Irish tended:

> to keep their cattle and to live themselves [spend] the most part of the year in boolies, pasturing upon the mountain and waste wild places and removing still to fresh land as they have depastured the former ... the very same that Irish boolies are, driving their cattle continually with them and feeding only on their milk and white meat. (Williams and Robinson 1983, 34-38)

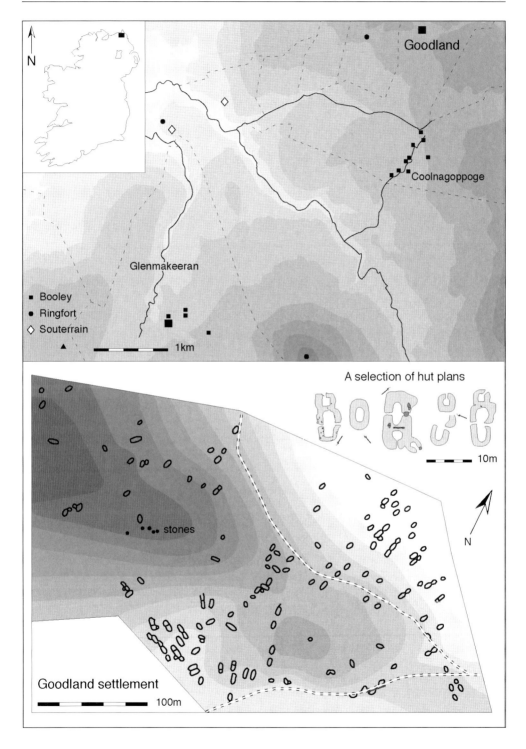

26   A map of the later-medieval booleying landscapes at Goodland and Glenmakeeran, high on the plateau of north county Antrim (after Williams and Robinson 1983)

On some sites sheep are at least as well represented as cattle, as at Ferns castle, county Wexford (Sweetman 1984a, 244), Shop Street in Drogheda, county Louth (Sweetman 1984b, 209-18), and the Four Courts in Dublin (McMahon 1988, 313-7). The Waterford excavations yielded massive amounts of sheep bones (McCormick 1997, 823). Sheep were prized for their fleece as much as for their meat. Pigs and goats were also farmed, and the record of some 2,000 'old hogs and goats' being lost to FitzWaren in 1282 (McNeill 1980, 40) provides a graphic illustration of how numerous these animals were on some manors. Alone among the major food sources, pigs could be reared in the backyards, and high numbers of young pigs and an absence of pigs over three years of age in the excavated urban sites suggests this was the case.

The early years of the fourteenth century, and especially the years from 1315 to 1322, saw Europe, including Ireland, in the grips of a 'great famine' of devastating intensity brought on in part by war and, in even larger measure, by inclement weather (Jordan 1996; Lyons 1989). Pollen diagrams record a decline in cereal pollens and a simultaneous rise in grass and weed pollens in Ireland around 1300 (Mitchell 1965), and these mark the beginings of a shift from arable farming towards pastoralism. Investment in animals was not a solution to the problem of bad weather — those animals needed to be fed, and sodden summer pastures and the lack of winter feed meant they too suffered in the famine — but animals were at least mobile, and that had clear advantages in a century of endemic social unrest.

Lesser species consumed on the manors included rabbits, which were actually introduced into Ireland by the Anglo-Normans. No warrens remain, but there was a warren at Dunfert in Kilkenny, according to its extent (O'Conor 1998, 34). Doves were also popular, but as a delicacy rather than a staple, as they provide little protein. The birds were encouraged to nest in the small cavities inside dovecots, and were 'harvested' in winter. Dovecots were found at virtually all manorial centres for which we have information. At Cloncurry, for example, a dovecot was part of a complex of buildings which included two eight-post barns, a corn-drying kiln, a cow-byre, and a threshing house (*Red Book of Ormond*, 27-31). However, comparatively few survive. The best-known examples are those associated with Ballybeg Augustinian priory, county Cork (**colour plate 10**), and Kilcooley Cistercian abbey, county Tipperary. The proximity of the dovecots to the monastic buildings is most surprising: canons sitting in the stalls on the north side of the Ballybeg choir would certainly have seen the birds fluttering around the open-top of the dovecot through the lancet windows opposite.

Fish were also consumed, and some of the edible molluscan species (oyster, cockle, periwinkle) are common on most sites, even on inland sites such as Ferns castle (Sweetman 1984a, 244). Fishponds of demonstrable medieval date are not common in Ireland. Thomas Westropp published a number of possible medieval examples in Clare and Limerick (1918), and to these the pond at Leamanagh castle, also in county Clare, can be added, although its date may be post-medieval. Valuable work on the mechanisms used to catch fish has been carried out by Aidan O'Sullivan (1995; 1997).

Manorial villages and manor houses

Collective open-field farming was most appropriate to communities living in nucleated settlements; such collective farming was not a realistic option if its potential participants were scattered across the countryside. Nucleation facilitated the organisation and regulation of the fields, and it enhanced the farmers' sense of shared identity. Lordship probably played a role in the actual creation of villages, but village communities were not dependent thereafter on a lord's imprimatur for their endeavours (Dyer 1988, 27-28).

Both villages and towns were associated with Anglo-Norman field systems in much of Ireland, particularly in the south-east. The towns were boroughs, places with urban constitutions which offered their inhabitants certain privileges. What is unusual, however, is that most of the villages for which we have specific historical or archaeological evidence seem also to have been boroughs, or at least to have been inhabited by burgesses. There are exceptions to this: for example 'villages' are recorded in east Cork in the thirteenth and fourteenth centuries (MacCotter and Nichols [eds] 1996), and several agglomerations of houses which might be described as villages have been investigated by archaeologists (Ó Ríordáin and Hunt 1942; Cleary 1982; 1983; Barry 1996). The fact remains, however, that the majority of Anglo-Norman villages in Ireland of which we have some tangible knowledge were boroughs, and that must be significant.

The concepts of borough and burgess status are explored in some detail in Chapter 4, but suffice it to say here that the medieval village community of much of contemporary England and north-west Europe was not a feature of Anglo-Norman Ireland: the villagers of Anglo-Norman Ireland invariably had burgess status, and that, in theory at least, gave them different entitlements than their fellow villagers elsewhere. From an archaeological perspective this matters little because burgess status does not have a particular morphological manifestation. But from historical and demographic perspectives this is extremely interesting: burgess status was used as a bait to attract settlers to Ireland, as we will see below (p92), and it seems from this that the Anglo-Normans felt that the nucleations necessary for the successful operation of the farming system could only survive and prosper if potential villagers were offered a form of tenure not enjoyed in contemporary, conventional manorial villages elsewhere.

Outside of south-east Ireland the pattern of settlement is slightly different. Nucleations in Meath and Ulster are very few in number. Tom McNeill has argued that the manorial centres of the earldom of Ulster were places of administration to which tenants went periodically rather than centres of population at which tenants lived permanently (1980, 84-8). The same interpretation might be offered of Anglo-Norman Meath where nucleations seem to have been very few; Brian Graham has suggested that there were once 98 villages in the lordship of Meath, each of them located where castles and churches are juxtaposed (1975, 224-8), but as yet there is little archaeological evidence of nucleated Anglo-Norman settlement at the majority of these places. Anngret Simms' suggestion, made specifically in the context of one of the Meath manors, Duleek (1988, 315), that the long-established townland structure militated against the creation of large nucleated villages in Ireland, is convincing.

Manorial extents give us some nominal information about buildings located at the administrative cores of these estates at the time that those extents were compiled (O'Conor 1998, 29-33). Lists of buildings are supplied to us, roughly in the order of their importance, but scribes unfortunately devoted as much of their energy to recording the existence of a dovecote as that of a hall or a chapel. Halls, not surprisingly, were features of most of the manorial centres, but some extents also list towers and chambers (Down 1987, 455), suggesting complex residential structures comparable with those in contemporary castles. The extents also inform us about gardens; at Knocktopher, county Kilkenny, for example, there were three fruit and herb gardens (Empey 1982-3, 332). Horticultural pursuits were probably very popular in manorial households, although the great experts in this area were monastic clergy, as Terence Reeves-Smyth's valuable survey (1999) makes clear.

None of the manor houses documented in the surviving manorial extents has been investigated, but a possible manor house was excavated in 1973 at Jerpointchurch, county Kilkenny (Foley 1989). Built on a mud platform at the edge of the small borough of Newtown Jerpoint, this was a substantial two-storeyed building of mortared stone with an internal width of about five metres and a length in excess of ten metres. Its date is uncertain — its floor was kept so meticulously clean that there were no diagnostic finds — but it was probably built late in the thirteenth or early in the fourteenth century. It was preceded on the site by a one-storeyed house of similar size but with mud walls; this earlier house has been dated to the early thirteenth century (O'Conor 1998, 50).

Tempting as it is to describe Jerpoint Church as the site of a manor house, in the absence of appropriate medieval documentation and good comparative evidence we should defer judgement. This may seem overcautious, but there is considerable difficulty in distinguishing between houses of manorial status and those of the higher orders of peasantry (Currie 1992, 85). Peasant houses in England, for example, could be quite sophisticated, and recent research (Dyer 1986) has overturned the older view that they were not permanent buildings. Moreover, there are instances in France where excavators were only able to distinguish manorial houses from nearby peasant houses by the range of objects — many of them are artefacts of leisure such as backgammon and chess pieces — which were found within them (Lorren 1977).

If the fastidiousness of the Jerpointchurch occupants has left us at a disadvantage, the fact that we have their house at all encourages us to believe that many more houses of Anglo-Norman rural settlers await discovery, either by systematic investigation or by chance. Farmhouses marked on the first edition Ordnance Survey six-inch maps of eastern Ireland may well occupy sites previously occupied by Anglo-Norman houses, even if there are very few such buildings in which fabric can be traced back to the seventeenth century or earlier. But the only rural sites where we can confidently expect to find colonial-era houses are those which are enclosed by moats, and to these we will turn presently.

Shrinkage and desertion of villages

Robin Glasscock, in a survey of three decades ago, listed six deserted Anglo-Norman towns, nine deserted and seven shrunken Anglo-Norman 'rural-boroughs' (settlements which were no more than villages despite having borough status), and eleven deserted villages (1971). Compared with England (Sheail 1971), the total of thirty-three sites is very low indeed, and while it could probably now be enlarged, it could not be enlarged significantly.

An assessment of the patterns and processes of shrinkage and desertion of villages in Ireland is fraught with two main difficulties. First, there is, as we have seen, a real difficulty in identifying settlements which can be classified as villages according to such reasonable criteria as the presence of a church, the existence of a street-plan, and a form of tenure which is not burgess-tenure. Secondly, if we include settlements with burgesses, as Glasscock did (1971), we must wonder if the low-level of settlement — or even the absence of nucleated settlement — at those places is because we are seeing them at the end of a cycle of foundation-growth-shrinkage/desertion or because they simply never developed in the first instance; as we will see in the next chapter, many places were ear-marked for nucleated settlement but simply never developed as their founders had hoped they would.

Moated sites

The distinguishing morphological features of moated sites in Ireland are rectangular areas generally less than 2,000 square metres in extent, with low banks defining these areas, and external, flat-bottomed ditches which either have standing water or have vegetation which indicates water-logging in wet seasons (**27**). Moated sites of circular plan are also known; figures are not available for Ireland for the obvious reason that circular moated sites cannot easily be separated from low-lying ringforts, but in England they are few in number (le Patourel 1978, 41) and this probably holds for Ireland as well. Rainfall was not the principal source of the moat-water. Rather, water was usually diverted to and from the moat by channels or leats from nearby springs or streams; in rare cases the spring was actually in the ditch or the stream formed one side of the enclosure.

The digging of moats required considerable physical effort. It is impossible to know how long it took to dig a moat because we do not know how many labourers were involved, nor what their pattern of work was, but we can still make an estimate of the magnitude of the effort. We can take Rathaspick, county Laois, a site surveyed and published by Kieran O'Conor (1998, 60), as an example. Here the moat, which is wrapped around a trapezoidal island, has a total length of 110m, a depth of a little less than two metres, and is about twenty metres wide all around. Using Green's calculations for the moat at Norton priory in Cheshire (Greene 1989, 35), we can calculate that the volume of clay which was dug out for the Rathaspick moat was a little less than 2000 cubic metres, that it weighed nearly 4000 tonnes, and that this was about 40,000 wheelbarrow loads; if, as Greene suggests, one man can move about forty barrow-loads a day, it would take a team of three men a full year of working flat-out to finish the job.

Despite some important publications in the 1960s (Hadden 1964), moated sites really only entered the consciousness of medieval archaeologists in Ireland in the 1970s, first with Robin Glasscock's seminal paper (1970), and then with Terry Barry's monograph on the subject several years later (1977). These and other studies have established beyond reasonable doubt that the majority of moated sites in eastern Ireland were constructed by Anglo-Normans in the thirteenth century. The evidence offered in these studies has three strands. First, there is the evidence of excavation; although less than 1% of known sites has been investigated, the results are consistent, as we will see. Secondly, there is the circumstantial evidence of their location relative to manorial centres. Barry has documented their distribution at the peripheries of the colony's administrative nuclei (1977). In the manor of Knocktopher, county Kilkenny, where this pattern of peripheral location is repeated, Empey (1982-3) has offered the convincing suggestion that the moats

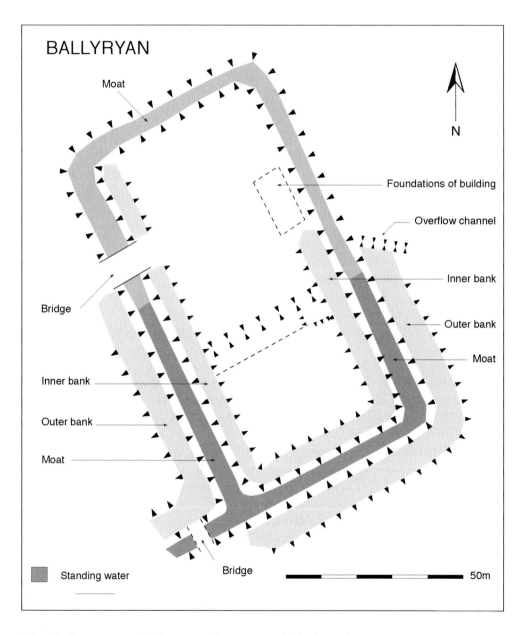

27   *Ballyryan, county Carlow, moated site, as recorded by the author in 1984*

are so distributed because they mark the colonisation of more marginal lands within the manor, and he attributes this 'secondary colonisation' to the period 1225-1325 on the grounds that the settlement of these marginal lands would have been recorded in the manorial extent had it been achieved in the late 1100s or early 1200s. Finally, the Irish moated sites can be broadly paralleled with the better-known moated sites of England, most of which date to the same thirteenth and early fourteenth-century period (le Patrourel and Roberts 1978, 47); moreover, many English moated sites were associated with the expansion of settlement into previously uncultivated land, as appears to have been the case in Ireland.

Distribution

It is remarkable that moated sites were neglected for so long by the scholarly community given that the Ordnance Survey actually identified many of the sites as archaeological monuments as early as the 1830s and hatchured them accordingly on their maps. The alarming rate of destruction of all classes of archaeological site in the past century and a half means that we depend very much on the Ordnance Survey cartographers for information on the number and spread of different monument types, and this is especially true for our distribution map of moats (**28**); many moated sites may have escaped identification to this day simply because, with their plan-shapes and networks of leats, they lend themselves so easily to incorporation in post-medieval systems of rectangular fields.

The distribution map presented here is not a map of settlement *per se* but a map of earthwork enclosures of a particular morphological character. We assume that the moats enclosed residential buildings and ancilliary structures, but without excavation we cannot know if the enclosures are contemporary with whatever it was that they enclosed; indeed, even on those sites which have seen excavation the exact chronological relationships between the moats and the structures within are not clear. It is interesting in this regard to note that at Ballyconnor, county Wexford, which was mentioned above (p62), it was recorded in 1280 that an existing *grangia* was enclosed by a palisade formed of sharpened tree-trunks set into a trench, and by an outer moat nearly 70 perches (about 350m) long; the moat, in other words, was an addition to an earlier settlement complex. Not only do we not know how common was such a sequence, but we do not know if the actual act of creating a moat around a rectangular area was a culturally-significant act: we understand a moat's pragmatic value as a defensive or protective barrier, but did a moat also have political or social 'meaning'? Did it communicate the tenurial status or cultural identity of its owner? These are questions for future research.

The distribution map shows strong regional differentiation in the spread of moated sites. In the south-eastern quadrant of the island they were far more densely distributed than elsewhere, but in the colonial lands of north Leinster, east Meath and Ulster they are not at all common. So closely does the distribution of moated sites in south-eastern Ireland match that of Anglo-Norman towns (**35**) that we must posit a relationship between them. If the moated sites are associated with the economic exploitation of the countryside, one assumes that the products of that exploitation were sold and distributed in the towns, and to that extent, then, the moated sites and towns were interdependent and, for some period of time at least, contemporary.

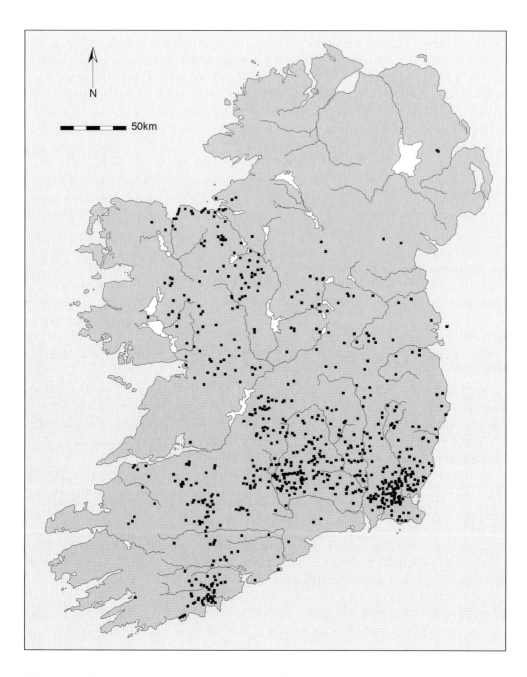

28   A distribution map of moated sites in Ireland (after O'Conor 1998)

A dense spread of moats in a wide north-south zone through the middle of counties Cork and Limerick effectively marks the western boundary of their distribution in southern Ireland. These counties ostensibly mark a defended frontier (Barry 1981), but this could also be an example of a favourable zone for settlement, a zone where colonial farmers and traders might well have benefited from contiguity with the Gaelic-Irish.

West of the Shannon there is an even distribution of moated sites across the landscapes of east Galway, east Mayo, north Roscommon and Sligo. The Galway sites may belong to the very start of the colonisation of Connacht in the second quarter of the thirteenth century (Holland 1988). Sites in Roscommon, however, have been attributed to Gaelic-Irish landowners (Graham 1988b; O'Conor 1998); this is an interesting and exciting idea, but it needs greater elaboration: none of the earthworks is specifically and unambiguously documented as Gaelic-Irish, so the possibility remains that the moated sites represent an otherwise undocumented attempt at colonial settlement in the district.

The evidence of excavation

The sites which have been excavated are all in the southern part of Ireland in areas which were unquestionably under Anglo-Norman control; two possible sites in county Antrim, Carnaghliss (Yates 1983) and Tildarg (Brannon 1984), have seen excavation, and it has been suggested that the latter is a Gaelic-Irish moated site (O'Conor 1998, 88-89). Two of the excavated sites in southern Ireland are in county Cork. Kilmagoura (Glasscock 1968) had a moated enclosure positioned in the corner of a larger, earthen-banked, enclosure. The latest of three phases of activity saw the erection of two buildings, one of them substantial enough to be regarded as a house or hall. Timber used in its bridge over the moat was dated by dendrochronology to AD 1225±70. Rigsdale (Sweetman 1981), dated numismatically to the close of the thirteenth century, also contained remains of a large, rectangular house or hall, oriented east-west and measuring 20m by 8m internally. The foundations were of stone but the superstructure may have been of timber. The interior of the house seems to have been sub-divided: the eastern quarter had a projecting garderobe turret and presumably contained private chambers, while the western three-quarters of the building had slot trenches suggestive of supports for the floor of an upper hall (**29**).

The partially-excavated moated site at Ballyveelish, county Tipperary (Doody 1987), was found to contain structures in a line inside the eastern arm of the moat (**30**). One of these was identified as a wattle-built house of square plan (4m x 4m) in the centre of a very narrow stone-walled yard, also of square plan. Beside it was a wooden building of rectangular plan which seems to have been subdivided by one or more timber partitions; this may have been a hall like that in Rigsdale. Finds from Ballyveelish included late thirteenth-century pottery, fourteen rotary querns, and considerable quantities of cereal grain, particularly wheat and oats.

Immigrants and entrepreneurs

Empey's argument that moated sites were not constructed at the time that the manors were laid out but represent a later, 'secondary' colonisation of the countryside (1982-3) is a convincing explanation for the heavily-manorialised lands of south-eastern Ireland (**7**).

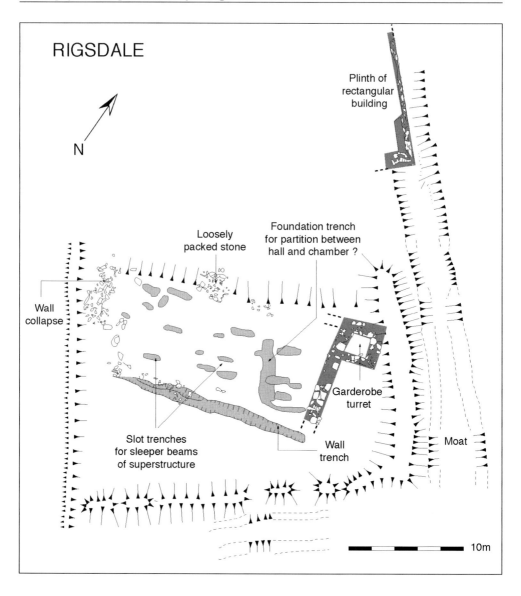

29   A plan of Rigsdale, county Cork, moated site (after Sweetman 1981)

But why was new land needed to be brought into use in the late thirteenth century, and who were the people who occupied this land?

Ireland's farmland had long produced a surplus, as we noted earlier, and it is unlikely that a rise in population in the thirteenth century was so great that land suddenly needed to be assarted — cleared from woodland and scrub for the purpose of cultivation — on a very large scale. The best evidence that the population of colonial Ireland did not increase dramatically may be the lack of significant growth in many of the towns during that period, as we will see below. The cereal grain which was produced in the fields

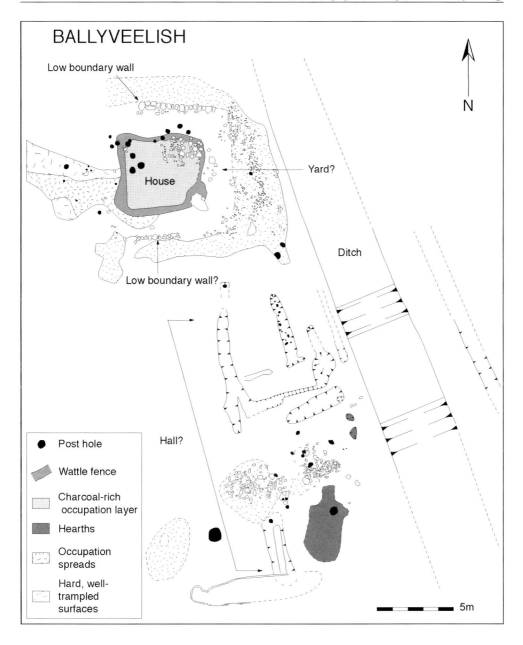

30   *A plan and interpretation of the structures excavated inside a moated site at Ballyveelish, county Tipperary (after Doody 1987)*

associated with the moated sites (and possibly dried in kilns and stored in barns on those sites) was probably not for consumption on the island at all. Who, then, were the consumers?

The crown drew freely, and with increasing demand, on Ireland's agricultural resources in the second half of the thirteenth century, and nothing illustrates this better than the royal request in December 1298 that 8,000 quarters of wheat, 10,000 quarters of oats, 2,000 quarters of crushed malt, 1,000 tuns of wine (presumably French wine which had been imported into Ireland), 500 carcasses of beef, 1,000 fattened pigs, and 20,000 dried fish, be exported from Ireland in readiness for a military campaign (Lydon 1987b, 197). This was not a unique request; similar demands were made of Ireland in other years. The dependence of the crown on Ireland for food to support its various wars probably explains the sudden expansion in land being cultivated. For those of an entrepreneurial bent there was certainly money to be made out of Ireland, as witness the Gaelic-Irish merchant who bought wheat locally at 5 shillings per crannock and then sold it in Gascony for a healthy profit at 22 shillings per crannock. But the population of the island, even in colonial areas, was hardly large enough to assart on the scale suggested by the moats. There is a case, then, for identifying the farmers in the moated sites as having come directly from England (O'Keeffe 1998b). Irish moats conform so closely to English moats in their morphologies that the idea of placing a moat around a farmstead complex of square outline must have been carried directly from England.

Rural settlement in Gaelic Ireland

We close this account of the medieval Irish countryside with an intractable problem: where did the majority of the Gaelic-Irish live in the later middle ages? The principal landowners of the fifteenth and sixteenth centuries manifest themselves in tower-houses and in their patronage of churches, but lower social levels are virtually invisible.

With respect to the relatively scarcity of Gaelic-Irish castles prior to the fifteenth century, Kieran O'Conor has suggested that the Gaelic-Irish used the natural topography rather than stone buildings as their fortresses of aggression and defence, stressing the mobility of Gaelic-Irish armies through inhospitable terrain. In Elizabethan State Papers there are numerous records of the Gaelic-Irish 'breaking' their castles before going to war to render them useless to opposing forces (Nicholls 1987, 405), the suggestion being that even these castles were not so permanent that they could not be rebuilt again. O'Conor has also suggested that the type of house favoured among the Gaelic-Irish could be dismantled and moved elsewhere when land was being redistributed according to native custom (1998).

A pastoral economy such as that which the Gaelic-Irish are known to have embraced certainly allows greater settlement mobility than a predominantly arable economy, and nomadism is documented in Gaelic Ireland in the later middle ages (Simms 1986), but a model of settlement mobility might not represent the whole picture; if the great field systems which cross the extensive Gaelic-Irish grasslands of eastern Connacht such as those recorded in the Rathcroghan and Carnfree areas (**31**) are indeed later medieval in date — a date in the twelfth century has been suggested by Michael Herity (1988) — they

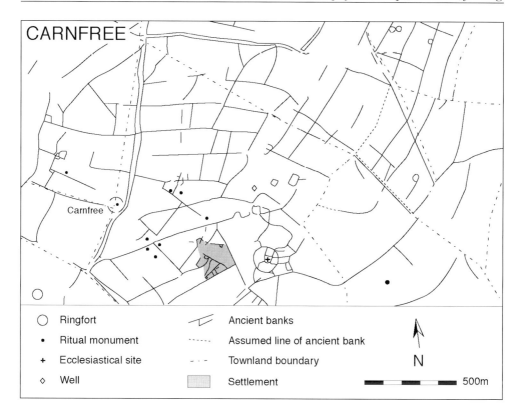

31 Part of the extensive field-system at Carnfree—a prehistoric cairn which was used as an inauguration place by the O'Conor kings in the fifteenth century—in county Roscommon (after Herity 1988). The long sinuous field-banks, which can be up to one metre high and several metres wide, indicate both a considerable investment of labour in the creation of the system and a carefully regulated distribution of the landscape resource; these, in turn, suggest that the system is a product of lordship control. An ecclesiastical site and a small settlement, both long-abandoned, are located in the system, but their chronological relationships with each other and with the fields are uncertain. A number of prehistoric ritual monuments, mainly burial mounds, survive in this landscape

represent a considerable investment of resources in the land, and we expect, drawing on parallels elsewhere, that they were accompanied by permanent, even nucleated, settlement. More work is clearly needed.

4 Towns and townlife

Nucleation is probably mankind's longest-established system of settlement organisation. It offers security and companionship, it allows collective retrieval and sharing of resources, and it creates a breeding pool and allows the family ties which result to be sustained. Whatever the case in prehistoric and early historic times, in the early middle ages the great majority of people in Ireland appear to have lived in the countryside, and that pattern may have continued into later medieval times despite the fact that both the Vikings and the Anglo-Normans were promoters of urban development. The phenomenal recent expansion of Dublin (and, to a slightly lesser extent, of Ireland's other cities) has now skewed that pattern, but most visitors to Ireland would still regard it as a rural country.

Urban archaeology has, not surprisingly, seen far more activity in the past three decades than any other specialisation in modern archaeology in Ireland. All the principal coastal towns have had some excavation, and fairly extensive parts of the historic cores of Dublin and Waterford (**32**) have been investigated. The best known of the urban excavations was that at Wood Quay, the area hemmed in between the cathedral of Holy Trinity (now Christ Church) and the river Liffey in Dublin. Wood Quay became a *cause célèbre* in the late 1970s when Dublin Corporation opted to construct modern offices on the site rather than preserve it (**colour plate 11**; Bradley [ed] 1984a). While the destruction of Wood Quay remains one of the most shameful episodes in the city's history, it at least focused attention on the value of heritage, and today all development, and not just in urban Ireland, must be preceded by an assessment of archaeological significance. The publication of the work at Wood Quay is on-going, but a series of important publications assessing elements of its archaeology and stressing its international significance has been published by Patrick Wallace (1985a, b; 1992a, b). Wood Quay is only a part of the vast jigsaw of excavations of early medieval Dublin (see also Ó Riordáin 1971; 1976; MacMahon 1988; Simpson 1994; 1995; Walsh 1997). There are published reports from investigations at other cities (for Cork see Hurley 1986; Cleary, Hurley and Shee Twohig 1997; for Waterford see Hurley, Scully and McCutcheon [eds] 1997) and coastal towns (for Carrickfergus see Simpson and Dickson 1981). Archaeology is not just excavation, and Ireland's urban heritage has been very well-served by survey (Bradley *et al* (eds) 1986-89), by case-studies of individual towns (Bradley 1977-80; Gosling 1991), some of them under the auspices of the Royal Irish Academy's Irish Historic Towns Atlas project (Simms, Clarke and Gillespie [eds] 1986-), and by a number of general studies (Bradley 1985; Bradley 1989; Thomas 1992).

32   A view of Waterford city from across the river Suir; the Hiberno-Norse settlement was at the tip of the peninsula to the left

Urban archaeology is the only branch of archaeology in Ireland in which synthesis cannot, at this moment at least, keep pace with discovery. While this chapter draws on information gleaned from archaeological excavations, its principal focus is on issues — the concept of 'town', and urban-planning, architecture and enclosure — for which generalisation is possible using above-ground evidence.

Towns in pre-colonial Ireland

The most common form of settlement in pre-colonial Ireland was the ringfort, which we discussed in Chapter 2; these qualify as dispersed rather than nucleated settlements, despite the clustering which is attested to on occasion (Ó Riordáin 1940). For decades it was supposed that clachans, the comparatively shapeless agglomerations of houses mapped by the Ordnance Survey in the mid-nineteenth century and associated with infield-outfield farming, had descended from unenclosed nucleations which co-existed with ringforts and embraced lower social classes, but there is no evidence to support this idea. The clachans themselves date from the recent rather than the ancient past (Leister 1976; Burchaell 1988), and most of them were depopulated and broken-up during the Great Famine of the mid-1800s.

Increasing lordship control was the circumstance that produced villages and their associated open-field systems in late Anglo-Saxon England (Hall 1988). Given that comparison between the Irish land divisions and those in contemporary Anglo-Saxon England is, as we noted in Chapter 2, both inviting and appropriate, one might expect the cultural landscape of Ireland *c*1000 to have experienced a transformation similar to that of England. There is some evidence for the ridging of arable in a configuration comparable with that found in the open-fields of England, although whether the land was open or not we do not know (see above, p62). But there is evidence, however, that a process of nucleation also accompanied the institution of the *trícha cét* in contemporary Ireland, and that this nucleation was associated with the abandonment of the ringfort (**7**). The clue is the word *baile*. The contexts in which this word was used in early medieval contexts in Ireland suggest it could mean a place or a settlement; we already noted its use at Dún Echdach or Duneight around AD1010 (p29); it was also used to describe Galway (in 1132), Athlone (in 1218), and Sligo (in 1257), each time in a context (O'Keeffe 1996, 147) which suggests a nucleation. In 1241, according to the *Annals of Connacht* [Freeman [ed] 1944), a *baile marcaid*, a market settlement or market town, was founded at Rockingham in county Roscommon. In the eleventh and twelfth centuries *baile* combines with *sráit* (*sráid* in modern Irish), 'street', to indicate a street-settlement (Doherty 1998, 315-6); Stradbally, county Laois, takes its name from *sráitbaile*, and the nature of the original settlement is still apparent in the remarkably long main street of the modern village.

Although *baile* is translated as 'town' in modern Irish, we know too little about the functions and morphology of the early medieval settlements to which *baile* was applied to justify translating it as 'town' in those contexts. The earliest indigenous nucleations which we *can* describe with some legitimacy as towns were those which clustered in and around the major church-sites from the tenth century onwards, as Doherty has argued from an exemplary integration of the evidence of documentary history and the methodology of social anthropology (1985). Their characteristics are large public buildings, public spaces, paved streets, and market places at which goods from far afield were traded. One of the best documented of these is Armagh (Edwards 1990, 108-11) where it is known that settlement was arranged within *trians*, or precincts, around the outside of the central enclosure: each of these — the *trian saxan* (the English *trian*), the *trian masain* (the middle *trian*), and the *trian mór* (the large *trian*) — contained streets. Annalistic references to conflagrations in the late eleventh and twelfth-century Armagh indicate very great numbers of timber houses. At Clonmacnois, county Offaly, another great monastic site, conflagrations claiming 105 and 47 houses were recorded in 1179 and *c*1205 respectively (Doherty 1985, 64-5), while at Derry, which was described as a *civitas* in 882, as a *cathair* (the modern Irish translation is 'city') in the eleventh century, and as a *baile* in 1532, over eighty houses were demolished in 1162 (Lacy 1988, 388).

Hiberno-Norse towns

The first recorded settlements of the Vikings in Ireland were in 841 at Annagassan, county Louth, and Dublin, and this was almost half a century after their first raids along Ireland's coasts. These settlements are described as *longphoirt*, protected or defended ports for ships. Another half a century later the Vikings established their urban centres in Ireland, beginning with Waterford in 914 and Cork in 915. Dublin was refounded as a town in 917, its *longphort* having been abandoned in 902. Limerick was founded in 922, and Wexford was founded by 935 (see Clarke 1998 for a discussion of the origins of Hiberno-Norse towns).

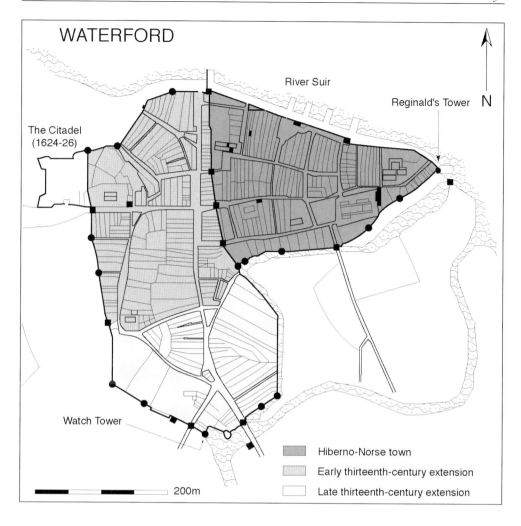

33   A map of Waterford city showing possible phases of growth (after Thomas 1992)

Extensive excavations in Dublin have revealed that the early tenth-century settlement had a rampart defining its river-side boundary, and this may have continued around the town as an enclosure. By the early twelfth century its area had expanded and it was enclosed by a stone wall. Waterford began its life as a Viking settlement on a promontory between the river Suir and a smaller tributary, St John's river. We know nothing of the town's extent in the early 900s, but by the time Raymond le Gros and the Anglo-Normans arrived in 1170 it enveloped much of the promontory, perhaps through incremental expansion (**33**). There was an earthen rampart at its wetern edge in the eleventh century, but this was replaced by a stone wall early in the twelfth century; Giraldus Cambrensis tells us in an apocryphal but illuminating account that when Raymond le Gros arrived in Waterford in 1170 he 'noticed a small building which hung down from the town wall on the outside by a beam', and that by cutting down this beam the Viking wall was made to collapse, thus allowing the Normans entry (Scott and Martin [eds] 1978, 67).

The houses inside the Hiberno-Norse towns were placed at the heads of long, narrow properties, and oriented at right-angles to the streets, with their doorways opening directly onto the streets. In the backyards were ancilliary structures, often of considerably less sophisticated architectural form. Although the houses were regularly replaced, the property boundaries proved very durable.

The houses themselves were originally of post-and-wattle construction, with sill-beam construction appearing somewhat later, and stone later still (**34**). The change from one mode of construction to another happened at different rates in different places. In Waterford the change from post-and-wattle to sill-beams and earthfast roof supports happened in the second half of the twelfth century (which is a little earlier than in Dublin), and fully-framed timber houses then became dominant in the early or mid-thirteenth century. The development in Cork seems to have been a little slower: close to the Christ Church site, for example, a post-and-wattle house no earlier than the middle of the thirteenth century was stratified beneath a sequence of three fourteenth-century houses, each of sill-beam construction (Cleary, Hurley and Shee Twohig 1997). The use of post-and-wattle construction even as late as the Anglo-Norman period underlines the continuity of population in these settlements.

The Hiberno-Norse communities of these coastal towns organised themselves in dioceses in the later eleventh century, and they chose as their bishops men who had been educated in southern England. The original cathedral churches in the Hiberno-Norse towns may have been of timber. They did not survive (above ground, at any rate) past the twelfth century when new cathedrals were erected (**colour plate 12**). The Hiberno-Norse towns also had parish churches, and they generally suffered the same fates as the cathedrals. However, one example, St Peter's in Waterford, is known to us from archaeological excavation (Hurley and McCutcheon 1997; Murtagh 1997). Unique among medieval Irish churches in having an apse, it suggests tantalisingly that these early urban communities looked to England, and possibly to the centres where their bishops were trained, for architectural inspiration: St Mary's, Tanner Street, Winchester (Biddle 1972, 104-7), close to the cathedral abbey where Malchus of Waterford was trained, is a good parallel for St Peter's.

The later medieval town defined

Before moving further we must ask how, within the spectrum of settlement nucleation, we can distinguish in general between medieval towns and medieval villages. The distinctions are complex, but they broadly can be categorised under three headings: settlement morphology, the activities and occupations of the inhabitants, and the legal status and institutional apparatuses of the settlements.

The first of these, morphology, relates both to the structure of a settlement as it might be recorded on a map, and to its landscape, which is what we observe as we move through a settlement. Common to most towns and villages, today as in the middle ages, are streets lined with terraced houses of fairly consistent width, market-places (or at least open, public spaces), commercial outlets, and churches. While the scale of a modern settlement may determine whether we chose to describe it as a town or village, scale is a very blunt

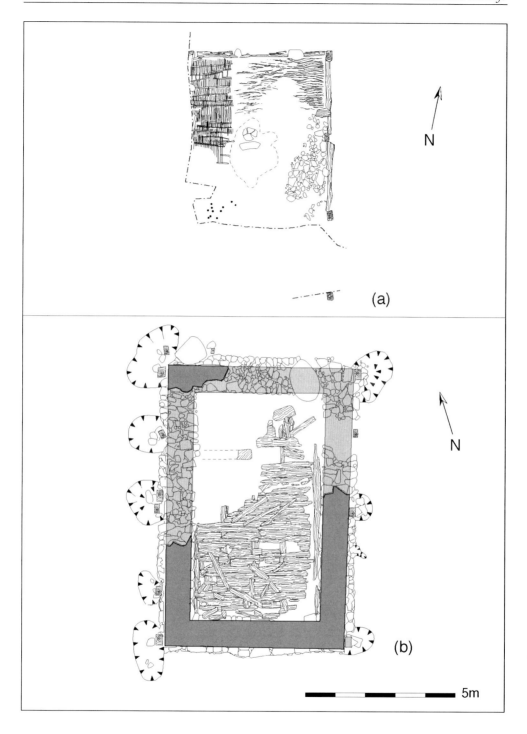

34   Two excavated Hiberno-Norse houses in Waterford: (a) a late twelfth or early thirteenth-century 'sill-beam' house; (b) a stone-walled house (AD 1150-1175), with part of its wooden floor still in situ *(after Wallace 1992a)*

analytical tool, particularly as we look backwards to the middle ages. With respect to Anglo-Norman towns, John Bradley has offered some resolution to this problem with a 'working definition' of town which emphasises physical and functional components:

> It is a settlement occupying a central position in a communications network, represented by a street pattern with houses and their associated land plots whose density is significantly greater than that of the settlements immediately around it (as seen in the burgage plot pattern); it incorporates a market-place and a church and its principal functions are reflected by the presence of at least three of the following: town walls, a castle, a bridge, cathedral, a house belonging to one of the religious Orders, a hospital or leper-house close to the town, an area of specialist technological activity, quays, a large school or administrative building, and/or suburbs (1985, 420).

Using this 'working definition' Bradley has identified fifty-six Anglo-Norman towns in Ireland, including the five Hiberno-Norse towns which continued to be urban places in the colonial era (1985, 418-20). This is a very useful tool, but two criticisms can be levelled at the method. First, the need for three (rather than two, or four) of the features to be present for a place to be regarded as a town is entirely arbitrary: Glanworth, county Cork, for example, is excluded from the list of towns despite being the capital of a manor and a central place within a communications network, and having a thirteenth-century castle, a market-place, and a main street with long properties running at right-angles from it, as well as a late medieval Dominican friary and a bridge. Secondly, the 'working definition' gives equal weighting to all the possible features which might be found in a settlement, but an enclosing wall or rampart — a town wall, in other words — must be regarded as having a greater significance than any single one of the other features. Town walls permitted careful regulation of commercial activity in settlements, including the monitoring of, and imposition of tolls on, those entering the settlements to engage in commerce. Also, the construction of town walls involved communities in collective statements of an identity which they shared to the exclusion of those living in the countryside. If we regard the features described by Bradley as being essential to any definition of a medieval town, but elevate the town wall to the status of principal criterion, we can add to Bradley's enumeration of Anglo-Norman towns in Ireland nearly a dozen medieval nucleated settlements with evidence of walling, or at least evidence that walling was intended (**35**).

The second criterion for distinguishing between medieval towns and villages concerns the people who lived in these nucleations. It is a loose definition, but we can regard as towns those settlements in which most people were fundamentally consumers rather than producers of food. Agriculture was the principal occupation of the inhabitants of medieval villages, but medieval townspeople engaged mainly in specialised craft, industrial and commercial activities. This is, on the whole, a reliable distinction between towns and villages.

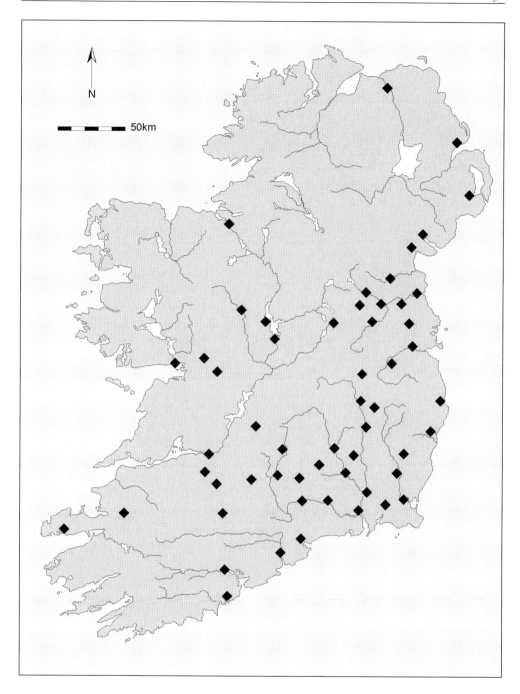

35   *A distribution map of later medieval towns in Ireland (after Bradley 1985 with additions)*

Boroughs

The third and final criterion for the defining of medieval towns is the one which has generated by far the most discussion among urban historians. This is the particular *mélange* of institutionalised freedoms and constraints which simultaneously bonded the occupants of the nucleations and separated them from their rural compatriots. The freedoms and constraints of which we speak here are those which were regulated by charter and legally-binding, and the towns of which they were a feature are known as boroughs. Burgesses — the inhabitants of boroughs — had plots in the town and a certain amount of land in the town-fields, and for the payment of an annual fixed money rent they enjoyed the proprietorship of this land, as well as exemption from the tolls paid by non-burgesses for the privilege of trading within the walls, and immunity from all jurisdiction save the king's (MacNiocaill 1985, 375-6).

Burgesses are first mentioned in Ireland at Dublin in the early twelfth century (Bradley 1994, 178); the existence of settlements with borough status is, along with the *caistél* sites discussed in Chapter 1, a good indication of how Ireland was changing in the century prior to Anglo-Norman colonisation. Killaloe, county Clare, is known to have had burgesses before *c*1200, and Bradley has recently and convincingly argued that this borough was a pre-colonial establishment (1994). Wexford had burgesses by 1172, and by 1200 there were burgesses to be found in at least a further eight settlements of which Drogheda (then part of Meath) was apparently the only settlement founded *ab initio* by the colonists (Bradley 1985, 411). Charters often post-date the foundations to which they referred: the earliest charter of New Ross, county Wexford, for example, dates from the 1280s, by which time the town — for 'town' it most certainly was, as it competed with Waterford to be Ireland's pre-eminent port — already had burgesses (Mac Niocaill 1964, 74, 300). Charters do not always survive, and in some cases they might not even have been issued, so the best indication that a settlement had borough status is a reference to burgesses.

Establishing a borough involved more than simply setting aside a small amount of land on which houses and a church might be built. Burgesses possessed land both inside and outside the settlements, and the latter holdings were generally of several acres. Given that a burgess's annual rent was customarily one shilling, for a lord to bring in a healthy annual rent from the borough he not only needed to attract a good number of burgesses but he also needed to set-aside sufficient land for them. The optimum time for establishing boroughs in Anglo-Norman Ireland was, therefore, at the start of the colonial period when the manors were being set-out and the land was being carved-up, and if a lord did not have the wherewithal to bring burgesses to his manor at an early date, he could at least calculate how many burgesses he would need for a reasonable income from burgage rents, and how much land they would need. At Gowran, county Kilkenny, for example, we know that twenty-one ploughlands were set aside for 680 burgesses (Empey 1982-3, 443), but Gowran's population never reached this size, as James White's attractive map of 1710-11 (**36**) makes abundantly clear. In the cases of the boroughs of Ferns, county Wexford, and Wexford itself, a third of the burgages were recorded in 1298 as being waste; whatever the situation at Ferns, an inland town without the benefit of a major river, the prosperous coastal port of Wexford is not likely to have had this level of abandonment before the end of the thirteenth century and one must conclude that these burgage plots were simply never occupied (Graham 1980b, 32).

36   *Gowran, county Kilkenny, surveyed in 1710-11 (NLI 21 F 55 [4]). One side of the town was protected by a Town Wall, the other by a rampart. This map creates the impression of a very tidy settlement in which all burgesses enjoyed possession of a reasonably-sized property, but this might be the direct result of seventeenth-century reorganisation: there were probably many derelict plots in Gowran, as in other Irish towns throughout the middle ages, and it is conceivable that these were redistributed among Gowran's burgess population after the middle ages*

Most of the settlements in later medieval Ireland which can be defined as towns according to functional and morphological criteria had borough status; the most obvious exceptions, such as Derry and Armagh, lay outside colonial control. Crucially, not all places with burgesses can be regarded as towns. There are several reasons for this. First, documentary evidence that there was land held by burgage tenure at a certain place does not presuppose that the tenant — or burgess — in question lived in a nucleation with the characteristics of an urban place; the tenant could, theoretically at least, be granted the privileges of burgess status without actually living in a borough, and the discrepancy between the dates of the charters and the earliest references to burgesses suggests that the privileges were attached to individuals before they were attached to the places. Secondly, burgesses were not always spared those agricultural or labour services which were owed by contemporary rural folk and which therefore allow us to separate country people from townspeople: for example, an undated (but presumably fourteenth-century) survey of the demesne of Kilmaclenine, county Cork, a manor of the bishop of Cloyne, mentions *betagii* as burgesses, and tells us that they were not allowed out of the *vill* except to pasture on the demesne lands (MacCotter and Nicholls [eds] 1996). Finally, many boroughs were speculative creations, as the Anglo-Normans sought to use burgess status as a bait to attract settlers to Ireland from rural England and Wales (Otway-Ruthven 1965). By Bradley's calculations only one in four boroughs actually developed into a proper town (1985, 425). Many of the others were mere villages — 'rural boroughs' is how Robin Glasscock (1970; 1971) described them — albeit with the urban privileges which we discribed above; some of these remained villages while others were eventually depopulated and disappeared. A number of the boroughs may never have reached any stage of nucleation which rendered them even worthy of being described as villages. One can only wonder if groups of settlers arrived ready to take up burgage tenure and were astonished to find their 'town' was a building site or, even worse, still a green-field site!

One example of a borough which did not develop into, or at least has not survived as, a settlement of any significance is Dunleckny, county Carlow. This was the capital of the barony of Idrone which Raymond le Gros, one of the first generation of Anglo-Normans in Ireland, granted to the Carew family. There were some burgesses here in 1207 (Brooks 1950, 60), but there is no mention of burgesses later in the thirteenth century. The only evidence today of Dunleckny's past importance is a convergence of roadways from all directions, one leading towards a thirteenth-century parish church and another towards a late twelfth-century motte and a nineteenth-century manor house (**colour plate 13**). We do not know why Dunleckny did not continue to develop as a nucleated settlement into the late middle ages and beyond.

The choice of site and the date of establishment were two major factors deciding the fates of individual boroughs. When located on hilltops and far from water sources, as was the case with Oughterard, county Kildare (Hall, Hennessy and O'Keeffe 1985), boroughs were severely disadvantaged and invariably failed to develop into settlements of any size or prosperity. Boroughs founded long after other boroughs in their vicinity had been founded were also disadvantaged: the borough of Rosbercon, county Wexford, for example, was founded around 1290 (MacNiocaill 1964) on the opposite bank of the river from the long-established New Ross and simply could not compete with it. A third factor determining the fates of boroughs was the extent to which they were promoted as good places to live. Many boroughs may have declined because potential burgesses in England and Wales were simply unaware of their existence. Unlike in the case of the east German lands in the twelfth century (Bartlett 1993, 121-2), there is no evidence of proactive estate agents or *locatores* operating between England, Wales and Ireland. This lack of promotion may explain the apparent discrepancies between the ideal (or anticipated) and the actual burgess populations at places like Gowran and Wexford.

To describe town and borough as synonyms, then, is clearly incorrect. In any case, the notion of town which is so deeply embedded in the modern psyche is one which is entirely without reference to the constitutions by which the customary entitlements of medieval townspeople to certain privileges were protected; in other words, not only does modern society not understand town as a legal construct, it has no memory of understanding it that way.

Anglo-Norman town-planning

We should distinguish at the outset between towns which we created afresh by the Anglo-Normans and those which were developed around older cores. Drogheda is the best example of the former; there is neither historical nor archaeological evidence of either early medieval or Viking settlement there. New Ross is another. Towns with older cores include the five Hiberno-Norse coastal ports, and the many places which had important churches in the pre-colonial era. Early ecclesiastical enclosures are sometimes reflected very clearly in the street-plans of the latter towns, as is the case at Duleek, county Meath (Bradley 1985, 438) and Kells, county Meath (Simms and Simms 1990); the Anglo-Norman settlement at Kilkenny (Bradley 1995, fig 19), however, was adjacent to an early ecclesiastical site but was laid out as an entirely new settlement.

Trim, county Meath, may have evidence of an enclosure around ecclesiastical land on both sides of the river (**37**): the Augustinian priory of St Mary may occupy a pre-colonial site (Gwynn and Hadcock 1970, 195-6), and the castle — the south curtain wall of which may preserve the line of the enclosure — was built on land belonging to the Church (Sweetman 1978, 133). The layout of Trim's streets is unusual. While there is no evidence that the town began as two separate settlements (as had Drogheda), the north and south sides of the town are laid out in different ways: the latter has a triangular arrangement of streets around the ancient site which is occupied by St Patrick's church, while the former has an H-shaped arrangement.

Most of the Anglo-Norman towns in Ireland are not quite so complex. The majority simply have long axial streets with lesser streets and lanes running off them at right-angles; these lesser accessways occasionally lead to a second axial street, parallel to the first, as at Carlingford, county Louth, and Loughrea, county Galway. Where streets of equal size and importance cross each other this can result in a simple crossroads-like plan (as at Callan, county Kilkenny), a double-crossroads (as at Carlow), or a grid-plan (as at Drogheda).

Market-places can occupy different positions within these towns. Sometimes the principal street was also the market-place, as at Nenagh, Carrick-on-Suir and Clonmel, all in county Tipperary, and Thomastown, county Kilkenny. Streets could even be widened slightly in the centre to accommodate the market, as at Athboy, county Meath. In a small number of cases the axial streets were widened gradually to create very extensive, triangular or funnel-shaped market-places, as at Naas, county Kildare, and Fethard and Thurles, both in county Tipperary. Cashel, county Tipperary, was very similar to Fethard, and virtually identical to Thurles; the similarity is not so obvious today as Cashel's great market-place was encroached-upon by a market-house and public water fountain in the nineteenth century. The wider end of these market-places was certainly the busy end, and activity fell away as the market-places narrowed to become streets. Market-places at the convergence of two streets tended to have a more compact triangular plan, as at Athenry, county Galway, and Fore, county Westmeath. The third plan-type among the market-places is square or rectangular, as at Kinsale, county Cork, and Tullow, county Carlow. The market-place and the churchyard were the two open-access spaces within a medieval town, and while they may appear to have been very different types of space — one was commercial, the other spiritual — many medieval

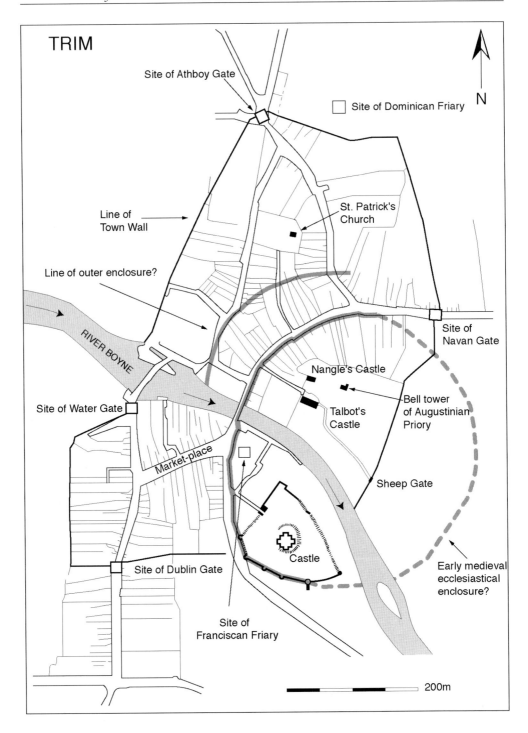

37   *A plan of Trim town, county Meath, showing how an ecclesiastical enclosure may have controlled the topographical development of the Anglo-Norman town (outline plan of town after Thomas 1992 and Bradley 1995)*

market-places had market crosses to remind traders and their clients that God's watchful eye was trained on their transactions.

Burgage plots and private buildings

Properties of consistent width along street frontages were a feature of Hiberno-Norse towns (Wallace 1992b), and the actual boundary lines between plots remained in use when these ports became important towns of the Anglo-Normans; indeed, the presence of equal-width plots in Hiberno-Norse towns other than Dublin may indicate that these settlements had, like Dublin, borough status before the coming of the Anglo-Normans. The sizes of the plots was very carefully regulated in both the Hiberno-Norse and Anglo-Norman settlements, and the borough charters of some of the colonial settlements actually specified what width they should be (Bradley 1985, 439). The basic unit of 3 or 3.5 perches (15-17m) which was used in England (Slater 1989) seems to have been used in Ireland. The narrowness of the plots meant that houses had to be turned with their gables towards the streets, and the houses were often narrower than the plots to allow a passage or lane to lead directly from the street to the backyard. Excavations of plots on the north island of Cork revealed such lanes alongside the thirteenth-century houses, and as the houses were replaced with larger buildings the lanes were encroached upon (Hurley 1997); at Fethard, county Tipperary, the lines of these lanes may have been preserved as passages running through the ground floors of late fifteenth or early sixteenth-century tower-houses (O'Keeffe 1999a). In the later middle ages the plots were often subdivided, probably under pressure of commerce, to maximise access to the street. We can see this at Trim (**37**) where the properties in the vicinity of the market-place are narrower than those on the north side of the town.

The need for consistency in the size of the plots in Anglo-Norman boroughs is no mystery: each burgess paid the same annual rent, so none should be disadvantaged with a smaller plot than his neighbour. But the length of plots was variable, as a perusal of Trim's town plan reveals. Some plots had a length:width ratio of 5:1, but plots close to the intersection of streets were inevitably shorter, as were plots which backed onto Church property or the river.

Excavations on the north island of Cork have yielded very good evidence for the development of both the street frontages and backyards of burgage plots. At the North Gate (Hurley 1997) the plots ran from the street frontage back towards the town wall, and each of the seven excavated plots measured between six and seven metres in width, although one was eight metres wide at the street and ten metres at the rear. These plots were laid out about the middle of the thirteenth century at a time when the north island had a stone quay wall at its north end but was still an unwalled suburb of the settlement on the south island; the north island was only walled in the late thirteenth or early fourteenth century. The street frontages had stone-footed sill-beam houses with a width:length ratio of about 1:2 and with their narrow sides facing the street. The backyards, which were separated from each other by rubble walls, were put to good use. Bake ovens, either open-air or in buildings, were a feature of some plots from the middle or late thirteenth century, and these possibly produced food stuffs for commercial purposes. One of the backyards contained the furnace of the water-powered forge in the late thirteenth or fourteenth century (see p104). Even more interesting is evidence for the early infill of the backyards: as early as the late thirteenth or early fourteenth century one of the north island plots had in its backyard three adjoining buildings, each of stone-footed sill-beam construction, and they occupied an area about 3.5m in width and 22m in length. Within half a century one of these buildings was replaced with a new, stone-walled building, again leaving the backyard of the plot almost completely in-filled.

Urban castles

Two principal groups of castles can be associated with towns: seigneurial castles of the Anglo-Norman magnates under whose auspices the towns were founded, and tower-houses. The former are features of about two-thirds of the towns, but only in four cases — Athlone, county Westmeath, Enniscorthy, county Wexford, Naas, county Kildare, and Ratoath, county Meath — could the castle be described as physically *within* the town; in the other cases the castles are either against the outside of the town boundaries or at very short distances from those boundaries. Both earth-and-timber and stone structures are represented among the seigneurial castles, but the majority are of the latter class.

Tower-houses were principally features of towns in the fifteenth and sixteenth centuries. Coastal settlements like Dalkey, county Dublin, probably had up to a dozen in the middle ages (**38**); as late as the seventeenth century the large inland town of Naas, county Kildare, still had ten (Simington [ed] 1931-61 x), while the small inland settlement of Newcastle Lyons, county Dublin, is known to have had six or seven (O'Keeffe 1986, 53). Ben Murtagh has counted 37 extant urban tower-houses in Ireland (1988, 536), but this is a small percentage of what must have existed late in the middle ages. Excavation by the late Dermot Twohig revealed the lower parts of one of Cork's many examples, Skiddy's castle, erected in the middle of the fifteenth century at a cost of £140 (Clearly, Hurley and Shee Twohig 1997).

These urban tower-houses, or fortified town houses as they are sometimes described, are generally attributed to merchants (Murtagh 1985-6; 1988; 1989), and most of them, particularly those in the coastal towns, were indeed probably owned by people involved in commerce. But one did not need to be a merchant burgess to possess a tower-house. Several tower-houses in Fethard, county Tipperary, for example, are known to have been owned by members of one important family in the political life of that town, the Everards, while one of the tower-houses there, the so-called Edmond Castle, might even have belonged to the Church (O'Keeffe 1999a).

Urban tower-houses generally conform to rural types in their morphology, but the fact of their location on restricted, street-fronting, sites sometimes necessitated alterations to the rural template. For example, their width was often conditioned by the width of the plot itself. Fifteenth-century tower-houses such as Hatch's Castle in Ardee, county Louth, surveyed by Ben Murtagh (1989), and Quirke's Castle in Cashel, county Tipperary, are very narrow buildings, presumably because they had to be hemmed into narrow plots; both these tower-houses faced onto market-places and the plots which they occupy may have been narrowed by subdivision under commercial pressure in the thirteenth or fourteenth century. But those property-owners with considerable wealth and political power did not always have to tolerate such restrictions. St Leger's Castle in Ardee, for

1   *Bannow Bay, county Wexford, where the Anglo-Normans landed in 1169. The ruined church in the distance marks the site of an abandoned Anglo-Norman settlement*

2   *The motte at Shanid, county Limerick. The heavily-ruined polygonal tower on its summit was erected early in the thirteenth century*

3   Clonmacnois Castle, county Offaly. The stone buildings are mainly of the early 1200s. The earthwork has been identified by some writers as a ringwork castle, and by others as a motte-and-bailey (Photograph: Dúchas, The Heritage Service, reproduced with permission)

4   Roscommon Castle, a royal fortress, was erected shortly before 1300. The insertion of large, mullioned windows in the late 1500s rendered it less formidable as a military fortress

5   *Inchiquin Castle, county Cork. This is one of a number of cylindrical great towers built by the Anglo-Normans in Munster in the early 1200s*

6   *Ballymoon Castle, county Carlow, from the air. The builder's intention was to have a continuous suite of rooms wrapped around a central courtyard; however, the castle seems never to have been finished (Photograph: Dúchas, The Heritage Service, reproduced with permission)*

7   *Barryscourt Castle, county Cork. Now undergoing restoration, this is a very fine fifteenth- and sixteenth-century tower-house with an adjoining hall and a bawn*

8   *The sixteenth-century tower-house of Cloghleigh, near Kilworth, county Cork, is among the finest examples in Ireland*

9   *Oughterard, county Kildare: the low ridge over which the wire fence runs is a plough headland, one of the few remaining traces of arable farming at this manor; a second headland is visable as a dark band further down the field. Similar features survive in the adjoining manor of Castlewarden*

10   The thirteenth-century dovecot at Ballybeg Augustinian priory, county Cork, is the largest surviving example in Ireland

11   Wood Quay, Dublin, June 1979, showing the Civic Offices of Dublin Corporation in the course of construction on part of the site of medieval Dublin; the stone-built town wall of c1100 snakes across the middle of the site (Photograph: Department of Archaeology, UCD)

12   Christ Church Cathedral, Dublin, viewed from the south; the transept is late Romanesque work of 1180-1200, the nave — the south side of which was rebuilt in the nineteenth century — is early thirteenth-century Gothic of western English character

13   *Dunleckny, county Carlow, had a settlement of burgesses in the early 1200s; although a parish church and motte survive from that period, the best indication of Dunleckny's former importance is the convergence of many roads at the site*

14   *Fethard, county Tipperary, is probably the best example of a small walled-town in Ireland: the part of the town wall in this view may be of fourteenth-century date, but the mural tower and the church tower both date from the fifteenth century when the town appears to have been especially prosperous*

15   St Laurence's Gateway, Drogheda, county Louth, is actually the barbican or forework which stood about ten metres in front of one of the now-destroyed gateways into the town. Comparable buildings are known to have been features of other major towns in Ireland, but none survives. The lower part of this Drogheda barbican is of thirteenth-century date, and the upper third dates from the fifteenth century

16   Although linked by popular tradition with Brian Boru, the tenth-century Irish king, this harp, preserved in Trinity College, Dublin, is probably fifteenth century in date. Decorative devices of so-called 'Celtic' type — interlace and marigolds — reflect the renewed interest of later medieval Gaelic-Irish patrons in their pre-colonial heritage (Photograph: reproduced with permission of the Board of Trustees, Trinity College Dublin)

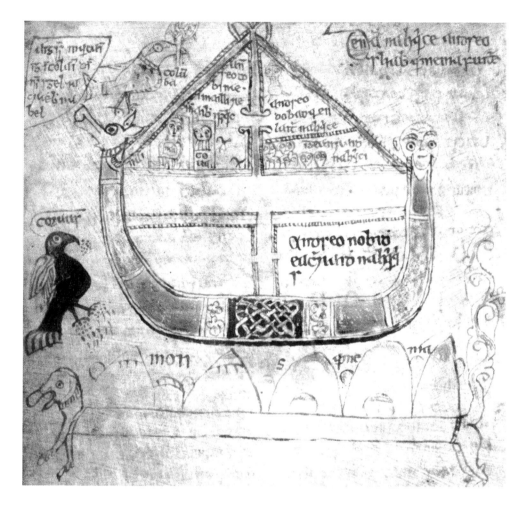

17   *The highly-stylised vessel in this fourteenth-century, Gaelic-Irish, depiction of Noah's Ark, may be an early form of hulk, a type of vessel capable of sea-travel. The image is entitled 'The construction of the Ark with the Armenian mountain below' (Ms G.3.f.16v; photograph: National Library of Ireland, reproduced with permission)*

18   *This cylindrical lighthouse on Hook Head, county Wexford, was erected in the early years of the thirteenth century to facilitate the entry of trading vessels into the estuaries of the rivers Suir, Nore and Barrow. It is one of the oldest lighthouses still in use in the world*

19   Jugs and a small bowl, all made in Saintonge, from the City Centre Excavations, Waterford, 1986-92 (exhibited at Waterford Treasures Museum, The Quay, Waterford)

20   A locally-made jug of Waterford 'A' ware from the City Centre Excavations, Waterford, 1986-92 (exhibited at Waterford Treasures Museum, The Quay, Waterford)

21   The west façade of Clonfert cathedral, county Galway, probably dates from the tenth century, but its Romanesque portal was inserted in the late 1100s, and the windows are fifteenth century

22   The (reconstructed) arch of the mid-twelfth-century Romanesque doorway of Dysert O'Dea church, county Clare, has details of English and western French origin on its second-largest and second-smallest arches respectively

23   Duiske Cistercian abbey, Graiguenamanagh, county Kilkenny, has a very plain, early thirteenth-century nave in keeping with the tradition of the Order

24   The chancel of Duiske abbey had an exceptionally well-crafted rib-vaulted roof in the early 1200s. The vault no longer survives

25   *Athassel Augustinian priory, county Tipperary, has a large and elaborate church of thirteenth-century date, the central (or crossing) tower of which was heightened in the 1400s; there are extensive remains of the cloister and its surrounding buildings*

38   This is one of only two fifteenth-century tower-houses still standing in the medieval port of Dalkey, county Dublin

example, which is the largest of all extant urban tower-houses (Bradley 1984b), was not only erected on a prime urban site but was projected into the market-place beyond the lines of the other buildings along the street. One possible explanation is that the owners of such buildings purchased these plots and, by political pull, managed to breach the integrity of the street frontages; alternatively, the corporations of these towns may have encouraged the building of defensible (but private) residences at strategic points.

Most of the urban tower-houses seem to have vaulted lower storeys, presumably for the storage and retailing of goods. The upper storeys, by contrast, were residential. This separation of private and commercial in an urban house had a long-established tradition in England from the thirteenth century (Faulkner 1966). The fact that one could not move freely from the basement to the upper storeys in many urban tower-houses suggests that the lower, commercial, storey was leased to a merchant (Murtagh 1988, 551; O'Keeffe 1999a, 20-21).

Urban churches

The Hiberno-Norse ports of Dublin, Limerick and Waterford were cathedral towns in the eleventh century, and they retained that status after the Anglo-Norman arrival; Dublin even acquired two cathedrals in the thirteenth century, one inside the town and the other immediately outside it. The towns of Cashel, county Tipperary, Downpatrick, county Down, Ferns, county Wexford, and Kildare and Kilkenny, also had cathedrals; in the case of Cashel that cathedral was sited on the outcrop known as St Patrick's Rock, and while this site was not physically a part of the town, without it the town would probably not have existed in the first instance as there is no river.

Most of the medieval towns in Ireland had coterminuous municipal and parochial boundaries; the towns were, in other words, self-contained parishes, and one church existed to meet the spiritual needs of the entire urban comunity. The small size of the towns militated against multiple parishes, largely because the communities were not sufficiently large to fund more than one church. Only the large towns with pre-colonial origins, such as Dublin, Kilkenny and Wexford, had more than one parish contained within their walls, and this reflects the structure of their pre-colonial pastoral organisation. Drogheda, county Louth, had two parish churches, but their location on either side of the river reflects that town's origin and early (pre-1412) history as two separate towns, one in Meath and one in Louth (Bradley 1977-80). The architecture of the parish churches will be discussed more thoroughly in the following chapter, but suffice it to say here that the largest of all Ireland's medieval parish churches are those which served the towns of New Ross, county Wexford, Youghal and Kinsale, county Cork, and Galway. One of the largest such churches is in Fethard, county Tipperary (**39**): its size is much greater than one might expect in what was quite a small town, and this may suggest that its patron envisaged the town growing to a larger size than actually transpired.

Monastic orders were drawn to urban settlements, but their houses were invariably outside the town walls. Franciscans and Dominicans usually occupied sites which abutted the exteriors of the town walls, thereby becoming magnets around which suburbs developed. Hospitals, which were run by religious communities, were also extra-mural, and for obvious health reasons. The Cistercians desired isolation in the siting of their

39   The parish church in Fethard, county Tipperary

houses, so they tend to be fairly distant from urban settlements, although St Mary's Abbey was erected across the river Liffey from, and within sight of, the walled town of Dublin. Hore Abbey, built in 1272 and the last of the medieval Cistercian foundations in Ireland (Stalley 1987), is quite close to the town of Cashel, but it occupied a site which is on the far side of St Patrick's Rock from the town and so it has a far greater separation from the settlement than the simple distance would suggest. The only monasteries which are found with any frequency within the towns are priories of Augustinian canons regular. Several factors explain this: their willingness to engage in pastoral work made them favourites among patrons, their space requirements were modest, and they, unlike the Dominicans and Franciscans, were present in Ireland at the time of colonisation (O'Keeffe 1999b).

Town walls

The town wall was a very powerful and evocative symbol of urban identity and wealth in the middle ages. Its construction was a venture which, to some degree, involved the entire urban community, and the protection which it offered to them was not only physical but economic. By wrapping towns in permanent embraces, town walls also contributed inadvertently to the development of suburbs, as populations gathered at the peripheries of the settlements, either in the vicinities of the monastic houses which were located there, or around the gateways where they might benefit from the coming and goings of traders. Extra-mural suburbs are mentioned in Dublin as early as 1200 (Thomas 1992 i, 11)

No less than 56 Irish towns had medieval walls around them, while a further 35 may have been walled or at least had walling planned for them (Thomas 1992 i, 3). The erection of a town wall was funded by a 'murage grant'. This is a somewhat misleading phrase since it suggests that money was simply handed over, when in reality it was simply a grant of permission to the townspeople to raise the money themselves by the collection of tolls; sometimes the grants permitted communities to divert certain duties or taxes which would otherwise have issued to the crown. The grants were not for indefinite periods but had strict time limits, and with urban communities unable to complete their construction work within the duration of one grant, it was normal for a whole series of grants to be made to the one town, sometimes in sequence and other times at intervals. At Fethard, county Tipperary, for example, there were murage grants in 1292, 1375-6, 1409, possibly 1456, and 1468, and in the case of the latter grant money left over was to be used for paving the streets; the circuit at Fethard is fairly complete (**colour plate 14**), and most of the fabric seems to be of fifteenth-century date. The inability of communities to wall their towns with money generated by a single murage grant may be because the sort of money raised by tolls was too low, but it might also be that the system was open to abuse, as is evident from records of embezzlement at Dundalk and Kilkenny in 1305 and 1383 respectively (Bradley 1985, 442). We must also remember that town authorities, conscious that their settlements might expand, may have erected town walls which had longer circuits than were actually needed: this may explain why there are empty areas inside the circuits of some town walls, as at Athenry, county Galway, for example.

Town walls were usually constructed of stone, but earthen ramparts were not unknown. In the case of Fethard the murage grant of 1375-6 specifically mentions a stone wall, suggesting that the boundary erected with a murage grant in 1292 was of earth and timber. Gowran, county Kilkenny, had a murage grant in the fifteenth century in which a stone wall was specified (Thomas 1992 ii, 114), but an early eighteenth-century map of the town (**36**) shows that one side of the settlement was protected by a 'rampart' which was presumably of earth. Some of the late town walls, such as Coleraine, Athlone West and Belfast, were merely earthen ramparts, although they were strengthened internally by stone.

The erection of town walls in Ireland was principally a phenomenon of the second half of the thirteenth century and of the fourteenth and fifteenth centuries. However, the Hiberno-Norse ports of Dublin and Waterford had been 'walled', first in earth and then in stone, in the pre-colonial period (see p85 above), but the mechanisms by which funding was raised for these projects are not known to us. Appropriately, these were also the first towns to be given murage grants in the colonial period.

Waterford's town walls

Waterford is a very interesting case-study (O'Keeffe 1995). The shape of the Hiberno-Scandinavian town was triangular. In the early thirteenth century the town possessed the same murage conditions as Bristol, a port with which Waterford enjoyed trading contacts, and this may have been to facilitate the renewal by the Anglo-Normans of walls around the pre-colonial town. In the early thirteenth century the Anglo-Normans extended the town westwards, and later in the thirteenth century the town may have been extended further to the south to rejoin the river; each extension was accompanied by campaigns of town wall construction (**33**). This extension of the town westwards and south-westwards did not, however, lead to the abandonment of the line of the western boundary of the original Hiberno-Scandinavian town; rather, that boundary was kept and was even provided with a series of new gates along its length. At the end of the thirteenth century the citizens of Waterford requested murage to repair the walls and gates of the city, so between 1291 to 1295 and between 1311 to 1326 provisions were made to raise money for this purpose, and from 1356 Waterford was granted permanent murage facilities to help the citizens maintain the walls. Two of the extant mural towers, the Double Tower and the Beach Tower, seem to be late medieval in date and may be attributed to this phase of continuous murage provisions. In the late sixteenth century Waterford was singled out by the government as a place likely to be chosen by invading Spaniards, so commissioners were appointed in 1587 to organise a new set of fortifications for the city. The new fortifications were comprised of ramparts outside the medieval walls on the south, south-east and west of the city, while alterations were made to towers on the medieval circuit; the Watch Tower (**40**) is entirely late sixteenth century in date, and the French Tower and Half-Moon Tower may be of the same date. In 1598, less than a decade after the construction of this new defensive system had begun, the Earl of Ormond considered these fortifications to be 'of small purpose' and thought that a better system could have been instituted at half the cost.

The oldest and most substantial of the mural towers to survive — and possibly the most substantial to have been built — is Reginald's Tower, located at the apex of the triangular area of the Hiberno-Scandinavian town. Giraldus Cambrensis referred to a 'Raghenald's Tower' (*Expugnatio Hibernica*) leading to the view expressed by some writers (Leask 1951, 111-2) that the present structure is of pre-Anglo-Norman date. This is not inconceivable: the stair connecting the two lower storeys is similar in construction — a cut newell and a plank-turned vault — to that in the south tower of the Romanesque church at Cashel, county Tipperary, which is known as Cormac's Chapel and which dates from the period 1127-1134. However, Reginald's Tower is best interpreted as an Anglo-Norman building of *c*1200: the internal arrangement of the tower indicates that, despite it being part of the town defences, it belongs firmly in the tradition of cylindrical *donjons*. In 1215 a royal castle is mentioned in Waterford in the same context as the royal castle of Dungarvan, which has a cylindrical *donjon*. Is it possible that Reginald's Tower acted as the *donjon* of that royal castle?

With one exception, the town gates of Waterford are known to us only from documentary and cartographic sources of post-medieval date, and the records of their morphology are not always reliable. That exception is St Martin's Gate, excavated in the 1980s. Comprised of two circular towers flanking a narrow passage, this existed by *c*1224 when reference was made to it in an inquisition. Of the other town gates, St John's Gate is the one for which we have the most reliable evidence of morphology. One of the principal gates into the medieval city, this was a large twin-towered structure with an external twin-towered barbican, rather like St Laurence's Gateway in Drogheda (**colour plate 15**). A channel of St John's River would have run between the inner and outer pairs of towers. Beyond the gate-house was the bridge, and this was probably connected to the barbican by a walled passage; in the late sixteenth century a star-shaped outwork of the type discussed in chapter 2 (see p55) was erected at the south end of the bridge for additional protection.

40   *The Watch Tower, Waterford City. This tower, at the southern tip of the town wall, has distinctive gun-loops intended for small cannon or hand-guns*

5 Craft, industry and trade

The archaeology we have considered so far is archaeology *in* and *of* the landscape, and it follows in a long historiographical tradition among medievalists concerned with the archaeology of Ireland in the second millennium AD. In Chapter 6, a review of churches and monastic buildings, we will be returning to archaeological evidence which survives as part of the landscape. Studies of artefacts in later medieval Ireland are not so far advanced, and in the only other synthetic work of this nature, Terry Barry's *The Archaeology of Medieval Ireland* (1987), artefacts appeared as a section on crafts and industries within a chapter on rural settlement. Whether craft and industrial produce would be better treated in a chapter on urban rather than rural settlement given that manufacturing is more an urban than rural pursuit could be debated, but the principal point to be made is that up to twelve years ago the study of medieval artefacts lagged far behind the study of buildings and settlement. Much of the work done on artefacts up to that date was a consequence of the discovery of material in the excavation of later medieval sites, rather than the sort of museum-based research which prehistorians have long practised on non-contextualised finds. Research on later medieval artefacts is still largely, though no longer almost exclusively, driven by the needs of excavators to understand their finds, and this means that the best commentaries on categories of medieval artefact are to be found not in research papers but in the finds-catalogues of excavation reports. The outstanding record of publication among excavators of urban settlements in Ireland has brought our awareness and understanding of material culture in later medieval Ireland to new levels. This chapter deals principally with the patterns and processes of production and distribution of this material culture, although the actual uses to which the artefacts were put, and the interpretations which they allow us to make about life in the middle ages, are also treated.

The areas within which that material culture was distributed are local, regional, national, and international, and 'trade' communicates the principal mechanism by which goods moved. The difference between 'craft' and 'industry' — the two words in the chapter title which relate specifically to production — should not detain us here. In a modern context we might regard the process of 'crafting' as hands-on and personalised, whereas 'industry' suggests depersonalised mass production; we can even think of the former in terms of specialist goods for limited markets, and the latter in terms of rather mundane goods for large markets. A similar distinction between 'craft' and 'industry' is appropriate for the middle ages, but we should not draw too heavily the boundaries between them: low-grade pottery for the mass market might be described as the product of an industry, but a household making the same low-grade pottery for its own use might be described as engaging in a craft activity. An analysis of the suitability of one term over another is not really appropriate to this discussion of the making of material culture in later medieval Ireland, so the 'craft' and 'industry' are regarded here as essentially the same things.

Metalworking

One of the many activities at which the aristans of pre-colonial Ireland, both urban and rural, excelled was metalworking, and their output included both mundane or everyday objects and spectacular *objets d'art* like shrines and reliquaries. Iron was the principal raw material of medieval metallurgists, and technical innovation in processing and manufacturing is a feature of Europe from the twelfth century onwards, and it is accompanied in the archaeological and historical records by an increase in evidence for smithing (Cipolla 1993, 139). The first step was the acquisition of the raw material itself. Once mined, it was normal in Ireland, at least until the sixteenth century (Rynne 1998, 89), to smelt the ore in a bloomery to produce the wrought — or 'pure' — iron from which the smith could then fashion artefacts. Imported iron was also available, but it came to Ireland not as bulky ore but already-smelted; much of this imported iron came in tandem with salt from Spain and Brittany (O'Neill 1987, 90-1).

Smelting and metal-working were both urban and rural pursuits. Substantial quantities of iron slag, which are indicative of on-the-spot smelting, have been found in association with iron artefacts in towns (Carrickfergus, county Antrim: Simpson and Dickson 1981, 80), in small house-clusters (Bourchier's castle, county Limerick: Cleary 1982; 1983), and at rural habitats (Lismahon, county Down: Waterman 1959; Coney Island, county Armagh: Addyman 1964).

Exceptionally good evidence of metalworking in an urban context comes from Cork where a water-powered forge, located in the backyard of a late thirteenth or early fourteenth-century plot close to the North Gate, was investigated (Hurley 1997, 45-9). Water was brought from the north channel of the river Lee, possibly via a timber-lined leat or channel; proximity to the river also allowed the easy off-loading from commercial ships of bar-iron and charcoal. The wheel-race brought the water to an undershot wheel, and this was connected to a bellow which, in turn, maintained the heat of the furnace on the platform. Once heated, the iron, which would have been smelted before being brought to the forge, was worked on the wooden anvil under a trip hammer activated by water-wheel. Very little slag was found near either the platform or anvil, and no metal-working tools were found. The forge continued in use for about half a century.

Iron was put to use in the manufacture of a very broad range of objects in later-medieval Ireland. These can be briefly outlined, but as examples are found on most excavated sites specific instances are not named here unless they are of particular interest. Tools were customarily made of iron, whether small carpentry axes, files, shears, knives or scissors. Keys and locks were also of iron, although some copper alloy keys are known. Some of the locks were mounted on doors but others were on caskets. Barrel padlocks seem to have

41 A tripod candlestick from Waterford (after Hurley et al 1997). A single candle would have shed little light, but the candlestick itself might have been a valued indicator of status; cresset stones (Moore 1984) provided a cheaper alternative

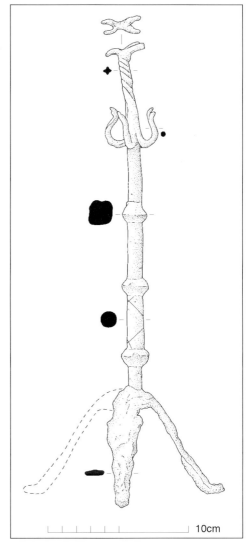

10cm

been especially common to judge by the finds from the excavations in Cork and Waterford. Household goods made of iron include candlesticks; these were mainly of pricket type, but a fine example of a tripod candlestick of early or mid-twelfth-century date from Waterford (**41**) shows how high-quality the metalwork could be.

Weapons were obvious items needing to be manufactured. The sword was the symbol of medieval chivalric society, and a number of Anglo-Norman and later medieval swords or fragments of swords survive in Ireland (Halpin 1986; Scott 1988). Swords and axes could be recycled if broken or blunted, but arrowheads for both bows and cross-bows could only be used once, so there was often a need for new ones to be made; the same may be true of spearheads (an especially popular weapon among the Gaelic-Irish: Harbison 1975-6). One can calculate from the accounts of Giraldus Cambrensis that archers represented 85% of those in the armed contingents at the beginning of the colonial period,

105

and the large numbers of extant bodkin-bladed arrowheads capable of penetrating armour is testimony to the importance of the archer in warfare in Ireland (Halpin 1997). It naturally follows from this that many of the arrowheads found on Irish archaeological sites might not have been made in Ireland at all.

Horseshoes were also made of iron, and examples are found at many urban and rural sites, sometimes with the characteristic nails (short, with square, block-like heads, as distinct from the long, flat-topped and square-sectioned nails used in more general contexts) still attached to them. Both shoes and nails seem to be especially prevalent in thirteenth-century levels. The appearance of the nailed shoe was one of the many developments in European agrarian economy around the end of the first millennium AD. The wear and tear on paved streets was increased when the animals were brought into settlements, but in compensation horseshoes increased the efficiency and thus the value of horses as beasts of burden and traction (Cipolla 1993, 138-9).

Iron was not the only metal in use in later medieval Ireland. Artefacts of silver and of various alloys are also known. Silver was used in coinage (see p116). It was also more popular than gold in the making of jewellery (Deevy 1998). The mining of silver is quite well documented. In 1276 Edward I initiated mining in what are now called the Silvermine mountains in county Tipperary, and in 1277 he ordered the opening of 'other mines of silver, copper, lead, or iron, or other metals lately found in Ireland' (O'Sullivan 1963; Cowman 1992). In the sixteenth century Clonmines, county Wexford, was identified as a potential source of silver and there was brief mining activity there (Cowman 1986-7).

Materials fashioned out of alloys of copper — an ore-type exploited in Ireland since prehistory — are especially prominant in the archaeological record, and all are fairly high quality objects. A crozier-head dating from between the twelfth and fourteenth centuries and found at the Four Courts in Dublin (MacMahon 1988, 308-10), a site directly across the Liffey from the medieval urban core, represents the prestige end of the market. Horse harness parts found on the Cork excavations were also of copper alloy (Hurley 1990, 70; Scully 1997, 186). Small personal items like stick pins were also made of copper alloy; at Waterford, for example, virtually all of the 232 pins made between *c*1000 and *c*1300 were of copper alloy, the remainder being of iron. Bronze, an alloy of copper with a significant (up to 30%) tin content, seems to have been the preferred material for one type of weapon in Ireland, the spiked macehead (Halpin 1988). Nineteen of these fearsome objects survive, and it is easy to imagine most of them in use in battle. At least one of the maceheads — that at Athenry, county Galway (**42**) — must have been used in ceremonial situations, and the relief decoration on the outside of its socket suggests that it was made outside Ireland or by an English craftsman in Ireland.

Stone

One of the major industries was the building industry, and its products are assessed elsewhere in this book. Given the great explosion of new buildings in the aftermath of the conquest, quarries must have been common sights and the sheering-off of great chunks of living rock must have been a common sound. Large-scale quarrying was necessitated

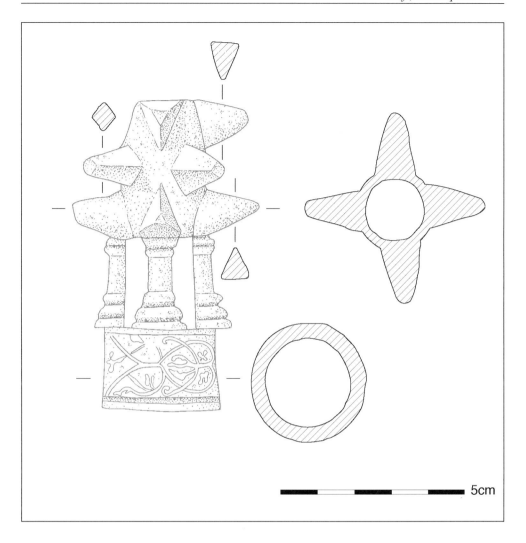

42   *A bronze macehead from Athenry, county Galway (after Halpin 1988)*

perhaps by the scarcity of native, stone-built Irish buildings which could be dismantled to make building material available. Churches may have been the only substantial buildings of stone in many parts of Ireland, and their stone was needed for their refurbishment or enlargement.

Local stone was used for general masonry, and so one finds, for example, castles and churches in granitic areas constructed of granite. Openings such as windows and doorways required dressed stone, and to produce the desired effect the masons of the period before 1400 often selected types of stone which were different in colour or texture from that which they used in the fabric of their buildings. Sometimes this special stone was imported: for example, oolithic limestone — a soft, chalky, light-coloured stone — was brought into south-east Ireland from the Dundry area of Somerset in the thirteenth

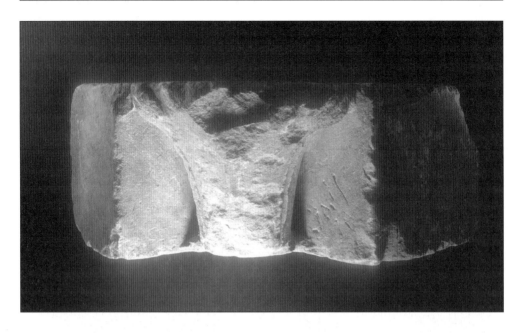

43   An ex situ *early thirteenth-century capital carved in Dundry stone from Bridgetown Priory, county Cork*

century (Waterman 1970; **43**). Although limestone was generally not favoured for architectural detail and sculpture in Anglo-Norman buildings, it was used in the making of tombs (**44, 45**).

Oolithic limestone was not imported into Ulster, but a comparable limestone from Cultra, county Down, was transported around south-east Ulster between the twelfth and fourteenth centuries for use on churches and castles, and on grave slabs (McNeill 1980, 45). A local arcosic sandstone, which is fairly indistinguishable from Dundry stone in its soft texture and light colour, was used around 1200 at Ballyderown castle, county Cork (O'Keeffe 1984), while local calcareous tufa was used in the castles of Dundrum and Greencastle, both in county Down (McNeill 1980, 43). Brick seems not to have been used very much for building prior to the seventeenth century (Craig 1982, 109, 145).

It was not only for the purposes of building that stone was imported. High-quality millstones which would allow the making of grit-free flour were often imported, either from Britain or France (O'Neill 1987, 92). Stone mortars, used for crushing nuts, herbs and other substances either for food or for medicinal potions, were also imported from southern England (Hurley 1997).

Animals as raw materials

One consequence of the considerable numbers of sheep and cattle in the landscape of medieval Ireland was the ready availability of source material for the making of textiles (**46**) and leather objects (**47**). Wool was a principal export of the Anglo-Norman economy

44   *An Anglo-Norman sarcophagus with its lid (see **Fig 45**), and a thirteenth-century grave-slab with figure sculpture, at Bannow church, county Wexford. Later in the middle ages grave-slabs became more elaborate, and by the sixteenth and seventeenth centuries they frequently bore long inscriptions and complex images including Symbols of the Passions, especially in the Pale and in Munster (see Gillespie 1994; Maher 1998)*

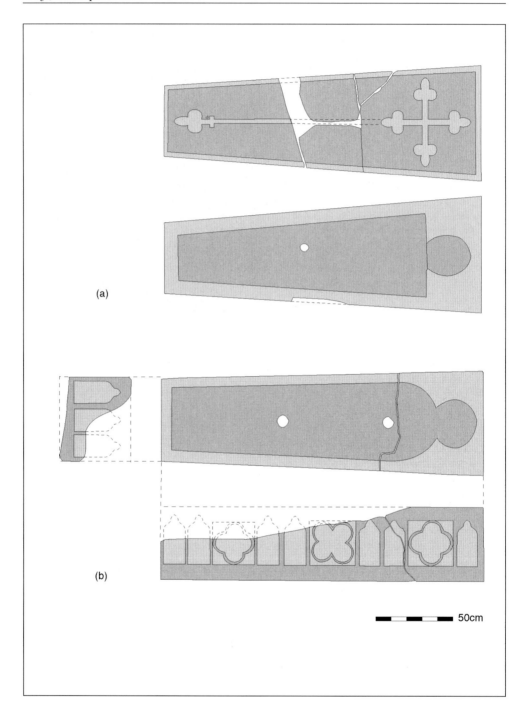

45   Two Anglo-Norman sarcophagi: (a) from Bannow, county Wexford; (b) from the Dominican friary, Kilkenny (after Bradley 1988). The identities of the occupants of such sarcophagi are rarely known, but the likelihood is that all of them were either senior clerics or secular patrons from local aristocracies

46   *An early fourteenth-century grave-slab at Athassel, county Tipperary. The people represented on this stone — a woman on the left and a man on the right — may be members of the de Burgo family, active patrons of Athassel in the colonial period. Both wear garments which are typical for their sexes in the years around 1300 (see Brennan 1990)*

47   *A leather scabbard from Essex Street West, Dublin (after Simpson 1995). Sheaths for knives are quite common on urban excavations in Ireland, but this particular example is unique in bearing five heraldic shields; these suggest it was the property of a Cheshire family*

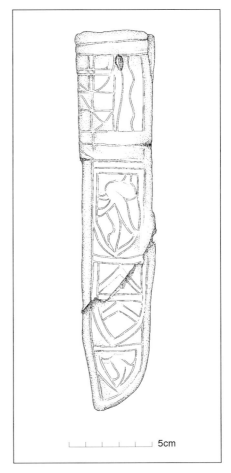

5cm

in Ireland; vast amounts of it were exported out of New Ross and Waterford between 1275 and 1294 (MacNiocaill 1964 ii, 527-8), with Italian merchant bankers controlling the collection of custom on those exports (O'Sullivan 1963). Not all of the wool was for exporting. Wool was spun in domestic contexts, and simple distaffs and spindles were used until at least the fourteenth century when the spinning wheel was first introduced (Hurley & McCutcheon 1977, 588). In the thirteenth-century the two-beam horizontal loom was introduced into Ireland, and it allowed longer pieces to be woven than had previously been possible (Rynne 1998, 86). A shuttle from a horizontal loom was recovered from a twelfth or early thirteenth-century context in Waterford, and there is a similar one in a thirteenth-century example from Cork (Hurley and McCutcheon, 1997, 583).

Spinning and weaving were carried out manually for much of the middle ages, but 'fulling' — ridding the cloth of the dirt and grease accumulated during the spinning and weaving — could be mechanised (Rynne 1998, 85-6). Fulling involved pounding the cloth, either in an alkaline stew of stale urine or with a special type of clay called 'fuller's earth'. Fulling resulted in the shrinking of the fibres and the thickening of the cloth. Fulling could be achieved by men trampling the cloth in great troughs, but the water-powered fulling mill was far more efficient and effective. So revolutionary was the development of the fulling mill that that textile workers in thirteenth-century France protested violently that mechanisation was detrimental to the quality of the product and was costing jobs (Cipolla 1993, 140). Fulling mills are recorded at Clones, county Monaghan, in 1211-12, while in the second half of the thirteenth century there were fulling mills near Youghal, county Cork (Rynne 1998, 86). Cloth which was fulled has been recovered from excavations in Dublin, Cork and Waterford (Wincott Heckett 1990, 81-5; 1997, 749). Implements for the making of garments have also been found (Hurley 1997, 119-21).

Leather shoes completed the medieval outfit, and substantial numbers of these survive in waterlogged contexts on urban sites (O'Rourke 1997, 149-51). They were normally 'composite turnshoes': two pieces of cowskin or calfskin leather stitched together to form the shoe, and then turned inside-out so that the stitching was on the inside. Bone, the other raw material extractable from dead animals, was also put to the service of personal appearances: finely toothed combs are well-represented on urban sites.

Bone and wood

One of the most interesting uses to which bone was put was in the making of dice and other items for the purposes of gaming and entertainment (**48**). The dice are different from modern dice only in the arrangement of the numbers: one is opposite two, three is opposite four, and five is opposite six. Two basic types of gaming piece are attested on many sites: one is a flat disc with dot-and-circle motifs, and the other a small dome-shaped object with a spike projecting from its underside. An oak-made gaming board of mid-twelfth-century date was found in Waterford (**49**).

Music was another form of entertainment. The instruments played in Gaelic-Irish circles were pipes, and lyres and harps. Each of these instruments is depicted in an example of high-status metalwork or manuscript-illumination: there is a piper on one

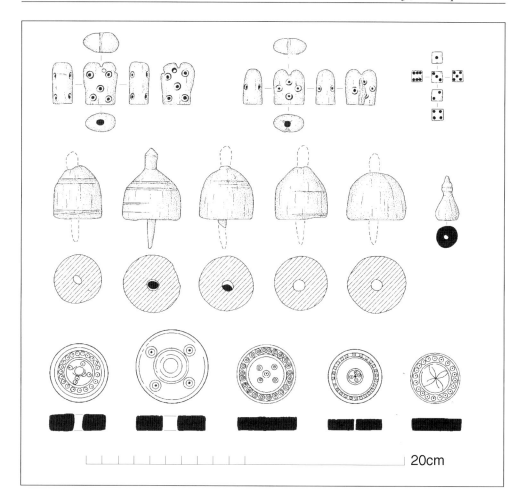

48   Gaming pieces. The two cylindrical pieces with incised dots in the top left-hand corner are from Jerpointchurch, county Kilkenny, and may be chessmen (after Foley 1989); the die, the six hemispherical gaming pieces, and the five flat discs, are all from Waterford (after Hurley, Scully and McCutcheon [eds] 1997); the hemispherical pieces may have been used in Hnefatafl, *a popular Viking-age game which was played on boards similar to that illustrated in* **49**

folio of a Cistercian ordinal (a book containing the outline of a liturgy) made *c*1500 (Henry and Marsh-Micheli 1959), a harpist (possibly King David) on the so-called Breac Maedhóg shrine of *c*1100, and a lyre player on the Shrine of the Stowe Missal, also of *c*1100. A magnificant, fifteenth-century harp of an unknown Gaelic-Irish aristocratic household is preserved in Trinity College, Dublin (**colour plate 16**); made of wood which is decorated with motifs which look back to the 'Golden Age' of Irish art in the eighth and ninth centuries, it also has brass and silver fittings. Irish harps were generally strung with bronze or brass wire (Rimmer 1969). The strings were tuned with keys of copper alloy rather than bone, and examples of these have turned up at urban sites such as

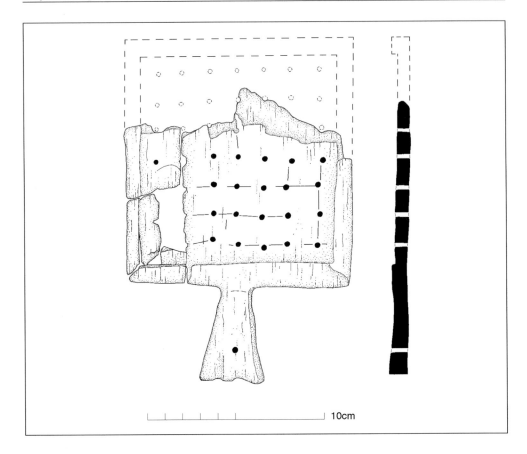

49   A small gaming board from Waterford (after Hurley, Scully and McCutcheon [eds] 1997)

Waterford (Hurley 1997) and Cork (Hurley 1996), as well as rural sites such as Clontuskert (Fanning 1976). An instrument popular among Anglo-Normans appears to be the jew's harp, and examples have been found at Trim Castle, county Meath (Sweetman 1978), Clontuskert (Fanning 1976), and Cork (Hurley, 1997, 123).

Glass

Glass was principally used in two contexts: in windows and in vessels. Prior to the seventeenth century all glass vessels used in Ireland, and that includes urinals, goblets, and stemmed wineglasses, seem to have been imported (Bourke 1997). No original medieval window glass is known to survive *in situ* in Ireland, but grooves in window-stones of post-1200 date indicate that glazed windows were quite common, especially in the eastern parts of churches and in the uppermost (and therefore most private) rooms of castles. Painted window glass has been found at quite a few sites, such as Mellifont Cistercian abbey, county Louth (de Paor 1969, 157), Kells Augustinian priory, county Kilkenny (Fanning 1973, 63), Clontuskert Augustinian priory (Fanning 1976, 149), Trim Castle, county Meath

(Sweetman 1978, 185), and Waterford city (Bourke 1997). The glass in the east window of the fourteenth-century chancel of St Canice's cathedral, Kilkenny, was apparently so impressive that in 1648 the papal nuncio sought unsuccessfully to purchase the entire window for £700; two years later the window was actually demolished (Rae 1987, 748). It is not known if any of this glass was made in Ireland, although it does seem likely.

Overseas trade

We can think about the movement of goods occuring at essentially two scales: local and international. At a local level within Ireland there was an economic symbiosis between town and country, as commodities needed by townspeople — hides, wool, grain, fuel — were brought in through the town walls, and commodities needed by rural dwellers — iron, fine cloth, salt, wine — were brought back out. Crucially, this exchange-system involved the participation of traders on the international market. The goods produced in the countryside were not only for consumption within the towns but were exported overseas, and some of the goods which ended up in rural households were themselves brought in from overseas and sold on stalls in urban market-places. This commercial choreography seems not to have been constrained directly by differences of politics or culture among merchants and consumers. Further research and reflection on the movement of goods across such boundaries may, however, reveal that in certain circumstances there were some goods which could not be offered for sale, or which would simply not sell, because they were so closely associated with one of Ireland's ethno-political populations.

The Irish of the middle ages were seafaring people (**colour plate 17**). The island's geographical location is both halfway along the great Atlantic littoral which spreads from the Arctic circle to the Straits of Gibralter, and at the western end of the sea route which, twisting around peninsulas and islands, brings one from the Baltic to the North Atlantic via the North Sea. This T-junction location gave Ireland's prehistoric people considerable influence in the development of contemporary European society, and many of the trade routes which emerged back in the Neolithic period or in the Bronze Age continued to have a life in the historic era. Late medieval, Italian-made portulan maps — maps which are constructed using bearings and distances complied by mariners — show clearly that the settlements and estuaries of Ireland's coasts were very familiar to sea-travellers in the 1300s and 1400s (Westropp 1913). The entry to Waterford and New Ross, the two principal (and competing) ports of the south-east corner of Ireland, was perhaps the most familiar of all, and this was in part because of the great cylindrical lighthouse on Hook Head (**colour plate 18**) which was erected around the start of the thirteenth century (Colfer 1984-5). The uses to which all these sea routes were put by later medieval traders, and the diverse goods in which they traded, have been discussed by Tim O'Neill in an invaluable survey (1989), while Alf O'Brien has published valuable accounts of Ireland's trade with France (1995).

Ireland's principal partner in foreign trade was England, and the ports of Chester and Bristol saw most of the traffic to and from Ireland. The best archaeological evidence in Ireland for incoming traffic is in the ceramic assemblages, as we will see below, but Bristol was also the port from which soft, white-coloured, oolithic limestone from the Dundry quarries was exported for use in several dozen Anglo-Norman buildings in Ireland in the thirteenth century (Waterman 1970). Ireland's very close trading connections with England were based on the political connection between the islands, their proximity to each other, and a reciprocated supply-demand relationship. There is also, of course, the matter of coinage (Dolly 1987).

Pre-Viking Ireland was coinless. Some Roman coins made their way to the island, but their value to the Irish would have been restricted to their gold, silver or copper content. English, Carolingian and Kufic coins came to Ireland with the Vikings and circulated among them until a mint — Ireland's first — was established in Dublin around 997. The coins which emanated from that mint were mainly copies of contemporary late Anglo-Saxon and early Norman coins from England. The first 'Irish' coins to be struck there in 1185 were silver halfpence bearing King John's name, and by early in the thirteenth century farthings and silver pence were also being struck there; the money minted in Dublin under King John had a wide circulation, and is more frequently found outside Ireland than in it. English-made money also came to Ireland, first as part of the baggage of the first generation of colonists in the immediate aftermath of the conquest, and then from the late 1400s when English money had great buying-power in Ireland because the coins already circulating on the island were so debased or so clipped that they had no real value beyond the island.

Dublin remained the centre of coin-production in Ireland throughout the later middle ages. Waterford was the only other city to have coins produced in it for long periods in the later middle ages. Limerick, Kilkenny, Downpatrick, county Down, and Carrickfergus, county Antrim, briefly had mints from end of the twelfth century, and Cork (and possibly also Roscommon) briefly had a mint at the end of the thirteenth century. In the 1460s new mints were opened in Limerick, Galway, Trim, county Meath, and Drogheda and Carlingford, both in county Louth, but by the start of the sixteenth century only Dublin, Waterford and Drogheda retained mints. Minting was not restricted to the colonists. Prior to the Anglo-Norman arrival bracteates — simple coins struck from a single die — were being made at mints established under royal patronage in Clonmacnois, county Offfaly, and Ferns, county Wexford. In the early fifteenth century the Gaelic-Irish of north Leinter and south Ulster were producing forgeries of English and Scottish coins.

Pottery

Ceramic material is remarkably durable; the rate of degradation of even the poorest pottery is so slow that we have probably not yet arrived at a stage where some phase of Irish antiquity seems to be aceramic because in reality its pottery has decayed. Also, while ceramic objects may have multiple uses, ceramic material does not lend itself to physical recycling, so that once a vessel is fashioned the clay is usually locked forever into a form, whether the vessel remains intact or breaks. And when a pot does break it is transformed from a single object into multiple artefacts, so the greater its fracturing the greater the chance that we might find evidence that it once existed.

Pottery-making was both a craft and an industry, and the tendency for potters at kilns to create forms which are uniquely their own, even when mass-produced, coupled with their use of local stone for gritting their vessels, makes it possible to trace the source areas of ceramic objects with some accuracy. The tens of thousands of sherds in the assemblages of ceramic materials from medieval sites in Ireland together constitute an extraordinary source for monitoring the endeavour of those born on the island to create their own ceramic fingerprints, and for reconstructing the patterns of contact between the mercantile communities in parts of medieval Ireland and the potters and merchants of other parts of Europe.

Such was the quantity of pottery produced in Europe in the middle ages that the lack of indigenous ceramic industries in most of Ireland throughout most of the first millennium AD and the first century of the second is remarkable. Only in the north-east corner of Ireland can we identify pottery from this period which was actually made on the island. Known as 'souterrain ware', these hand-made pots (Ryan 1973) are neither technically nor aesthetically accomplished. However, we should not be too critical of the craftsmen who made these pots: vessels which we identify as cooking pots — they may just as readily be used for storage — were not designed to be seen, so no effort was made to make them visually attractive. Indeed, when the Anglo-Normans moved into Ulster in the late 1100s and found themselves too busy with the processes of subjugation and colonisation to worry about establishing their own kilns, they had no hesitation using these native cooking pots. In the thirteenth century Irish-made cooking pots in Ulster began to acquire everted rims in the manner of English cooking pots, and they continued to have a market among the region's Anglo-Normans; significantly, these everted-rim pots also had a market among the Irish communities of central and southern Ulster (McNeill 1980, 109-12), and there they represent the ancestry of the so-called 'crannóg ware', the late medieval Gaelic-Irish pottery which was first published a century ago by Wood-Martin (1886).

Pottery industries were founded on Irish soil by the colonists in the thirteenth century, but in the initial stages of colonisation they depended on imports for their tableware and, outside of Ulster, their cooking pots. The pottery which they eventually produced themselves was clearly influenced by the pottery they were importing, and even when they were very adept at producing their own ceramic material in Ireland they retained a taste for English-made or overseas-made vessels. One suspects that those imported vessels were as prized for the messages they communicated about wealth and status as they were for their practical value.

Before considering the wares produced in Ireland, and their patterns and processes of production, we must look at the vast amount of imported ceramic material which made its way into the kitchens and onto the tables of peasants and aristocrats, and clerics and inn-keepers. The key references for any consideration of the pottery made in or imported into Ireland are those descriptions and analyses by specialists — among them Claire McCutcheon and Maurice Hurley — which appear in the published excavations of urban sites in Cork, Waterford and Dublin; while it is not possible to reference each of these individually here, their contribution to elucidating this important aspect of later medieval culture in Ireland cannot be understated.

Ceramic imports from England

The majority of those imports came from England and France, and particularly from south-west England and western France, but wares from the Low Countries, northern Germany and the Rhineland, and from the Mediterranean, are also present. Most of the imported material we possess was made in the twelfth and thirteenth centuries. Fifteenth- and sixteenth-century wares are not so well represented, and while this probably reflects a diminution in ceramic importation in that era, we should be conscious that stratified deposits of this date do not generally survive in urban contexts.

Much of the ceramic material of English origin which circulated in colonial Ireland was produced in Bristol or its vicinity. That trade started in the century before the Anglo-Norman arrival, during which time it clearly targeted urban centres. Considerable quantities of Saxo-Norman cooking pots and spouted pitchers from Bristol and Gloucester made their way in eleventh- and twelfth-century Hiberno-Norse Dublin (Vince 1988). These cooking pots were replaced during the twelfth century by two new series of English cooking pots. The earlier series — 'Proto-Ham Green' ware — was imported from the Bristol area, possibly in the first half of the twelfth century; its place of manufacture is not known. The more enduring series of cooking pots came from the kilns at Ham Green, located to the north-west of Bristol; these vessels first appeared around the middle of the twelfth century and they continued to be imported until late in the thirteenth century. Nearly 250 cooking pots are known to have been imported into Waterford in the late eleventh and early twelfth centuries from south-western England (Gahan and McCutcheon 1997), and while the place of manufacture of many of these is unknown, nearly half of the vessels are of 'Proto-Ham Green' type.

Whatever food was consumed in Dublin and Waterford in the twelfth century, and in both urban and rural settlements of south-east Ireland in the early thirteenth century, it was invariably washed down with water, ale or wine poured from glazed pitchers and jugs which had been fired at Ham Green. Two hand-made jug types from Ham Green — types 'A' and 'B' — were imported into Ireland (**50**); the former tend to have wide, sagging bases and an external glaze of brown-green colour, while the latter tend to be taller vessels with narrow bases, and their external walls (which are usually decorated with linear motifs and occasionally with figurative motifs) bear a green glaze which is sometimes quite dark. The types are sequential, with 'A' jugs having been made between *c*1120 and *c*1175 and 'B' jugs between *c*1175 and *c*1250 (Ponsford 1991). It is likely that jugs of these types were being imported into Ireland from the time their production started in England, and that the greater number of 'B' jugs attested to in excavated assemblages can certainly be attributed to the stimulus which the Anglo-Norman arrival in Ireland gave to Irish Sea trade.

The Ham Green kilns continued to yield pottery in the later thirteenth century, but their output was superseded after 1250 by the wheel-thrown vessels produced at Redcliffe in Bristol, and this shift in the ceramic industry of Bristol was reflected on tables in Ireland in the second half of the 1200s. While the Redcliffe jugs shared some of the formal characteristics of their hand-made Ham Green B predecessors — bridge spouts, strap handles, a tendency to be large — they were generally more decorative, with strips of clay applied in patterns to their walls and sealed beneath glazing. Redcliffe products found in Waterford include an aquamanile (an ewer, usually in the form of an animal or bird) and

50   Ham Green jugs found at Skiddy's Castle, Cork: (a) an 'A' jug; (b) a 'B' jug (after Cleary, Hurley and Shee Twohig 1997)

a costrel (a bottle with lugs which allow it to be hung). Redcliffe wares would probably be better represented in the assemblages were it not for the ever-inceasing popularity of wares from the Saintonge region of south-west France during the thirteenth century.

Vessels from other kilns in south-west England were also present in colonial Ireland, but their number seems to have been relatively small and their distribution apparently restricted to the ports, suggesting perhaps that they cost a little more to purchase on the stalls of quayside traders. Cooking pots made somewhere in the Somerset-Wiltshire area in so-called Bath Fabric A were imported into Dublin and Waterford around 1100, while Waterford also simultaneously acquired some Cornish cooking pots. Waterford and Cork had some cooking pots from western Wales (so-called Dyfed Gravel-tempered ware) from the middle of the twelfth century. The same three Irish port towns had pitchers and jugs with tripod bases imported from south-east Wiltshire, possibly also in the early 1100s, and from Minety in north Wiltshire later in the twelfth century; Cork had a small number of jugs from Laverstock in Wiltshire. Some spouted pitchers in the Dublin assemblages, also later twelfth century in date, have been attributed to a south Gloucestershire production-site, while a three-handled, tripod pitcher (**51a**), possibly twelfth century, can best be paralleled among Dorset and Hampshire wares (Barton 1988, 284-5). South-western English wares even penetrated, albeit gingerly, the hitherto aceramic markets of Gaelic Ireland, as is testified by the fragments of a Ham Green jug and a Minety-type pitcher from a crannóg at Strokestown, county Roscommon (Hurst 1988, 229).

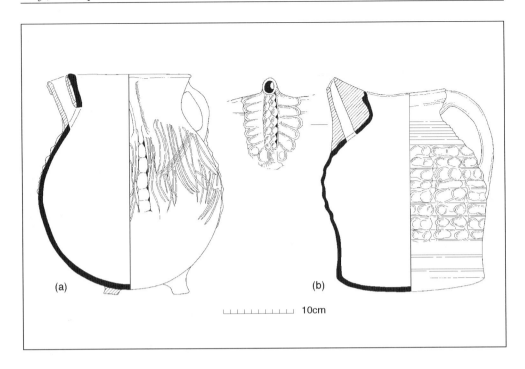

51   English ceramic types imported into Dublin: (a) a tripod pitcher from Gloucester; (b) a Cheshire frilled-spout jug (after Barton 1988)

Pottery from further afield in England also made its way to Ireland. The Anglo-Normans of the Earldom of Ulster looked to northern England and even to south-west Scotland, rather than to south-west England, for their ceramic imports. Wares from Chester and its vicinity are especially well-represented in Ulster and as far south as Drogheda, but they are also present in Dublin (**51b**). Ulster's trade connections with the north end of the Irish Sea should not surprise us: de Courcy's family estates were in Cumbria, and his wife, Afric, was from the Isle of Man. Scarborough ware, which dates from the mid-thirteenth to the mid-fourteenth century and disseminated in vast quantities along the east coast of Britain from Kent to the Northern Isles (McCarthy and Brooks 1988, 95), also appears in Ulster, as well as in Dublin and Cork. Smaller quantities of pottery from other places in England are also attested, such as the jug fragments in thirteenth-century Waterford from Yorkshire, London, Hedingham, Stamford, Worcester, and possibly Grimston, but they are not indicative of any regular trade.

Late medieval wares brought into Ireland, such as the fifteenth and sixteenth-century Surrey-made Tudor Green pottery in Cork or the sixteenth-century North Devon pottery in Dublin, should be regarded not as a continuation of the earlier patterns and processes of importation but as representing the early stages of the vibrant post-medieval ceramic trade.

Ceramic imports from France

Various other parts of western Europe contributed material to Ireland's ceramic assemblages between the twelfth and seventeenth centuries. Small numbers of ceramic goods, mainly coarseware and lustreware, from Portugal and Spain (Seville and Valentia) came to Ireland from the middle of the thirteenth century onwards, and while the coastal ports have the best assemblages (Meenan 1992), some of this western Mediterranean material occasionally turns up on rural sites, even in parts which were under Gaelic-Irish control and far from the ports (Hurst 1988, 227). Northern Europe, including the Low Countries, also exported pottery to Ireland during this period. Flemish jugs, for example, are attested in thirteenth-century levels in Cork and Waterford, although they are rather scarce in Dublin; pottery from the Paffrath area to the east of Cologne is found in some early thirteenth-century levels in Ireland, as at Waterford and Ballyfounder, county Down (Waterman 1958), while vessels from elsewhere in Germany are found in sixteenth and seventeenth-century levels in the coastal ports of Carrickfergus, Waterford, Cork and Dublin.

But Ireland's major trading partner, other than England of course, was France. Rouen, the hub of a thriving slave-trade between the Norse communities in Ireland and Normandy in the tenth and early eleventh centuries (Holm 1986), and a centre of religious contact in the twelfth century, had a monopoly on merchandise traded between Ireland and northern France until 1204 when the French king Philip Auguste captured the city from the English (O'Brien 1995, 32). Trade with northern France did not terminate at this point. Rather, other ports of the Seine — Fécamp and Dieppe, for example — became involved in trade with Ireland. Jugs from Orléans, Paris and Rouen were imported in the twelfth and thirteenth centuries; the Rouenais jugs are particularly interesting in having a distribution which is not restricted to the main ports of Dublin, Cork and Waterford but extends into such rural habitats as Rathmullen motte, county Down, and Kells Augustinian priory, county Kilkenny (Hurst 1988, 244). Occasional finds in urban contexts of red-painted cooking pots from Normandy and *céramique onctueuse* cooking pots from the Morbihan area of Brittany indicate that northern French trade in ceramics was not confined to table ware.

A steady escalation in trade between south-west France and Ireland during the thirteenth century — in part a consequence of Gascony remaining English long after the rest of France had been lost to the French early in that century — reduced the relative amount of northern French ceramic material in Ireland, and by the second half of the thirteenth century virtually all French pottery coming into Ireland had been made in the Saintonge region to the north of Bordeaux. Excavations of thirteenth-century levels on sites in Ireland invariably yield pottery from Saintonge, and that includes Gaelic-Irish settlements such as Clonroad, county Clare (Hunt 1946; Hurst 1988, 229) and the town of Armagh (Hurst 1988, 246).

Ireland's connections with the wine-producing regions of western France were long-established. There was no nearer, nor no more convenient, a place from which to import wine to Ireland than here; wine had been produced in southern England in the early middle ages but this was in decline from the end of the eleventh century (Clarke 1983, 19), and, in any case, the early medieval Irish seem not to have been interested in English viticulture. La Rochelle had been the principal port of export for the wine until its loss to

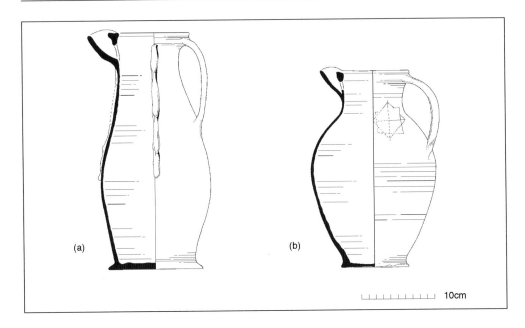

*52   Two jugs from Saintonge area found in Waterford: (a) green-glazed jug; (b) a bib-glazed jug
with the owner's marks on its neck*

the French in 1224; thereafter the wine brought to Ireland was loaded on the dock at
Bordeaux to the south, and the merchants of that city were assisted by royal licence to
export to Ireland (and to England and Wales) without payment of additional duties
(O'Brien 1995, 52-3). The wine was probably imported in perishable wooden caskets or
hogbacks, and the tableware and other ceramic products came with that cargo.

The kilns at which these ceramics were produced were located in the vicinity of the
quaintly-named La-Chapelle-des-Pots and its neighbouring communes, all situated high
on the limestone plateau overlooking the navigable stretch of the river Charente and
several kilometres to the north-east of Saintes, the city which gives its name to the district.
The wares were brought to Port Berteau, a short distance downriver from Saintes, and
they were shipped from there to the two principal ports — La Rochelle, also on the river
Charente, and Bordeaux — from which they were then transported northwards to
England and Ireland. The ceramics exported from Saintonge were not surplus to local
needs but were made to be distributed beyond the region: we note, for example, that the
cargoes retrieved from wrecked boats excavated at Port Berteau contained high-quality
glazed pots in contrast to the unglazed pottery which is most common around the kilns.
Cargoes may also have been assembled with a particular destination in mind: glazed
ceramic horns, examples of which have been found in Waterford, Dublin and
Carrickfergus, are so rare in Britain that Jean le Patourel has suggested that they were
made specifically for the Irish market (1992, 162).

Saintonge jugs are invariably tall, elegant and green-glazed, with parrot-beak spouts,
undecorated rolled strap handles, and flat bases (**52**). They first appear at the end of the

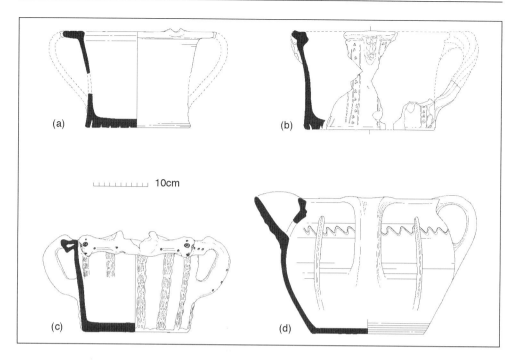

53   *Three ceramic mortars and one pitcher (pégau) made in the Saintonge area: (a) and (c) are mortars from Waterford; (b) is a sgraffito mortar from North Gate, Cork; (d) is a redware pégau from Waterford (after Hurley, Scully and McCutcheon [eds] 1997; Hurley 1997)*

twelfth century and thereafter dominate the assemblages imported from France; when the importation of jugs eventually ended in the middle of the fourteenth century it was not because they had fallen out of fashion but because the Hundred Years War had devastated their source area. The other products brought into Ireland from Saintonge in smaller numbers include baking dishes, three-handled pitchers known as *pégaux*, costrels (round or oval bottles of fairly flat section with handles or 'ears' which allow them be suspended from the waist), mortars for grinding substances (**53**), and the horns which have already been mentioned.

The Saintonge jugs are all fine, white or cream-coloured micaceous earthenware vessels. Decoration distinguishes one type from another. A small percentage was not glazed, just as some of the *pégaux* were not glazed. Of those that were, the most numerous are the jugs with mottled green glaze; the horns were similarly glazed. Some jugs were completely covered externally with green glaze (they are described as 'all-over-green'), and some of these were even glazed internally. Other jugs had sgraffito decoration, which was achieved by applying iron-rich (red) clay to the vessel and then scratching or paring away the design before glazing; mortars were customarily decorated with sgraffito. Finally, the most appealing of all the Saintonge vessels must be the polychrome jugs, with their painted designs of birds, shields and trefoils, which were imported into Ireland in the late thirteenth and early fourteenth centuries.

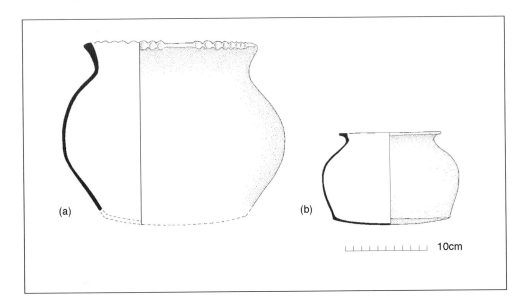

54   'Leinster cooking ware': (a) from Jerpointchurch, county Kilkenny (after Foley 1989); (b) from Essex Streeet West, Dublin (after Simpson 1995)

Saintonge imports reappear from the middle of the fifteenth century when that region recovered from the vissitudes of war. Fewer kilns were in operation, but a similarly diverse range of products — polychrome ornamental wares and plain household vessels — came from them, and the catchment area for the export of these ceramics had now enlarged to take in the New World (Musgrave 1997). Excavations in Dublin (Meenan 1994, 54), Carrickfergus (McNeill 1981, 74-5; Simpson and Dickson 1981), Cork (Hurley 1996) and Waterford (Hurley 1997) have yielded quite an amount of late Saintonge material, particularly chafing dishes.

Pottery made in Ireland

The most widespread pottery known to have been manufactured in Leinster between the middle of the twelfth century and the fourteenth century is so-called 'Leinster Cooking Ware' (**54**; Ó Floinn 1988). The vessels, which are generally plain with everted rims and sagging bases, were hand-built using a clay rich in mica, quartz grits and other inclusions, and were dried on sandy material — hence their pitted bases — prior to firing. The distribution of Leinster Cooking Ware matches closely that of medieval ceramic tiles in Ireland. Those tiles, the forms and chronology of which were discussed at length by Elizabeth Eames and Tom Fanning (1988), were largely used in churches.

The major towns also had their own contemporary pottery-making industries. The products of Dublin's industry included both hand-built and wheel-thrown wares, and glazed jugs are especially common among the latter. Waterford and Cork were centres of production of pottery, but only from the thirteenth century (**55**). Both wheel-thrown and hand-made vessels (mainly glazed jugs but also unglazed cooking pots) fashioned out of a

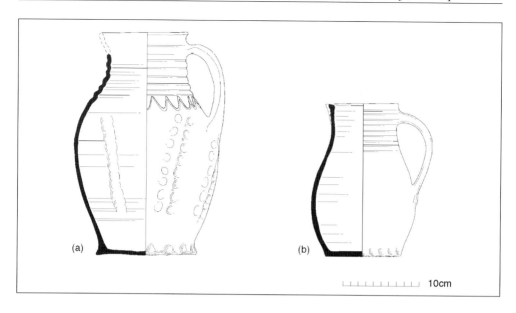

55   *Waterford jugs: (a) type 'B'; (b) type 'A' (after Hurley, Scully and McCutcheon [eds] 1997)*

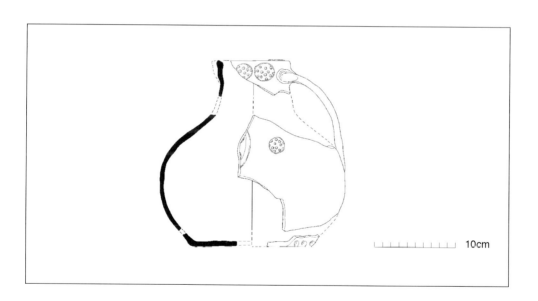

56   *A Cork-type jug, from North Gate, Cork (after Hurley 1997)*

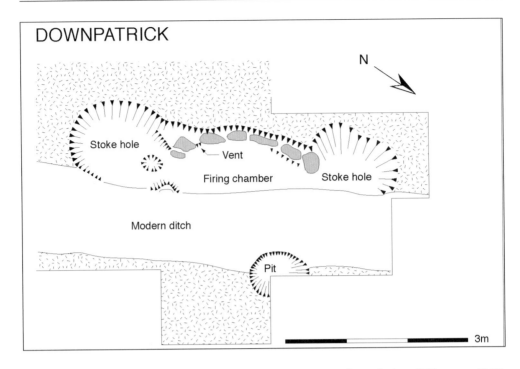

DOWNPATRICK

N

Stoke hole

Vent

Firing chamber

Stoke hole

Modern ditch

Pit

3m

57   *A medieval pottery kiln from Downpatrick, county Down (after Pollock and Waterman 1963)*

micaceous, sandy clay, constitute so-called Waterford 'A' wares; a similar range of vessels is attested among the Waterford 'B' wares, so-distinguished because they were made using a different clay source. The 'Cork-type' wares were made using clay from the vicinity of that city, and jugs with glazing seem to have been the principal products (**56**).

Local wares were produced at several centres in Ulster, but their geographical dispersal is fairly limited (McNeill 1980, 107-9). Wheel-thrown glazed jugs of rather soft fabric were made at the kiln excavated at Downpatrick, county Down (Pollock and Waterman 1963; **Fig. 57**); jugs which are likely to have been produced at Downpatrick, although not necessarily from the excavated kiln, have been found at Ballynarry (Davison 1969), Clough (Waterman 1954), and Lismahon (Waterman 1959), all in the Lecale district of county Down. The Downpatrick kiln was also used for the production of cooking pots and pipkins (skillets). Jugs were also produced at Carrickfergus, where a kiln has been found (Simpson and Dickson 1981). The influence of Cheshire potters is not just apparent in the Downpatrick and Carrickfergus vessels: it seems likely that the industries were established by actual men from Chester or Rhuddlan. There was a third production centre for jugs, at least, supplying vessels in the Antrim and Down areas. The third group with its unidentified source was made, according to McNeill, by men who had worked in Leinster.

6 The Church

Ireland was in the vanguard of both intellectual and artistic life in Europe for most of the second half of the first millennium AD, and whatever reasons may be adduced for that so-called 'Golden Age' coming to an end — the Vikings are a popular target for blame, but the reasons are surely more complex — Ireland never again achieved such cultural pre-eminence. If we wish to measure the achievements of the Irish against those of other people in medieval Europe after AD 1000 we will find that the competition from the Continent was much stronger than it had been in earlier post-Roman centuries. Once the millennium turned Europe moved quickly towards the age of great cathedrals and great universities. The first truly international movement of art and architecture, Romanesque, emerged somewhere in western Continental Europe within half a century of the start of the millennium; Gothic emerged in north-eastern France in the 1130s to become the second international movement. The finest works of Romanesque and Gothic architecture were great cathedrals and monastic churches, a fact which underlines how central was Christianity to Europe's post-millennium *zeitgeist*. The Irish, with a longer record of unbroken Christian practice than most of their European neighbours, embraced both styles and even created with them some churches of considerable originality, but the fact that no church edifice in post-millennium Ireland can be said to have had a significant impact on architectural practice anywhere in England or on the Continent illustrates how an island which was part of the core of early medieval Europe had become part of the periphery of later medieval Europe.

Students of medieval church architecture in Ireland are fortunate to have Harold Leask's three books (Leask 1955-60) as basic source material. Drawing on earlier research from many scholars, especially Arthur Champneys whose *Irish Ecclesiastical Architecture* (1910) remains outstanding, and from his own work as an Inspector of National Monuments in Ireland, Leask forged a synthesis of a thousand years of architectural development. Despite many conceptual weaknesses, especially marked in the content of the first volume, it remains an essential compendium. There have also been detailed studies of the architecture of specific monastic organisations such as the Franciscans (Mooney 1955-7) and Cistercians (Stalley 1987), as well as excavation reports on a small number of sites such as Mellifont Cistercian abbey, county Louth (de Paor 1969) and Clontuskert Augustinian priory, county Galway (Fanning 1976), and a number of monographs on individual buildings, among them St Canice's cathedral, Kilkenny (Empey *et al* 1985), Kilmallock Dominican priory, county Limerick (Hogan 1991), and Bridgetown Augustinian priory, county Cork (O'Keeffe 1999b).

This review begins with an assessment of the great changes in the architectural traditions of the Irish Church in the twelfth century, and it then explores, in turn, the impact of the Anglo-Normans on architectural style, the arrival in Ireland of thirteenth and fourteenth-century English styles, the *floruit* of friary architecture in the fifteenth century, and the architecture of the ubiquitous parish church.

Irish ecclesiastical buildings before the Anglo-Normans

Ireland's stone churches of pre-1100 date are small and have little structural sophistication. If we believe the testimony of the Venerable Bede, the majority of early medieval churches in Ireland of this date were constructed in wood, not stone, and if we believe the testimony of the excavator's spade those wooden churches were principally simple post-built structures (for a summary see Thomas 1971). When the Romanesque tradition infiltrated Ireland in the early decades of the 1100s it did not effect a widespread or significant change in the size or structure of Irish churches; rather, the Romanesque features were, as we will see below, simply integrated into the long-established, indigenous architectural format.

We do not know why the early medieval Irish opted for very simple architecture for their churches, and it is not really a matter within the scope of this book, but we can at least be confident that they erected simple churches because they chose to, not because they were incapable of building anything better. The Round Towers, the most remarkable buildings of medieval Irish Christianity, make it clear that the Irish could build with great aplomb when they so desired (**58**). The first of these towers were built before the middle of the tenth century, and the fashion for them continued throughout the twelfth century, with one reference in the *Annals of Connacht* to a tower being built as late as 1238 at Annaghdown, county Galway, just as the Anglo-Norman were establishing their Connacht colony (Freeman [ed] 1944).

Reconsidering Round Towers

It is not just because they happen to fall within the chronological span of this book that Round Towers merit discussion here. Rather, it is because these towers are intrinsically interesting monuments which tell us much about the relationship between architecture and ritual, and perhaps also between secular and ecclesiastical power, in the native Irish Church in the centuries leading up to the Anglo-Norman arrival (see O'Keeffe *forthcoming* a for a more comprehensive discussion).

We know that bells were rung from Round Towers because they are described as bell-houses in annalistic sources. The sheer effort devoted to constructing the towers suggests that they must have fufilled other functions as well, but the only other function for which we have good documentation was the storing of relics, and this we know because it was recorded that fires, accidental or deliberate, destroyed relics or treasures in towers, as at Slane, county Meath, and Monasterboice, county Louth, in 950 and 1097 respectively.

Two observations about their architecture suggests that Round Towers were more than simply treasuries from which bells were rung. First of all, the doorways into the Round Towers are almost always a couple of metres or more above ground level (**59**), but they did

58   *The Round Tower at Roscrea, county Tipperary. The lower of the tw openings is the doorway, which is round-arched; there is a triangular-headed window which is almost as large as the doorway, at the level of the second-floor (Photograph: Dúchas, The Heritage Service, reproduced with permission)*

not need to be so elevated for the structural stability of the towers, as witness one of the tallest of Irish Round Towers, Scattery, county Clare, which has a doorway at ground level. It could be argued that doorways high off ground level offered some security if relics and treasures were stored inside the towers, and this may indeed be part of the explanation for their elevation, but there remains a problem: why were the doorways in many twelfth-century Round Towers (Timahoe, county Laois, and Donaghmore, county Meath, for example) elaborated with sculpture such as might be found on the entrance doorways of contemporary churches when that detail was too high up in the towers to be seen very clearly? The treatment of these Round Tower doorways may actually suggest that the interiors of the towers were sacred spaces of the same order as the interiors of the churches, and that entry into the Round Towers was as ritualised as entry into the churches; this suggestion receives circumstantial support from the observations that the Round Towers are sometimes locked into a metrical relationship with the churches associated with them, and that the doorways of both buildings almost always faced towards each other.

If Round Towers contained relics we can speculate that they also contained altars, and therefore chapels, and that these were either at their summits (where there are windows facing in the cardinal directions) or at the floor level immediately above the entrance (where there is often a large window: **58**). Some corroboration for this suggestion that there were chapels inside Round Towers comes from the records of the deaths inside towers of considerable numbers of people, as at Tullyard, county Meath, in 1171, or of important people such as Murchad Ua Maeleachlainn, the newly-crowned king of Tara who was killed by a rival inside the Round Tower at Kells, county Meath, in 1076. These fatalities indicate that Round Towers were places of refuge, but not refuge in the sense that a castle or fort provides refuge. Rather, we might consider them places where, because of the presence of a chapel, sanctuary was sought. Why else would people fearing for their lives actually *hide* inside a Round Tower, if not to seek sanctuary? We should note that the violent deaths of large numbers of people inside conventional churches is also recorded in annalistic sources, and these we might also interpret as failed attempts to secure sanctuary.

The second observation about Round Towers relates to their windows. Although the towers were ascended by means of wooden ladders rising almost vertically through the multiple storeys, the windows in the towers, which are restricted to one per storey, tend to be arranged in a clockwise manner as the towers rise. Each of these windows allows a different view of the landscape around the church-site, and because their pattern imitates the clockwise pattern of processions, it seems likely that the towers were themselves used in processions. We can easily imagine, then, that in the course of a procession an abbot or bishop stood brandishing relics in a Round Tower doorway and in full sight of the community. Kings might also have been involved in such rituals — we know that secular powers were increasingly involved in Church affairs in Ireland from the tenth century onwards — and the holding of relics was a device by which claims to kingship were authenticated.

The idea that a king might have occasion to stand in the doorway of a Round Tower looking outwards and being looked at is not at all outlandish, and we do not need to travel back in time and place to the Carolingian world to find appropriate parallels. Instead, we need only look to Anglo-Saxon England and such square Anglo-Saxon tower-churches as

59   *The doorway of the Round Tower of Kilree, county Kilkenny*

Earl's Barton and Barton-on-Humber. These were estate-churches of pre-Conquest English magnates, and they have upper 'doorways' which open out into the landscape, allowing the lord to view and to be viewed. In tenth and early eleventh-century England a church was regarded as an essential element of the ideal thegnly (or lordly) residence, and one of the critical historical sources for that indicates that such private estate-churches could sometimes be described as bell-houses (Williams 1992). Could it be that the idea of the Irish Round Tower actually originated in this context? This is not entirely unlikely: a link with the Anglo-Saxon architectural tradition of the eleventh century is suggested by the triangular-headed windows which are common in many eleventh and twelfth-century Irish Round Towers (**58**).

Europe's embrace: Ireland and the Romanesque style

The Roman past was near enough in time and space to the world of later medieval Europe that it could be regarded not as ancient history but as living heritage, and eleventh and early twelfth-century Europeans happily cherry-picked its complex legacy for foundation material for a whole range of artistic and intellectual ventures, among them the Romanesque style of art and architecture. The term Romanesque was coined not in the middle ages but in the nineteenth century (Waldeier Bizzarro 1992). The formal definition of the style is extremely difficult and it cannot detain us here, but we can acknowledge that the emergence of the multifarious forms and concepts which modern scholars designate Romanesque is inextricably linked to the Gregorian Reform of the mid-1000s. It is not that those forms and concepts articulate in an explicit way the ideals of the reformers; rather, they provided a visual metaphor for reform, first by virtue of representing a new departure in art and architecture just as reform represented a new departure in Christian practice, and secondly, by virtue of their deployment in Christian buildings erected by patrons supportive of reform (O'Keeffe 2000a).

The movement to bring the practices of the Irish Church into line with the Church elsewhere in Europe achieved its goal in the twelfth century with a series of synods and councils, the most important of which were those of Rath Breasail in 1111 and Kells/Mellifont in 1152 (Gwynn 1992). This reform brought to Ireland a system of dioceses; the early medieval Irish Church already had bishops for sacramental duties, but now there was a territorial framework in which bishops could exercise power over clergy. Although modelled on the structure of the contemporary English Church, the geography of the Irish dioceses set up in the early twelfth century generally reflected the geography of local and regional secular power; the new diocese of Kilfenora, for example, was co-terminous with the kingdom of Corcomroe in north Clare (Ní Ghabhláin 1996).

New dioceses meant new cathedral churches, and here two choices faced the patrons of reform: change the rank of an existing church, or erect a new building. It is difficult to know which was the preferred path because the cathedral churches on many sites were rebuilt in later, often post-medieval, periods, but in many cases, and probably the majority, existing churches simply became cathedral churches, and sometimes structural alterations were not made for several generations. The cathedral churches of the twelfth-century dioceses of Clonmacnois, county Offaly, Glendalough, county Wicklow, and Clonfert, county Galway (**colour plate 21**), for example, were actually buildings of tenth-century

60   *Ardfert Cathedral, county Kerry: the west façade of the Romanesque cathedral church (shown here prior to restoration) is preserved in the west wall of the thirteenth-century Gothic cathedral*

date, and they appear not to have been physically altered in line with their new status until the second half of the twelfth century. The original church at Clonfert had a simple façade flanked by *antae*, projections of the side walls past the gable wall; *antae* are very common in pre-Romanesque Irish churches, but their function is not known with certainty. Around the third quarter of the twelfth century Clonfert's original doorway, which we presume to have been lintelled, was replaced by a great portal in the Romanesque style.

Two of the earliest examples of cathedral architecture in the Romanesque style are at Roscrea, county Tipperary, and Ardfert, county Kerry (**60**). The former site was not recognised as a diocesan centre by the synodians who determined such matters in 1111 and 1152, but it claimed diocesan status nonetheless, and its church was almost certainly built to be a cathedral. Ardfert was not designated a diocesan centre in 1111, but it, like Roscrea, soon claimed to be one and the Romanesque church which is of interest to us here was probably built to be its cathedral; in 1152 Arfert's claim to be a diocesan centre was upheld. The early twelfth-century façades of both of these churches have a very distinctive design of a central portal flanked on each side by a pair of blind arches. Roscrea's doorway and blind arcades are covered by pediments, there are *paterae* or stone rosettes arranged symmetrically around the façade, and, in a clear expression of the continuity between the pre-Romanesque and Romanesque traditions in Ireland, the entire façade is flanked by *antae*. Ardfert's façade is somewhat simpler in that it lacks the *antae*, the pediments, and the *paterae*. Neither of these churches is dated historically, but we can infer from the chronology of their claims to be diocesan churches that they were built around the 1120s (O'Keeffe 1994).

Also in Munster is the finest and most celebrated of all Ireland's Romanesque churches, Cormac's Chapel in Cashel, county Tipperary. Erected between 1127 and 1134, it bears the name of its patron, Cormac MacCarthaig, the king of Munster, and can be interpreted as a royal chapel. Cormac's Chapel has a barrel-vaulted nave and a rib-vaulted chancel, and both vaults have above them large chambers with arched-stone ceilings, external to which are steep stone roofs. Two tall, square towers flank the east end of the nave, one terminating in a pyramidal roof and the other in a simple parapet. Internally and externally the chapel is covered with arcading, and on the exterior south wall that arcading is arranged in several horizontal levels. The chapel was entered from the north and south, the former being the principal entrance. The architectural pedigree and significance of Cormac's Chapel has been discussed in print in some detail (de Paor 1967; Stalley 1981; O'Keeffe 1994). The modern consensus seems to be that the building's architecture and sculpture need to be seen as western English in character but that the building's personality, as expressed in its small scale and its high, stone roofs, is a product of the Irish building tradition. From an international perspective Cormac's Chapel is extremely interesting because the rib-vaulting in its chancel is among the earliest examples of that type of construction north of the Alps. We should remember in this regard that the chapel was consecrated one year after the 1133 completion of Durham cathedral, the most celebrated of northern European rib-vaulted Romanesque churches; we might also remember, however, that the east end of St Denis in northern France, the cradle of the Gothic architectural style, is almost contemporary with Cormac's Chapel.

The Irish Romanesque style was clearly inaugurated in the archdiocese of Cashel, possibly at Cashel itself (de Paor 1967) or perhaps at Lismore, county Waterford, an important site at which (and in the vicinity of which) there are some early twelfth-century Romanesque remains (O'Keeffe 1994). The style seems to have spread northwards and north-eastwards from the south-west corner of Ireland during the middle decades of the 1100s, and as it spread it changed from being used on entire façades and elevations (as it was at Ardfert, Roscrea and Cashel) to being restricted to doorways (**61**), windows and chancel arches.

Influence from the English Romanesque tradition was apparent from the very beginning, with the chevron, the most popular motif in twelfth-century England, featuring prominently at the Munster churches already discussed. Chevrons remained extremely popular as the Irish Romanesque spread outwards from its Munster birthplace. From the middle of the twelfth century chevrons were accompanied by motifs of animal interlace borrowed from the repertoire of the artists in the Hiberno-Scandinavian towns: particularly popular were motifs of the so-called 'Urnes style', an umbrella term for compositions in which small and large animals are intertwined in a graceful choreography. In the Shannon valley there are even some motifs of western French origin: at both Dysert O'Dea, county Clare (**colour plate 22**) and Clonfert, for example, there is one arch-ring with a scalloped effect, and the parallels for this, which are closest to Ireland geographically are in the west of France (O'Keeffe 1996).

61 The Romanesque doorway of Killeshin, county Laois. A now-defaced inscription on this doorway of c1150 records the name of a king Diarmait, who is certainly Diarmait Mac Murchada, the king of Leinster who invited the Anglo-Normans to Ireland

Cistercians in twelfth-century Ireland

Reform also created the environment which drew to Ireland some of the new monastic ideas and groups of the eleventh and twelfth-century Continental Church. The new monastic orders which appeared in Ireland during the 1100s were Cistercians, Augustinians, Benedictines and Clunaics. The first two of these played a central role in Irish ecclesiastical history (Stalley 1987; O'Keeffe 1999b); the others were far less important. The Benedictines had a small number of establishments, and the only Benedictine house of which there are substantial remains is at Fore, county Westmeath; founded by Hugh de Lacy around 1180, it retains an original, if modified, church.

The Cistercian Order came to Ireland in 1142, fifty years after its foundation in Burgundy. The first Cistercian community in Ireland was at Mellifont, county Louth, and it had both French and Irish brethren; by the time of the Anglo-Norman arrival there were no less than twelve Cistercian abbeys in Ireland, and by 1272, the date of the last medieval foundation (Hore, county Tipperary), another 22 had been added thanks to both Anglo-Norman and Gaelic-Irish patronage (Stalley 1987).

The earliest examples in Ireland of monastic planning which involves a central cloister or courtyard may be the Cistercian houses (**62**). This type of layout, which we describe as *claustral*, was in use in Continental Europe from the early ninth century if not earlier. Its spatial principle was very simple: the main monastic buildings were arranged around the cloister. The church was on an opposite side (normally the north side) of the cloister from the dining hall or refectory, the Chapter House (the place where a chapter of the monastic rule was read daily and monastic business discussed) was on the east side of the cloister, and the monastic community's dormitory was upstairs along the same eastern range as the Chapter House; lay brethren were accommodated in Cistercian houses, and their dormitory was upstairs on the west side of the cloister.

Claustral plans were common to all the major monastic organisations, and not just to the Cistercians, and the arrangement of their elements is very consistent across the medieval world. What made claustral planning so attractive was its efficiency. It was not just that daily routines were played out within the four ranges of buildings which ran around the outside of the cloister, but that distances between parts of the monastery were maximised or minimised according to the relationships between the activities carried out in them: the church and refectory, for example, were directly opposite each other because one was a place of worship and the other a place of eating, and the dormitories of monks and lay brethren were also positioned on opposite sides of the courtyards, while monks' dormitories were as close to the choirs of churches as they could be to allow the monks to reach their stalls as quickly as possible as the daily cycle of prayer began.

Although executed within the context of a universal conception of monastic planning, twelfth-century Cistercian architecture in Europe has a quite distinctive personality. Its austerity is what strikes the visitor most forcibly: for example, the wall surfaces of Cistercian churches of the period are quite unadorned, and that includes important external walls such as façades. In terms of plan, the churches are simple cruciform buildings with flat-ended rather than apsidal presbyteries and transeptal chapels. Karl Heinz Esser christened this plan-type 'Bernardine' (1953) after the Order's most prominent individual, St Bernard of Clairvaux, whom he believed — incorrectly, in all probability — to have devised it. The 'Bernardine' plan is found in Ireland (**62**).

The rapidity with which the so-called 'Bernardine' plan spread across Europe after 1135 — the date at which St Bernard's own church, Clairvaux, was rebuilt — should not, however, be taken as evidence that the design was mandatory in the family of Cistercian monasteries. The General Chapter — the body which was charged with the running of the Order from the mid-1120s — made no ruling on the matter. Indeed, its first ruling on matters of architecture was as late as 1157 when it issued a prohibition on the building of church towers; this ruling, incidentally, was ignored in twelfth-century England and by the end of the 1100s it was being ignored in Ireland as well.

136

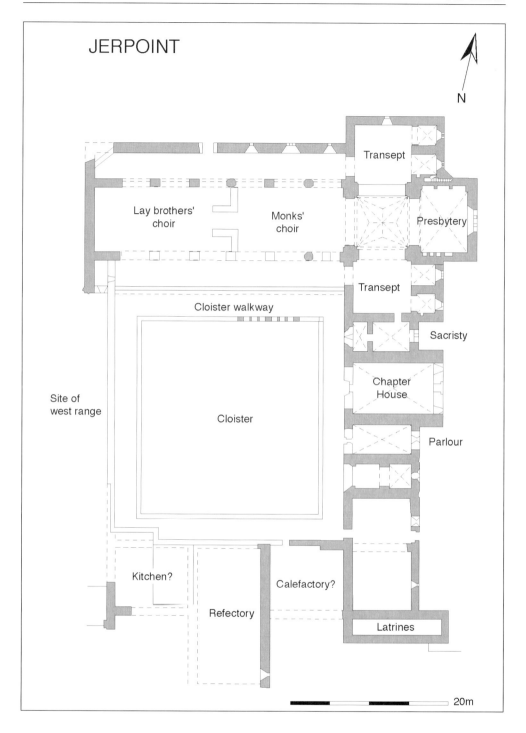

62   Jerpoint Cistercian abbey, county Kilkenny (after Stalley 1987). This monastic house has a claustral plan, and its church has a plan of the so-called 'Bernardine' type

63   The nave of Jerpoint abbey, looking west. The piers which carry the arcading are of alternating plan, and the clerestory windows — the windows which lit the nave from just beneath the roof — were placed above these piers to allow a fairly low roof. Churches like this were subdivided internally to accommodate many different liturgical activities; the partitions were normally made of perishable timber, but foundations of one stone-built partition still remain at Jerpoint and these are visible in this picture

It is curious that the first two Cistercian churches to have been built in Ireland are quite atypical by the contemporary and later standards of the order. Mellifont, the first, had a Clairvaux monk, Robert, oversee its construction, and his builders produced a church very different to anything in Burgundy in having apsidal chapels flanking flat-ended chapels in each of its transepts. Baltinglass, county Wicklow, founded as a daughter house of Mellifont in 1148 by Diarmait Mac Murchada, was unusual in having flat-ended transeptal chapels projecting separately from each other. However, the Cistercian churches of the next generation in Ireland — Jerpoint, county Kilkenny, and Boyle, county Roscommon — had rather more typical eastern ends, complete with barrel-vaulting comparable with that found in Burgundy. The naves of Jerpoint, Boyle and Baltinglass were built towards the end of the twelfth century and display influence from contemporary Cistercian architecture in England (**63**).

The masons involved in building and giving modest decoration to some of Ireland's Cistercian abbeys also found employment outside of Cistercian contexts. Two such places were the parish church of Carrickfergus, county Antrim, and the Augustinian priory church at Dungiven, county Derry, as Tom McNeill has demonstrated (1980, 47-50). The most striking example may be the cathedral of St Mary's in Limerick, founded in 1172 by

Domnall Mór Ó Briain, king of Munster from 1168 to 1194. This bears the very strong imprint of early Cistercian architectural style: square piers carry the four bay nave arcade, arches sprung north and south from those piers to divide the aisles into bays, and the roof of the entire church appears to have run the entire length of the building without interruption. Domnall Mór was an energetic patron of the Church, and no less than five, and possibly six, Cistercian monasteries owed their existence to him, but little pre-1194 architecture is now visible at those sites and St Mary's is, therefore, the best place in Munster to experience twelfth-century Cistercian architecture. Arches over aisles are also a feature of the early thirteenth-century parish church of Fethard, county Tipperary, and they may also have been inspired by Cistercian architecture.

Augustinians in twelfth-century Ireland

Twelfth-century Ireland also had canons regular of St Augustine, priests who lived in community in accordance with the strictures of the Rule of St Augustine (O'Keeffe 1999b). In the pre-colonial era the Augustinian communities in Ireland were simply indigenous monastic communities which had adopted the Rule of St Augustine as a way of life, but canons from England and Wales appeared in Ireland in the aftermath of the conquest of the late 1100s. Many of the pre-Anglo-Norman Augustinian houses were founded with royal patronage, as in early twelfth-century England (Dickinson 1950, 129), but the Anglo-Norman foundations more frequently had lords rather than kings as their patrons. There is no evidence for the use of the claustral plan in Augustinian priories of the pre-1170 period in Ireland.

The Rule had an interesting history. The eleventh-century reformers advocated that secular clergy should, for the good of their morality, spirituality and intellect, live in community according to a monastic regime, and the writings of St Augustine, one of the early Church's great intellectual heavyweights, provided authority for this view. Even though Augustine did not compile a set of specific monastic regulations as had St Benedict, his writings were moulded by these eleventh-century reformers into a monastic rule — the Rule of St Augustine — which allowed ordained clergy (canons) live a monastic life without hindering the prosecution of their pastoral duties. The Rule of St Augustine proved remarkably flexible, and there was considerable diversity in its application, with some Augustinian communities identifying their mission as pastoral and others pursuing a contemplative life.

Augustinian houses far outnumbered the monastic houses of other orders in Ireland. Their popularity over Cistercians in twelfth and thirteenth-century Ireland was partly because their pastoral mission made them far more attractive to patrons than cloistered monks, and partly because establishing an Augustinian monastery did not require the land or labour resources which a Cistercian monastery demanded.

The 'school of the west'

The most remarkable of all the regional traditions of architecture in medieval Ireland flowered west of the Shannon in the last decade of the twelfth century and the first three decades of the following century. Leask termed it 'the school of the west' and interpreted it as 'Transitional' between Romanesque and Gothic (1955-60 ii, 53). Both phrases continue to be used in the literature. Most of the buildings which qualify for inclusion were located in the kingdom of Connacht and many of them can be attributed directly to the patronage of Cathal Crobderg Ó Conchobair, effectively the king of Connacht from 1195 to 1224, but there were also examples in the kingdom of Thomond, and there the patrons were Domnall Mór Ó Briain and his sons.

In terms of affiliation, the churches with 'school of the west' detail constitute a very heterogeneous group. The two kingdoms of Connacht and Thomond embraced several dioceses, and each of the cathedral churches in those dioceses was either rebuilt or significantly altered in the decades around 1200. Reformed monastic communities were also welcomed in the two kingdoms, and they have left for us some of the finest Cistercian and Augustinian architecture in Ireland. Finally, at the lower end of the spectrum, a number of 'local' or parish churches were built, and while these did not enjoy royal patronage they did at least benefit from the skills of masons who had worked on the prestigious buildings. The architecture of these foundations is also as varied. For example, the Cistercian monasteries — Boyle, county Roscommon, Abbeyknockmoy, county Galway, and Corcomroe, county Clare — were claustral, and their churches conform to that Order's pan-European tradition in the twelfth century of flat-ended and vaulted presbyteries, and transeptal chapels. The abbey of Cong, county Mayo, and the priory of Ballintober, county Mayo (**64**), both Augustinian, were also designed as if they were Cistercian, but the Augustinian priory churches at Kilmacduagh (O'Heyne's Church), county Galway, and Inishmaine, county Mayo, had nave-and-chancel plans. The finest of the surviving cathedral churches is at Killaloe, county Clare, and its cruciform plan with an elongated eastern arm bears no comparison with any of the monastic churches.

What binds these diverse buildings together are the details and profiles of mouldings, and the sculpture on capitals and corbels, all of which suggest some fusion of Romanesque and Gothic. Common to a number of the larger churches, for example, are pointed doorway and chancel arches, wall-ribs and chancel arch responds which are carved as clusters of triple shafts, and window splays which are framed by continuous mouldings. Chevrons were still in use, but they were frequently of tubular form. The sculpture on capitals and corbels is largely comprised of highly-stylised plant ornament, but zoomorphic and anthropomorphic motifs are also found. One can certainly detect the movement among these sites of one stone-carver, or of a group of carvers under the watchful eye of a master (Stalley 1971, 116-7).

The three-ordered south doorway of the small church at Drumacoo, county Galway (**65**), is a minor masterpiece of the 'school of the west,' and it illustrates perfectly how the tradition straddles both the Romanesque and Gothic styles. The pointed arch and the bowtell moulding (a type of moulding in which a roll of stone is flanked by very deeply-cut hollows) on its outer arch-ring, and the bands (small horizontal rings of stone) and fillets (small, flat-topped ridges of stone running along the mouldings) on the detached shafts of the two outer orders of the door jambs, suggest this is a Gothic doorway. But the chevron and lozenges on the arch-rings are of Romanesque origin, the lack of sculptural embellishment on the doorway's inner arch-ring and jamb can be paralleled on many Irish Romanesque doorways, and one of Drumacoo's capitals bears a register of small, snarling

64   The east end of Ballintober Augustinian priory, county Mayo, built in the early thirteenth century. The flat-ended (as distinct from apsidal, or curving) east wall with its three windows is very reminiscent of Cistercian architecture (Photograph: Dúchas, The Heritage Service, reproduced with permission)

animal heads which is a Romanesque motif (O'Keeffe 1996) which travelled from western France to the Nun's Church at Clonmacnois, county Offaly, and Clonfert Cathedral.

The description of this western Irish architectural tradition as 'Transitional' is unfortunate because it embodies a misunderstanding of the concept of 'style'. Architectural styles were created in the middle ages when technological and aesthetic challenges manifested themselves during the making of great buildings such as cathedrals. The Gothic features of the doorway at Drumacoo do not represent a new architectural idiom *in embryo* but merely the selection and adaptation of Gothic forms and motifs out of the vast repertoire which was created for, and were on display in, large and prosperous buildings. We can interpret the doorway at Drumacoo as Romanesque which displays the influence of Gothic, or as Gothic which retains elements of Romanesque, but we cannot see in it a metamorphosis from Romanesque to Gothic, which is precisely the interpretation conveyed by the concept of transition. On balance, we should probably regard Drumacoo and the other churches of the 'school of the west' as representing the last stages of the Irish Romanesque. Indeed, they represent one of the last expressions of Romanesque in Europe.

65   The south doorway of Drumacoo church, county Galway (Photograph: Dúchas, The Heritage Service, reproduced with permission)

Gothic in Ireland, 1190-1300

The appearance of the Gothic style in Ireland can be attributed to the Anglo-Normans but its establishment did not immediately follow their arrival. The seminal Gothic work in England — the new choir of Canterbury Cathedral — was only built in the 1170s and early 1180s under the guidance of a Frenchman, and it took until the end of the twelfth century for England to develop her own Gothic architectural aesthetic (Wilson 1989). While Gothic was taking root in England and developing 'English' characteristics in the closing decades of the 1100s, the Anglo-Normans in Ireland were still working within the Romanesque idiom. Nowhere is this clearer than in the late twelfth-century transepts of Christ Church Cathedral (formerly Holy Trinity Cathedral) in Dublin (Stalley 1973; O'Keeffe 2000b), but there are also some examples of Romanesque work in Anglo-Norman castles erected early in the thirteenth century (O'Keeffe 1984). The first Gothic works in Ireland date from the very end of the twelfth century, but the great masterpieces of the style were the cathedrals and monastic churches which the Anglo-Normans built as their colony took shape in the early thirteenth century. The building of churches in the Gothic style in Ireland then continued throughout the 1200s and into the early 1300s, but the second half of the fourteenth century saw a fall-away in new construction before an extraordinary revitalistion of the building industry in the 1400s. The principal types of church already discussed — cathedrals, Augustinian and Cistercian monastic churches, and 'local' or parish churches — were still, of course, being built after 1200, albeit with Anglo-Norman patrons in eastern parts of Ireland. After the first quarter of the thirteenth century there is a new addition to the ecclesiastical landscape: the friary. Dominican friars appeared in 1224, followed by Franciscans about seven years later, by Carmelites around 1270, and by Augustinian friars in 1282.

Before looking at the architecture it should be noted that these monastic groupings do not represent the entire spectrum of monasticism in later medieval Ireland. There were also monastic houses of other groups, among them Premonstratensians, Trinitarians, Carthusians, and both Knights Templars and Knights Hospitallers (Gwynn and Hadcock 1970). Few of these have received appropriate attention, either in the historical or archaeological literature. There were also nunneries, but little has been done on these; the nunnery which is perhaps the most interesting from an architectural-historical perspective is Monasternagalliaghduff ('the monastery of the Black nuns'), near Shanagolden, county Limerick, a house of Augustinian canonesses with a long church projecting from the middle of the east wall of the cloister (O'Keeffe 1999b, fig. 99), but this, sadly, is neglected.

Turning now to the genesis of the Gothic style in Ireland, two Cistercian abbeys, Inch, county Down founded as a daughter house of Furness in Lancashire in 1187, and Grey, also in county Down, colonised from Holm Cultram in Cumberland in 1193 (Stalley 1987, 245-6), can claim to be the first examples of this tradition on the island. Despite their chronological primacy, these buildings do not represent the fountainhead — the stimulus, the inspiration — of Irish Gothic; it is a matter for debate whether any single structure has that distinction, but the early thirteenth-century nave of Christ Church Cathedral in Dublin would be quite a strong candidate. It was not their location in Ulster which denied Grey and Inch the opportunity to be hugely influential buildings but the fact that, as Cistercian churches, they were quite modest exercises in the new style; at any rate, perhaps they were probably too closely identified with that Order and its very particular *modus operandi* to be considered potential blueprints for churches elsewhere.

Christ Church Cathedral and St Patrick's Cathedral in Dublin are the best places in Ireland to experience the Gothic architectural aesthetic. The former (Stalley 1979; O'Keeffe 2000b) is the earlier foundation of the two, having been established by the Hiberno-Norse when Dublin was a pre-reform see. The transepts, which we mentioned above, are among the few works of ecclesiastical architecture in the Romanesque style to have been built under Anglo-Norman patronage. The nave, however, is a fine example of western English Gothic architecture (**66**); it was built in the first three decades of the thirteenth century using a ground plan which had been determined by the builders of the Romanesque crypt which underlies almost the entire cathedral. Augustinian canons regular served as Christ Church's monastic chapter, but nothing other than the rebuilt foundations of their Chapter House, a small but opulent building of *c*1200, remains of the cathedral's claustral buildings.

Located just outside Dublin's town wall and within sight of Christ Church is St Patrick's cathedral, a building which began life in the 1190s as a collegiate church and was promoted to cathedral status two decades later in an attempt by Dublin's then-archbishop, Henry of London, to wrest control of the diocesan nerve-centre from the Augustinians. The church is very large by Irish standards, with a eight-bay nave, aisles, transepts, and a flat-ended, four-bay presbytery with an ambulatory. Its sculpture belongs within the same English repertoire as its rival, Christ Church. Its interior also displays the same western English character as its neighbouring cathedral (Rae 1979; Stalley 1984, 73).

A third building of the same quality was Waterford Cathedral. Virtually none of its fabric survived a rebuilding in the late eighteenth century, but there are illustrations of its interior and exterior, and in his analysis of these Roger Stalley has drawn attention to western English characteristics (1981).

Other cathedrals of the early 1200s are less important and impressive but are no less interesting. Three worthy of note are Kilkenny (Barry 1985) and Newtown Trim, county Meath (O'Keeffe 1999b, 123-7), both with Anglo-Norman patrons, and Cashel, county Tipperary (Stalley 1971, 84-7), located in an area of Anglo-Norman control but erected while Gaelic-Irish bishops held the see. The first of these, Kilkenny, is the most complete. Under construction for the entire first half of the thirteenth century and only completed around 1260, it is a large church with an aisled nave and a long choir flanked by two chapels on either side; its interior walls are not subdivided into bays, and there was no vaulting over any of its main spans prior to the fifteenth century. Its west door is unmistakeably English in design, with an especially good parallel at Wells Cathedral (Stalley 1971, 77-78), and this tells us that the western English influences which were so strong in the big metropolitan cathedrals in Ireland in the early 1200s were still important in the 1250s. The second of these cathedrals, Newtown Trim, was begun after the bishop of Meath moved the diocesan centre from Clonard to a site downriver from the great de Lacy castle at the start of the thirteenth century. Like Christ Church, this cathedral had Augustinian canons regular serve as its monastic chapter, so a great cloister was attached to its south side. The complex of buildings is now very incomplete but it must have been

66   *A bay in the Gothic nave of Christ Church Cathedral, Dublin (after Street and Seymour 1882)*

magnificent by Irish standards: the cathedral church's east end (the presbytery) had rib-vaulting, probably of stone but conceivably of timber, and the east end of the nave — perhaps it was the west end of an extended choir? — had mural passages and complex rib-vaults of stone. Cashel Cathedral, finally, was rebuilt over many decades during the thirteenth century to a design which is without exact parallel in Ireland. Roofed in timber throughout, its choir (**67**) is extremely long, but it is also narrower than the nave and transepts, which creates a very unusual sensation of space when one stands at their junction; indeed, that sensation is exaggerated somewhat by a nave which is now absurdly short because it was never completed to its intended length. Each of the transepts at Cashel has a pair of chapels projecting as separately-roofed structures, a feature for which near-contemporary parallels in Ireland may be found in the transepts of the early twelfth-century Baltinglass Abbey, county Wicklow, and the north transepts of mid-thirteenth-century Buttevant Franciscan friary, county Cork. The Cashel transepts also have wall passages which allow circulation between them just below what was the level of the roof.

Duiske Abbey in Graiguenamanagh, county Kilkenny (**colour plates 23, 24**), has the only extant Cistercian church to rank alongside the best of the Gothic cathedrals. A daughter house of Stanley in Wiltshire, it was founded in 1204 and was laid-out in typical Cistercian fashion. The claustral buildings are fragmentary and inaccessible, but the church survived the middle ages so intact that it could be restored for worship in the late 1970s and early 1980s. In keeping with Cistercian tradition, the nave and transepts are rather plain, but the east end was vaulted with a fine flourish of slender ribs. Duiske actually exhibits a mild schizophrenia, balancing a presbytery of quintessential Gothic design with a nave which is still essentially Romanesque in having plain walls and round-arched windows. The early thirteenth-century Cistercian church of Mellifont, county Louth, was probably as impressive as Duiske but only its foundations remain; the church of St Mary's Abbey in Dublin, the richest of all Irish monastic houses, probably surpassed both of them but is long gone.

The Augustinian monasteries of the Anglo-Normans were not especially wealthy, but a small number of them possess architecture of the first rank. Athassel Priory, county Tipperary, is certainly the finest (**colour plate 25**). The great church, which is now in ruins, was a large cruciform structure, timber-roofed throughout except for vaulted nave-aisles. The architectural details of the building suggest it was built over many decades: the choir belongs to the decades after 1200, but it took until the second half of the thirteenth century for the priory's builders to get as far as the west façade. Late in the middle ages the crossing tower, which is probably mid-thirteenth century in date, was heightened and transformed into a comfortable residential space. Perhaps the greatest loss among the Augustinian houses is St Thomas's Abbey in Dublin. This was founded as a priory in 1177 but was upgraded to an abbey in 1192, and its great wealth in the later middle ages was probably reflected in its architecture. Both it and the Cistercian abbey of St Mary's may have rivalled Dublin's cathedrals of Christ Church and St Patrick's for sophistication and opulence.

Although the richest and most spectacular ecclesiastical buildings had been erected by 1250, in the half-century that followed the ecclesiastical-buildings industry in Ireland lost none of its energy, even if it did lose some of its capacity to surprise us with idiosyncratic

67   *The choir of Cashel Cathedral. The high altar in this great liturgical chamber was lit by a large east window (now destroyed) and by a row of lancets along the south wall*

68   Rathkeale Augustinian priory church, county Limerick. The east wall of this Anglo-Norman foundation was provided with a four-light window with switchline tracery in the fifteenth century

works: most of the major building activity after 1250 was for the Dominican and Franciscan friars, and while their friaries provided ample opportunities for the masons and craftsmen to practice their arts, the friars' simple lifestyle meant they could not aspire to the grand architecture of the monks, canons or bishops. Even allowing for this, late thirteenth-century friary churches are elegant and attractive, with claustral ranges which were appropriately simple and workmanlike in execution; the urban sites in which a small number of the friaries were located — see, for example, the Franciscan friary in Waterford — did not, in any case, facilitate extensive buildings. But the whole effect in these friaries is strangely anachronistic, both in conception and in detail. For example, in the later 1200s rows of lancets — sometimes single lights, sometimes mullioned — lit the choirs at places like Ardfert Franciscan friary, county Kerry, or Kilmallock Dominican friary, county Limerick, just as they had at places like Athassel at the start of the century. Graded lancets were still preferred for east windows, even though no self-respecting senior cleric in contemporary England would allow anything other than tracery in such important openings.

The Decorated and Perpendicular Styles in Ireland

Tracery did eventually make an appearance in Ireland, but probably not much before 1300, if even that early. The simplest form of tracery is 'switch-line' in which the lines of arches cross each other as if railway tracks; this appeared as early as the first decade in the Franciscan friary at Castledermot, county Kildare, and did not go out of fashion thereafter

69   Fethard Augustinian friary, county Tipperary. This was founded around 1305 but heavily modified in the fifteenth and nineteenth centuries. Two original fourteenth-century windows in the north wall of the church choir are fine examples of Decorated style craftsmanship

(**68**). More elaborate tracery involving such features as cusps, trefoils, quatrefoils, cinquefoils, and small dagger-shaped openings (*mouchettes*), appeared simultaneously with 'switch-line' tracery, and its inspiration was that English Gothic tradition of the late 1200s and early 1300s which is known among modern scholars as the Decorated style (Bony 1979; Coldstream 1995). Among the earliest examples of Decorated style windows are two fairly simple three-light windows in the south wall of the choir of the Augustinian friary at Fethard, county Tipperary (**69**), founded in the first decade of the fourteenth century. Impressive four-light east windows are found at Athenry Dominican friary, county Galway, and the parish church of Fenagh, county Leitrim, both dating from the second quarter of the fourteenth century. There are also imposing five-light windows in the choir of Tuam Cathedral, county Galway, and in the south transept of the Dominican friary in Kilkenny, both early fourteenth century in date.

It seems that the years between 1350 and 1400 saw comparatively few new churches being built in Ireland, but this fall-away in construction activity did not have a significant affect on the popularity of Decorated style tracery in Ireland. On the contrary, this tracery had a far longer life in Ireland than it had in England where the Perpendicular style achieved dominance over it in the first half of the fourteenth century. The best examples of the tracery are fifteenth century in date, as witness the extraordinary variety of windows of that date at places like Holycross Abbey, county Tipperary. Twin-light windows with comparable tracery appear in castles after 1400, with the best examples to be found at Newcastle West and Askeaton, county Limerick. Windows with cusped-ogee arches are

70   A fifteenth-century cusped-ogee window in the medieval parish church of Leixlip, county Kildare

found in very great numbers all across Ireland in fifteenth-century castles and churches (**70**), and while they are very simple manifestations of the Decorated style aesthetic, they do express far better than anything else the extraordinary life-span of this style in the later medieval Ireland.

The Perpendicular style, perhaps the most English of all expressions of the Gothic style, had a lesser impact on Ireland, and that impact is not manifest before the fifteenth century, by which time England was already several decades into its Perpendicular phase. We can see elements of English Perpendicular very clearly in the traceried windows of some churches in the region known as the English Pale in the fifteenth and sixteenth centuries, as at Killeen, county Meath, built in the first half of the fifteenth century (**71**), but even here the survival of the Decorated style aesthetic is still strong. Other manifestations of Perpendicular in churches in Ireland include the shallow but complex mouldings around

71   The west window of Killeen church, county Meath. The short vertical bars of stone in the centre of the arch of this elaborately traceried window suggest influence from the English Perpendicular tradition

some fifteenth-century doorways, such as Dean Odo's door of 1461 in Clonmacnois Cathedral, county Offaly (**72**), and the doorway of 1471 erected in the west wall of Clontuskert Augustinian priory, county Galway. The arcades of many fifteenth-century cloisters in Ireland, and particularly the mid-century cloister at Holycross, county Tipperary, also possess such strong Perpendicular characteristics as rectangular frames around arches, slender mouldings, and capitals and bases of polygonal shape.

The fact of the appearance of Decorated style tracery in Ireland around 1300 and in the following decades is testimony to the close contacts between the two islands even as their political relationship was being transformed by a combination of ethnic stress and economic crisis in the smaller island. The appearance of some Perpendicular forms in the 1400s also reflects the continuing transmission of stylistic ideas across the Irish Sea in an age when most of Ireland could claim full political automony from England. How exactly

the Decorated and Perpendicular forms were transmitted from England to Ireland is not known to us, but it is probable that some stone-carvers from England were present in Ireland, at least in the early stages of Ireland's involvement with both styles; in the case of the Decorated style we can be confident, based on its post-1300 chronology, that these men were in Ireland not as incidental members of that immigration entourage from late thirteenth-century England of which we spoke in Chapter 3 (pp59-60, 80 above) but had travelled here at the behest of patrons. The same may be said of the stone-carvers working within the Perpendicular idiom, and their earliest commissions may have been in the Pale where connections with England were especially strong and where families like the Plunketts, Talbots and Cusacks might have been attracted to Perpendicular because it was a style favoured in court circles in England.

More important than establishing the chronology and mapping the diffusion of these styles may be the matter of their 'meaning' in Ireland. Did contemporary viewers of traceried windows and other architectural features in fourteenth and fifteenth-century Ireland know that the designs were of English origin? Would they have even observed that the designs was radically different from what had appeared previously in churches (and castles), and if they made such observations would they have thought of asking themselves where it had come from? These are questions we cannot answer, but if we use Ireland's experience of the Romanesque style as a point of comparative reference, we can offer some speculation. All these stylistic traditions were alien importations, all were largely restricted to architectural openings rather than made manifest in entire architectural conceptions, and both Romanesque and Decorated (if not also Perpendicular—more work is needed on it) seem to have undergone a development from fairly 'pure' forms in their early stages to more idiosyncratic, 'gaelicised' forms in the later stages. Perhaps the Decorated and Perpendicular styles were first adopted by old Anglo-Norman families in Ireland precisely because they expressed links with England, just as Romanesque was adopted because it expressed the alignment of its patrons with the spirit of Church reform.

The architecture of the fifteenth-century friars

Although friars first appeared in Ireland during the thirteenth century, the period after 1350 saw the number of their houses greatly expand, largely as a result of Gaelic-Irish patronage, and the fifteenth century saw the erection of their most noteworthy and original buildings. All the friars, regardless of whether they were Franciscan, Dominican or Augustinian, were divided into 'Conventual' and 'Observant' congregations. Here, 'Conventual' refers simply to the act of living in a convent (a religious community), and it is essentially a blanket-term for medieval monastic life, but 'Observant' refers to the Observant reform movement which, from the fourteenth century when it started its sweep through communities of friars, demanded strict adherence to the letter of their monastic rules. If generalisation is possible, the friaries founded under Anglo-Norman patronage in the later thirteenth and fourteenth centuries were Conventual, but most of the newly-founded friaries of the fifteenth century seem to have been Observant. Also, most of them were located in the western half of Ireland — counties Cork, Kerry, Limerick, Clare, Galway and Mayo — and had Gaelic-Irish patrons.

Some general observations may be made about friary architecture in this period. The friary churches tend to be long and aisleless, but there is often a large transept leading southwards off the nave; sometimes the transept is aisled, and sometimes its aisle continues along the south side of the nave. The transepts are frequently additions, made to increase the amount of space available for lay worship. What impresses visitors from afar are the slender and beautifully-constructed bell-towers which rise between the nave and choirs of the churches (**73**). Nineteen of these still stand (Craig 1982, 84). Unlike the towers which were added to many Cistercian abbeys around the same time, these friary towers are not 'crossing towers' in any conventional sense as they do not co-incide with the intersection of naves, choirs, and transepts; rather, they simply rise above the place where screens would have blocked the view into the choir from the nave. The towers can sometimes be rectangular, with their narrow axis from east to west, as at the Franciscan friaries of Muckross, county Kerry, and Creevelea, county Leitrim, or the Dominican

73   *The friary of Rosserk, county Mayo. This exceptionally well-preserved complex of mid-fifteenth-century date is dominated by a slender bell-tower (Photograph: Dúchas, The Heritage Service, reproduced with permission)*

friary at Cashel, county Tipperary. Far more popular, however, and particularly among the Franciscans, was the square tower which rose on great arches and was narrower than the church below.

The friaries are arranged around cloisters; two friaries, the Franciscan Ross Errilly, county Galway, and the Dominican Rathfran, county Mayo, even had two cloisters each. Friary cloisters are generally much smaller than cloisters in the abbeys of Cistercian monks and the priories of Augustinian canons regular. In the case of Quin, county Clare, the cloister's size was restricted by the fact that this early fifteenth-century friary was constructed within the ruins of a late thirteenth-century fortress (**74**). Elsewhere, however, there were no such restrictions, and yet the cloisters were still kept small. A second feature of the friary cloisters is that they are invariably to the north of the churches, a position which was normal for cloisters in nunneries but not for the cloisters of male religious communities; we do not know why the friars chose north-side cloisters, but we might suppose that they attached some symbolic significance to the darkness into which the cloisters were plunged when the evening sun settled behind the friary churches. Askeaton Friary, county Limerick, is exceptional in having its cloister to the south of the church; it is also one of the few friaries with a refectory running at 90° to the south side

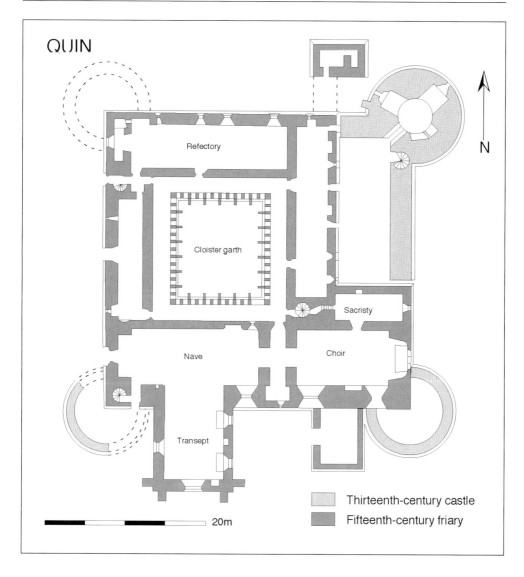

QUIN

Refectory

Cloister garth

Sacristy

Nave

Choir

Transept

20m

Thirteenth-century castle

Fifteenth-century friary

N

74   *A plan of Quin Franciscan friary, county Clare, showing how the friary was accommodated within the plan of a long-abandoned fortress*

of the cloister in the manner of many thirteenth-century Cistercian refectories. The final feature of note is that the cloister ambulatories in the friaries rarely have lean-to roofs; with few exceptions (Rosserk, county Mayo, Creevelea, county Leitrim, and Sherkin and Kilcrea, county Cork, all of them Franciscan), the ambulatories had stone-vaulted roofs which also supported the first-floor rooms of the claustral buildings. Consequently, while the cloister courts seem rather cramped, the rooms upstairs seem very spacious indeed.

Parish churches

The parish church, the last of the principal categories of churches which we will examine, is by far the most neglected among students of medieval Ireland, despite being the category of church with which medieval people had greatest familiarity. Before we consider the architecture, there are matters of definition and chronology to be resolved. The Anglo-Normans were responsible for considerable numbers of new parish churches in eastern Ireland. However, the parochial system in medieval Ireland was apparently not, *contra* some earlier views (Otway-Ruthven 1964), newly-created by them, as its two main features — a network of 'local churches' and a system for collection of tithes based on units of land (Sharpe 1992; Doherty 1998, 314) — are clearly attested to in pre-colonial Ireland. There was a rise in the number of new churches in southern Ireland in the two decades after the Synod of Kells/Mellifont in 1152, and given that most of these were apparently not monastic churches, it may be appropriate to offer them as evidence of an emerging, if not an already-emerged, parish system (O'Keeffe 2000a).

Returning to the Anglo-Normans, discussions of the process of their conquest and colonisation have long stressed, not unnaturally, the role of their castles, but the considerable evidence that they were erecting new churches in the first decades after 1169 has generally not been remarked upon. The evidence is both historical and archaeological. First, Anglo-Norman patronage is well-documented for large, urban, parish churches; perusal of the few surviving records of monastic houses also makes it clear that smaller, rural, parish churches were, from an early stage in the history of the colony, being granted by Anglo-Norman lords to monasteries in accordance with contemporary custom. Secondly, examination of the fabric of many churches, both urban and rural, reveals windows, doors and walls of probable early thirteenth-century date.

Much more work needs to be done on the matter of Anglo-Norman parish churches, and there is probably scope for a refinement of their chronology so that we can distinguish between churches built at different times in the thirteenth century. On the whole, however, thirteenth-century Anglo-Norman parish churches do seem to be longer and larger than pre-colonial churches. With a few cathedral churches as exceptions, the relationship of length to breadth in pre-colonial churches did not exceed 2:1; indeed, proportions of 2:1 seem only to have appeared in Romanesque churches, whereas in earlier, eleventh- and tenth-century Irish churches proportions could be as short as 1:1.4, which is essentially the $1:\sqrt{2}$ proportion which was so beloved of Classical and medieval builders across Europe. Anglo-Norman parish churches, however, could have proportions up to 4:1 or 5:1, which are similar to the proportions which they used in their cathedral, abbey and priory churches. The Anglo-Normans also made use of the $1:\sqrt{2}$ proportion, but it was generally to lay-out *parts* of their churches.

The largest Anglo-Norman parish churches were those in town parishes. The largest seems to have been St Mary's at New Ross, county Wexford, founded by William Marshall the Elder, lord of Leinster from 1189 to 1219. Only the choir and transepts remain. Neither is vaulted, but each is embellished with fine architectural sculpture. Its grand scale rivals that of contemporary cathedrals in Ireland. Other substantial parish churches include St Mary's in Youghal and St Multose's in Kinsale, both in county Cork and both port towns like New Ross. Inland towns sometimes also had large, aisled churches. The parish church at Fethard, county Tipperary, has already been mentioned in the context of possible Cistercian influence. Gowran and Thomastown, both in county Kilkenny, are also large town churches, and both have design elements in common with the mid-thirteenth-century nave of the cathedral in Kilkenny; Roger Stalley has argued that the same man, whom he calls the 'Gowran master', is responsible for all this work (Stalley 1971, 75-80). Even in its ruined condition, Gowran, which was run by a college of priests, is a particularly splendid building, packed with high quality architectural and effigial sculpture; among its many treasures is the inscribed mid-seventeenth-century tomb of James Keally and his two wives: 'Both wives at once alive he could not have; Both to annoy at once he made this grave'!

The finest of the post-1300 parish churches is unquestionably that of St Nicholas in Galway (Leask 1936). A collegiate church like Gowran, this was built around 1330 to a far more complex plan — a four-bay nave, transepts, a choir without aisles — than was customary for non-cathedral churches. At the end of the fifteenth century the south aisle was widened, and the piers of the crossing were strengthened to take a tower; in the sixteenth century the church was enlarged under the patronage of the Lynch family (patrons also of Lynch's Castle, described on p49 above), and one consequence of its enlargement is that it now has a three-gabled façade. Other large churches with substantial fifteenth-century fabric include the collegiate church of SS Peter and Paul at Kilmallock, county Limerick, and St Mary's at Callan, county Kilkenny.

Ireland has ruins of many hundreds of small rural churches, many of them now wrapped in impenetrable ivy and briars. Until such time as a national inventory is compiled, complete with descriptions, we will not know exactly how the pattern of church-building at this local level ebbed and flowed through time, but there is little doubt that in the fifteenth century many older churches had changes made to them, particularly new doorways and windows, while many other older churches may have been rebuilt.

The Plunkett churches in Meath

In our discussion of castle architecture in Chapter 3 we noted that the English Pale was home to a very distinctive tradition of tower-house design. The only hint of a comparable tradition in church architecture is a propensity for residential towers at the west ends of the churches, although these are not confined to the Pale (one of the best is at Taghmon, county Westmeath, which is outside the Pale). Few families in the Pale had as high a profile as the Plunketts, and different branches of the family erected many of the finest monuments of the Pale, such as Killeen castle, county Meath (now hidden inside a Gothick mansion), and Dunsoghley castle, which we already mentioned (p50). Three marvellous churches of the early fifteenth-century in county Meath, Killeen, Dunsany and Rathmore (**75**), can be attributed to the patronage of scions of the one branch of the family. These are not conventional parish churches but estate churches, and their patrons are buried inside them. Killeen and Dunsany are quite identical in all but detail, and Rathmore diverges only slightly from their form. The size of their chancels, at least in relation to the size of the naves, underlines the essentially private nature of these churches.

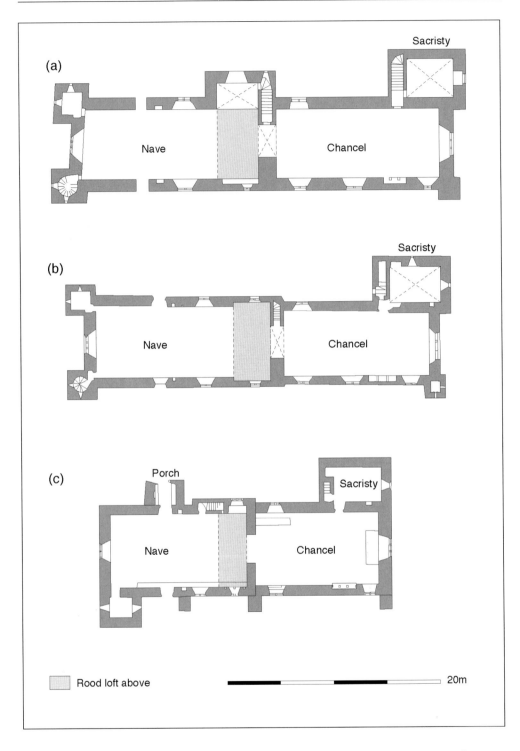

75   *The plans of three Plunkett churches in county Meath: (a) Dunsany; (b) Killeen; (c) Rathmore (after Leask 1955-60 iii)*

Fine art, furnishings and tombs

Comparatively little remains of the non-sculptural decoration, furnishings, and altar plate of Ireland's later medieval churches. There are traces of painted plaster at dozens of sites, but frescoes which are sufficiently complete and well-preserved for us to read their iconography are comparatively few. The best survivals are probably those in Cistercian contexts, as at Holycross, county Tipperary, where the fifteenth-century fresco depicts a hunting scene, or Abbeyknockmoy, county Galway, where the sixteenth-century fresco depicts the medieval tale of the Three Live Kings and the Three Dead Kings, the martyrdom of St Sebastian, and possibly St Michael weighing the souls. Wooden furnishings are gone from virtually all the churches. The late fifteenth-century misericords — the undersides of the seats in the choir stalls — in Limerick cathedral are the only notable survivals; carved in black oak, they bear plant ornament and a selection of animals from the medieval bestiaries, and the manner in which the plant ornament flanks the main image in each misericord is characteristic of English work. There are some thirteenth-century statuesque sculptures in wood which were presumably displayed in churches. The representations, which are attractive but rather stiff, include the Virgin and Child, as at Kilcorban and Clonfert, both in county Galway, and St Catherine, also at Kilcorban, St Molaise, at Inismurray, county Sligo, and God the Father, at Fethard, county Tipperary.

There are also few surviving examples of altar plate and other items of liturgical metalwork. There are some chalices, such as the so-called De Burgo O'Malley Chalice of 1494, and the chalice found in excavations at Mellifont (Stalley 1987). An exceptional late-Gothic processional cross of 1479, decorated with evangelist symbols and the crucified Christ, as well as plant motifs, remains from Lislaughtin Franciscan friary, county Kerry. Another exceptional item to survive is the crozier made in 1418 for Cornelius O'Dea, bishop of Limerick; made in silver-gilt with coloured enamel, the figures which decorate it include assorted local, national and international saints. The same bishop's mitre also survives.

Shrines or reliquaries associated with churches have a better survival rate, thanks in part to their custody within the same families over many generations. The shrines of the twelfth century are especially spectacular (Henry 1970; O Floinn 1996). They include the Cross of Cong, made in 1124 to house a portion of the True Cross, the Shrine of St Patrick's Bell, made about the same time to encase a bronze bell associated with the saint, and the Shrine of St Lachtin's Arm, made in the early twelfth century in the shape of the corporeal relic it was intended to contain. New shrines were made later in the middle ages, such as the Domhnach Airgid, made around 1350 at the behest of the abbot of Clones, county Monaghan, to contain a gospel book of eighth or ninth-century date.

Remembering the dead

The enclosed areas outside the churches were foci of community burial. In modern Ireland care is taken not to intercut burials, and so cemeteries are naturally expansive; many modern cemeteries in Ireland are extra-mural extensions of older cemeteries, or brand new cemeteries without churches at all. In the middle ages there does not seem to have been the same concern about intercutting, so the cemeteries are less extensive and rather more crowded.

76   *Kilfane, county Kilkenny. This effigy, known locally as 'Long Cantwell', is the finest of about a dozen such effigies to survive in Ireland. Comparable effigies in England date from the middle of the thirteenth century, but details of this knight's attire, particularly his spurs, suggest a date about a century later (Stalley 1994)*

Valuable data on the evolution of a later medieval cemetery was retrieved in the excavation of St Peter's church in Waterford (Hurley and McCutcheon 1997). In the period around 1100, immediately prior to the construction of the Hiberno-Norse church, there was a cemetery of inhumations in east-west oriented graves — the heads were to the west — which were either in simple pits or wood-lined. There were two coffin burials. Between the early twelfth and mid-thirteenth centuries the density of burial increased and stone-lined graves (some of them coffin-shaped) first appeared. The construction of the church gave spatial definition to the cemetery: some individuals were buried inside the nave, but most were buried outside the apse and along the south side of the church. That church was partly demolished and reconstructed in a new form in the thirteenth century. Between the time of this reconstruction and *c*1600 the cemetery expanded again, but the south side of the church area remained the focus for burials, most of which were in simple pits, while burials were still being allowed into the church. Simple pit burials, apparently

77   *The tomb of Piers fitz Oge Butler in Kilcooley Cistercian abbey, county Tipperary, carved by Rory O'Tunney and bearing an inscription* Roricus O Tuyne scripsit *(Photograph: Dúchas, The Heritage Service, reproduced with permission)*

without coffins, were also identified in the thirteenth and fourteenth century cemetery excavated at the Dominican priory in Drogheda (Halpin and Buckley 1995).

The churches themselves were certainly the preferred places of burial. It seems that in the Anglo-Norman period it was mainly the patrons or founders of churches who were allowed burial in churches, and especially in the choir areas where their remains would forever be close to the high altars. The tombs of patrons, benefactors and senior clergy were vehicles for the display of very high quality sculpture (Hunt 1974).

Effigial sculpture was particularly popular on the tombs of both bishops and knights in the thirteenth and fourteenth centuries. Among the earliest knight-effigies is that of Robert fitzRichard de Valle at Timolin, county Kildare, dating from the early thirteenth century. The finest of all effigies is that of a knight at Kilfane, county Kilkenny (**76**), carved in the fourteenth century; his crossed legs can be paralleled on other tombs, as at Hospital, county Limerick, and while it might signify the knight's participation in crusades or his death in battle, it does impart to the figure a certain vitality, and thus it celebrates his life as effectively as it marks his death. Effigial sculpture was also used in parts of Gaelic Ireland in the thirteenth and fourteenth centuries, as in the cases of King Felim Ó Conchobhair at Roscommon and King Conor na Suidaine Ó Briain at Corcomroe, county Clare, both carved around the year 1300.

In the early fifteenth century the Plunketts of Killeen, Dunsany and Rathmore, the three county Meath churches which we discussed above (p157), had effigies of knights and their ladies carved on top of free-standing tomb-chests; the sides of those chests were decorated with Passion and Crucifixion scenes, as well as with assorted saints, apostles, and family coats-of-arms. The patronage of the Plunketts may have provided the impetus for a *floruit* of effigial sculpture in the lands of the Pale in the 1400s; in this part of Ireland the sculptor's art was also put at the service of limestone fonts (Roe 1968) and, around the end of our period, wayside crosses (King 1984). Comparable tombs with carved sides and effigies on their top surfaces appeared later in the fifteenth century in south-east Ireland, with the finest works being made in Kilkeny and Tipperary in the sixteenth century by the O'Tunney craftsmen — we know their identities because they signed their works (**77**) — and the anonymous craftsmen of the so-called 'Ormond school'. Further west in Ireland the tomb-chest contained within a wall recess and covered by fine tracery was preferred for the burial of high-status individuals.

9 Looking back, looking forward

The bibliography at the end of this book contains 348 items, of which 291 references — 84% — relate directly to Ireland. References from the 1980s and 1990s amount to 33% and 31% of this total respectively. The bibliography is not exhaustive, and it includes some material which is specifically historical in nature, but a more comprehensive list of archaeological references would probably increase rather than decrease these percentages. We can reasonably conclude from this measure of the expansion of relevant literature that later medieval archaeology in Ireland is no longer in that infancy stage to which Terry Barry referred a dozen years ago (1987, 1). But it is not so easy to assess what level of maturity it has actually reached. It should be apparent from the preceding chapters that there are issues about which we have comparatively little information, and that as a consequence there are imbalances in our understanding of later medieval Ireland as a whole. For example, we know more about the archaeology of Ireland in the colonial period (from 1169 to the early 1300s) than in the late middle ages (the 1400s and 1500s), and we have a better general understanding of landscape, settlement and architecture than of material culture, or environmental conditions, or health and mortality. Most surprisingly, perhaps, we are far more familiar with the archaeology of the colonists than that of the contemporary Gaelic-Irish people. A perusal of the archaeological literature will provide the hard evidence on which these statements are based. Of course, these imbalances are not as pronounced as they were twenty years ago, and in twelve years from now, which is the distance in time between Terry Barry's *The Archaeology of Medieval Ireland* and this book, there may no longer be such imbalances.

Progress is partly contingent on the excavation of appropriate sites, particularly with respect to both material culture and the general archaeology of the fifteenth and sixteenth centuries. How, though, do we make progress in the study of the later medieval Gaelic-Irish? Excavation of sites associated with them is needed, but locating such sites has long been a problem: settlements of the lower social ranks have generally not been located, and discussion of the settlement archaeology of the higher social ranks, especially in the pre-tower-house period, still largely revolves around the question of the medieval ringfort. One strategy for the study of Gaelic-Irish archaeology is to look at the modern landscapes of those parts which remained outside colonial control. These landscapes were home to the medieval Irish, and they reveal that to us everytime we travel across them: they are clear of forest, enclosed with fields, made accessible by roads, and divided into named townlands. All of these conditions were achieved by the time of the first Ordnance Survey maps in the 1840s, and most of them had been achieved by the end of the middle ages. It is by studying the maps of these landscapes, followed by detailed field-survey and recording of the micro-topography, that we can hope to break into the landscape and settlement histories of medieval Gaelic Ireland.

If we are ever to write an archaeology of the medieval Gaelic-Irish we must also address directly the matter of ethnicity. Up to the 1960s most prehistoric archaeologists assumed that recurring assemblages of archaeological traits — burial practices, pottery types, and domestic building types, for example — allowed the identification of cultures, and sometimes of ethnic groups, within certain regions. This assumption has been challenged repeatedly in recent decades, and most recently by Siân Jones (1997). The details of the debate about archaeology and ethnicity lie outside the scope of this book, but issues raised in that debate need to considered in future research on Gaelic-Irish archaeology. What, after all, do we mean by 'Gaelic-Irish'? Does it refer to a 'culture', or to a 'race', or to both? How would we identify a 'Gaelic-Irish' site?

Finally, progress in later medieval archaeology in Ireland is contingent on progress in what we might describe as the 'intellectual methods' employed by medieval archaeologists in bridging the gap between the physical remains of the past and the visualisation of actual people interacting with those physical things in the past. The principal challenge of 'intellectual method' facing medieval archaeology is surely that of establishing its role in relation to medieval history. To a degree, historians of the middle ages engage in the same exercises as medieval archaeologists, albeit by using a different range of skills on a different range of source materials, but the fact that historical materials seem to articulate the story of the past in a language more immediately intelligible to us than the language of mortared stones, glazed pots and rusting metal has long given the historian an advantage, or at least a head-start, over the archaeologist in making sense of the middle ages. However, archaeologists cannot take the view that their job is to contextualise their archaeological data in the historian's version of the past, if only because historical interpretations of the past are themselves constantly shifting. In any case, the historical record excludes more often than not the observations which would help answer the questions which archaeologists ask. Indeed, much of this book relates to matters about which we know very little from the historical record: we may, for example, have a written record of the names of the builders of certain castles and churches, and we may know both the circumstances in which they were built and their cost, but archaeology offers insights into why those buildings appear as they do.

What of the argument that many of the problems discussed in this book, such as the origins of the tower-house, the relationship between 'town' and 'borough', or the relative chronologies of Bristolian and Saintongeais ceramic imports, are problems about *things* rather than about *people*, and that bringing them to resolution does not, of itself, bring us any nearer to reconstructing in our minds' eyes exactly what life was like in the later middle ages? The answer is that resolving these problems helps us understand the structure of the world in which medieval people lived. We can easily empathise with individuals of the middle ages whoever they were and whatever their status because we understand from our own experiences in the modern world how landscapes, buildings and objects communicate complex ideas about society and identity, and how changes of fashion or innovations in technology simultaneously create dilemmas and offer opportunities. We can understand, then, the pride of a wealthy merchant expressing his status in a new tower-house, just as we can understand the disappointment of a minor lord in the countryside having to pour his wine from a tall French-made jug because the Bristol-made jugs to which he was accustomed were simply no longer available. Even if the great majority of Ireland's population in the five centuries covered in this book were not actually responsible for those endless transformations in the forms of buildings, landscapes and material goods which we see in the archaeological record, they were never unaffected by it.

Appendix: a note on published historical sources

Much primary evidence relating to colonial Ireland has been translated and published in calendared form: there are, for example, five volumes of the *Calendar of Documents Relating to Ireland 1171-1306* (H.S. Sweetman [ed] London 1875-86), and three volumes of the *Calendar of Justiciary Rolls, Ireland, 1295-1314* (J. Mills and M.C. Griffith [eds] Dublin 1905-56). Other material relevant to Ireland and published in calendared form appears in the multi-volume *Calendar of Inquisitions Post Mortem* and in the *Calendar of Papal Registers*. Important primary material relating to the two urban settlements of Dublin and Kilkenny is published in the *Calendar of the Ancient Records of Dublin* (J.T. Gilbert [ed] Dublin 1889-1944) and *Liber Primus Kilkenniensis* (C. McNeill [ed] Dublin 1931) respectively. Borough charters have been compiled and published by Gearóid MacNiocaill in *Na Buirgéisí* (Dublin 1964). Manorial extents and related records of landholding patterns have been published in calendared form in the *Calendar of Archbishop Alen's Register* (C. McNeill [ed] Dublin 1950), which relates to the Dublin region, the *Calendar of the Gormanstown Register* (J. Mills and M.J. McEnery [eds] Dublin 1916), which relates principally to north Dublin and Meath, the *Dowdall Deeds* (C. McNeill and A.J. Otway-Ruthven [eds] Dublin 1960), which relate to county Louth, and the *Calendar of Ormond Deeds, 1172-1603* (E. Curtis [ed] Dublin 1932-43), which relates to the earldom of Ormond in Tipperary and Kilkenny. Rentals and deeds of the earls of Ormond are also recorded and published in the *Red Book of Ormond* (N.B. White [ed] Dublin 1932), while the *Red Book of the Earls of Kildare* (MacNiocaill [ed] Dublin 1964) contains comparable material relating to the great FitzGerald family.

Some records relating to ecclesiastical properties survive. Those pertaining to four exceptionally wealthy monastic houses in Dublin — St Mary's Cistercian abbey (J.T. Gilbert [ed] London 1884-6), the Augustinian abbey of St Thomas the Martyr (J.T. Gilbert [ed] London 1889), the cathedral priory of Holy Trinity (J. Mills [ed] Dublin 1891), and the Hospital of St John the Baptist (E St J Brooks [ed] Dublin 1936) — have been published. Also available are charters of Duiske abbey, a Cistercian house in county Kilkenny (C.M. Butler and J.H. Bernard [eds], *Proceedings of the Royal Irish Academy* 35C 1918-20, 1-188), the Register of the Augustinian priory at Tristernagh, county Westmeath (M.V. Clarke [ed] Dublin 1941), and the cartularies of the Irish possessions of Llanthony Prima and Secunda in Wales (E St J Brooks [ed] Dublin 1953). The Ecclesiastical Taxation of the early fourteenth century, the only such taxation for which information survives, has also been published in the *Calendar of Documents Relating to Ireland 1171-1306* (HS Sweetman [ed] vol 5 [1886], no. 693). An extremely valuable source is the so-called Pipe Roll of Cloyne, a compilation of extents, rentals and inquisitions of episcopal manors in the diocese of Cloyne; long unavailable except in an inadequate recension, a new and comprehensively cross-referenced translation is now available (P. MacCotter and K.W. Nicholls [eds] *The Pipe Roll of Cloyne [Rotulus Pipae Clonensis]* Cloyne 1996).

Contemporary medieval narratives include the two books of Giraldus Cambrensis, the Welsh cleric who visited Ireland in the 1180s and whose brothers were participants in the invasion. The earlier of the two, *Topographia Hibernica* (J.J. O'Meara [ed] Harmondsworth 1982), describes the topography of the island, and his more celebrated *Expugnatio Hibernica* (A.B. Scott and F.X. Martin [eds] Dublin 1978) describes the process of invasion in colourful detail. Among the most important narratives in poetry is *The Song of Dermot and the Earl* (G.H. Orpen [ed] Oxford 1892), Dermot being Diarmait Mac Murchada, and the earl being Strongbow, one of the early Anglo-Norman adventurers.

Irish chronicles provide valuable information on both the colonial and Gaelic-Irish worlds. The most comprehensive of all the Irish chronicles, both in terms of chronology and geographical spread, is the *Annals of the Kingdom of Ireland by the Four Masters*, compiled from diverse sources in the seventeenth century (J. O'Donovan [ed] Dublin 1848-51). The *Annals of Clonmacnois* are known only in a seventeenth-century version (D. Murphy [ed] Dublin 1896). Annalistic compilations which throw light on the twelfth, thirteenth and fourteenth centuries include the *Annals of Ulster* (W.M. Hennessy and B. MacCarthy [eds] Dublin 1887-1901; the earlier, pre-1131 material in this edition is now available in a new and more reliable edition: S. MacAirt and G. MacNiocaill [eds] Dublin 1984), the *Annals of Connacht* (A.M. Freeman [ed] Dublin 1944), the *Annals of Inisfallen* (S. MacAirt [ed] Dublin 1951), the *Annals of Lough Cé* (W.M. Hennessy [ed] Dublin 1939), and the chronicles of Friar Clyn and Thady Dowling, published together in the same edition (R. Butler [ed] Dublin 1849).

One of the principal bodies of source material for archaeologists of later medieval Ireland belongs to the mid-seventeenth century and was created as part of the process of land redistribution which followed the Cromwellian reconquest of Ireland in 1649. The *Civil Survey*, published in ten volumes (R.C. Simington [ed] Dublin 1931-61), covers the entire country other than the western counties of Sligo, Mayo, Roscommon, Galway and Clare, and it provides invaluable information on the structure of landholding and the monuments within. Sir William Petty's *Down Survey* maps of 1654-56, preserved in the National Library of Ireland (MSS no. 715), cover less of the country and provide a little less detail.

References

Aberg, F.A. (ed) 1978 *Medieval Moated Sites*. London

Addyman, P.V. 1965 'Coney Island, Lough Neagh; prehistoric settlement, Anglo-Norman castle and Elizabethan native fortress', *Ulster Journal of Archaeology* 28, 78-101

Annals of Connacht, ed A.C. Freeman, Dublin 1944

Allen, R.C. 1992 *Enclosure and the Yeoman*. Oxford

Astill, G. and Grant, A. (eds) 1988 *The Countryside of Medieval England*. Oxford

Barrett, G.F. and Graham, B.J. 1975 'Some considerations concerning the dating and distribution of ring-forts in Ireland', *Ulster Journal of Archaeology* 38, 33-45

Barry, S. 1985 'The architecture of the cathedral', in Empey (ed), 25-48

Barry, T.B. 1977 *Medieval Moated Sites of South-East Ireland*. Oxford

Barry, T.B. 1981 'The shifting frontier: medieval moated sites in counties Cork and Limerick', in F.A. Aberg and A.E. Brown (eds), *Medieval Moated Sites in North-west Europe*. Oxford, 71-85

Barry, T.B. 1983 'Anglo-Norman ringwork castles: some evidence', in Reeves-Smyth and Hamond (eds), 295-314

Barry, T.B. 1987 *The Archaeology of Medieval Ireland*. London

Barry, T.B. 1996 'Rural settlement in Ireland in the middle ages: an overview', *Ruralia* I, 134-41

Barry, T.B. 1993 'The archaeology of the tower house in late medieval Ireland', in H. Anderson and T. Wienberg (eds), *The Study of Medieval Archaeology*. Stockholm, 211-17

Barry, T.B. 1995 'The last frontier: defence and settlement in late medieval Ireland', in T.B. Barry, R. Frame and K. Simms (eds), *Colony and Frontier in Medieval Ireland*. Dublin, 217-28

Barthélemy, D. 1988 'Civilising the Fortress: Eleventh to Thirteenth Century', in G. Duby (ed), *A History of Private Life* II *Revelations of the Medieval World*. Cambridge, Mass., 397-421

Bartlett, R. 1993 *The Making of Europe. Conquest, Colonization and Cultural Change, 950 1350*. London

Barton, K.J. 1988 'The medieval pottery of Dublin', in Mac Niocaill and Wallace (eds), 271-324

Bennett, I. 1984-5 'Preliminary archaeological excavations at Ferrycarrig ringwork, Newtown townland, Co. Wexford', *Journal of the Wexford Historical Society* 10, 25-43

Beresford, M.W. and Hurst J.G. (eds) 1971 *Deserted Medieval Villages Studies*. London

Biddle M. 1972 'Excavations at Winchester, 1970: ninth interim report', *Antiquaries Journal* 52, 93-131

Bony, J. 1981 'Durham et la tradition saxonne', in S.M. Crosby, A. Chastel, A. Prache and A. Chatelet (eds), *Etudes d'Art Médiévale offertes à Louis Grodecki*. Paris, 79-92

Bony, J. 1979 *The English Decorated Style*. Oxford

Bourke, E. 1997 'The glass', in Hurley, Scully and McCutcheon, 381-9

Bradley, J. 1977-80 'The topography and layout of medieval Drogheda', *County Louth Archaeological Journal* 19, 98-127

Bradley, J. (ed) 1984 *Viking Dublin Exposed: the Wood Quay Saga*. Dublin

Bradley, J. 1984 'Ardee: an archaeological survey', *County Louth Archaeological Journal* 20, 267-96

Bradley, J. 1985 'Planned Anglo-Norman towns in Ireland', in Clarke and Simms (eds), 411-67

Bradley, J. 1989 'Recent archaeological research on the Irish town', in H. Jäger (ed), *Stadtkernforschung*. Köln-Wien, 321-70

Bradley J. 1994 'Killaloe: a pre-Norman borough?', *Peritia* 8, 170-79

Bradley J. 1995 *Walled Towns in Ireland*. Dublin

Bradley, J. *et al* 1984-90 *Urban Archaeological Survey*. 24 vols. Dublin

Brady, N. 1993 'Reconstructing a medieval Irish plough', *I jornados internacionales sobre tecnologia agraria tradicional*. Madrid, 31-44

Brannon, N.F. 1984 'A small excavation in Tildarg townland, near Ballyclare, County Antrim', *Ulster Journal of Archaeology* 47, 163-70

Brennan, P. 1990 'Incised effigial slab at Athassel Priory', *Tipperary Historical Journal*, 193-5

Brooks, E. St John 1950 *Knights' Fees in Counties Wexford, Carlow and Kilkenny*. Dublin

Brown R.A. 1976 *English Castles*. London

Brunner, K. 1995 'Continuity and discontinuity of Roman agricultural knowledge in the early middle ages', in D. Sweeney (ed), *Agriculture in the Middle Ages*. Philadelphia, 21-40

Burchaell, J. 1988 'The south Kilkenny farm villages', in W.J. Smyth and K. Whelan (eds) *Common Ground: Essays on the Historical Geography of Ireland*. Cork, 110-123

Byrne, F.J. 1987 'The trembling sod: Ireland in 1169', in Cosgrove (ed), 1-42

Cairns, C.T. 1987 *Irish Tower-houses. A Co. Tipperary Case-study*. Athlone

Caithréim Thoirdelbhaigh, ed S.H. O'Grady, Dublin 1929

Caulfield, S. 1969 'Some quernstones in private possession in Co. Kerry', *Journal of the Kerry Archaeological and Historical Society* 2, 59-73

Champneys, A. 1910 *Irish Ecclesiastical Architecture*. London

Charles-Edwards, T.M. 1993 *Early Irish and Welsh Kinship*. Oxford

Cipolla, C.M. 1993 *Before the Industrial Revolution. European Society and Economy 1000-1700*. London

Claffey, J.A. 1980 'Rindown windmill tower', in Murtagh (ed), 84-8

Clarke, H. 1983 'The historical background to North Sea trade *c.*1200-1500', in P. Davey and R. Hodges (eds), *Ceramics and Trade*. Sheffield, 17-25

Clarke, H.B. 1998 'Proto-towns and towns in Ireland and Britain in the ninth and tenth centuries', in Clarke, Ní Mhaonaigh and Ó Floinn (eds), 331-380

Clarke, H.B., Ní Mhaonaigh, M. and Ó Floinn, R. (eds) 1998 *Ireland and Scandinavia in the Early Viking Age*. Dublin

Clarke, H.B. and Simms, A. (eds), 1988 *Comparative Urban Origins in Non-Roman Europe*. 2 vols. Oxford

Cleary, R.M. 1982 'Excavations at Lough Gur, Co. Limerick: part II', *Journal of the Cork Historical and Archaeological Society* 87, 77-106

Cleary, R.M. 1983 'Excavations at Lough Gur, Co. Limerick: part III', *Journal of the Cork Historical and Archaeological Society* 88, 51-80

Cleary, R.M., Hurley, M.F. and Twohig E.A. (eds) 1987 *Archaeological Excavations on the Cork-Dublin Gas Pipeline (1981-82)*. Cork

Cleary, R.M., Hurley, M.F. and Shee Twohig, E. 1997 *Excavations by DC Twohig at Skiddy's Castle and Christ Church, Cork, 1974-77*. Cork

Coldstream, N. 1994 *The Decorated Style*. London

Colfer, B. 1984-5 'The tower of Hook', *Journal of the Wexford Historical Society* 10, 69-78

Colfer, B. 1996 'In search of the barricade and ditch of Ballyconnor, Co. Wexford', *Archaeology Ireland* 10, 2, 16-19

Colloque de Caen: 'Les fortifications de terre en Europe Occidental du Xe au XIIe siècles', *Archeologie Médiévale* 11 (1981), 5-123

Condit, T. 1996 'Rings of truth', *Archaeology Ireland* 10 (37), 30-33

Cosgrove, A. (ed) 1987 *A New History of Ireland*, Vol. II *Medieval Ireland, 1169-1534*. Oxford

Coughlan, M. *Forthcoming* 'Public power, private worship', *Archaeology Ireland*

Cowman, D. 1986-7 'The German mining operation at Bannow Bay 1551-52', *Journal of the Wexford Historical Society* 11, 67-82

Cowman, D. 1992 'The metal mines of Tipperary', *Tipperary Historical Journal*, 105-115

Craig, M. 1982 *The Architecture of Ireland*. London

Cunningham, G. 1987 *The Anglo-Norman Advance into the South-west Midlands of Ireland 1185-1221*. Roscrea

Currie, C.R.J. 1992 'Larger medieval houses in the Vale of the White Horse', *Oxoniesia* 57, 81-244

Davies, R.R. 1990 *Domination and Conquest. The Experience of Ireland, Scotland and Wales 1100-1300*. Cambridge

Davies, O. and Quinn, D.B. 1941 'The Irish Pipe Roll of 14 John 1211-1212', *Ulster Journal of Archaeology* 4 supplement

Davison, B.K. 1961-62 'Excavations at Ballynarry Rath, Co. Down', *Ulster Journal of Archaeology* 24-25, 39-87

De hÓir, S. 1982-83 'Guns in medieval and Tudor Ireland', *The Irish Sword* 15, 76-87

De Paor, L. 1967 'Cormac's Chapel: the beginnings of Irish Romanesque', in E. Rynne (ed), *North Munster Studies*. Limerick, 133-45

De Paor, L. 1969 'Excavations at Mellifont Abbey, Co. Louth', *Proceedings of the Royal Irish Academy* 68C, 109-64

Deevy, M. 1998 *Medieval Ring Brooches in Ireland*. Bray

Dickinson, J.C. 1950 *The Origins of the Austin Canons and their Introduction into England*. London

Dickinson, C.W. and Waterman, D.M. 1959 'Excavations of a rath with motte at Castleskreen, Co. Down', *Ulster Journal of Archaeology* 22, 67-82

Dickinson, C.W. and Waterman, D.M. 1960 'Excavations at Castle Skreen, Co. Down', *Ulster Journal of Archaeology* 23, 63-77

Doherty, C. 1985 'The monastic town in Ireland', in Clarke and Simms (eds), 45-75

Doherty, C. 1998 'The Vikings in Ireland: a review', in Clarke, Ní Mhaonaigh and Ó Floinn (eds), 288-330

Dolley, M. 1987 'Coinage, to 1534: the sign of the times', in Cosgrove (ed), 816-26

Doody, M.G. 1987 'Moated site, Ballyveelish I, Co. Tipperary', in Cleary, Hurley and Twohig (eds), 74-87

Down, K. 1987 'Colonial society and economy in the High Middle Ages', in Cosgrove (ed), 439-91

Du Bouard, M. 1967 'Quelques données franaçises et normandes sur le problème de l'origine des mottes', *Château Gaillard* II, 19-26

Duffy, P.J. 1981 'The territorial organisation of Gaelic landownership and its transformation in county Monaghan, 1591-1640', *Irish Geography* 14, 1-23

Dyer, C. 1983 'English diet in the later middle ages', in T.H. Aston, P.R. Cross, C.C. Dyer and J. Thirsk (eds), *Social Relations and Ideas*. London, 191-214

Dyer, C. 1986 'English peasant buildings in the later middle ages', *Medieval Archaeology* 30, 19-45

Dyer, C. 1985 'Power and conflict in the medieval village', in D. Hooke (ed), *Medieval Villages*. Oxford, 27-32

Dyer, C. 1988 'Documentary evidence: problems and enquiries', in G. Astill and A. Grant (eds), 12-35

Eames, E.S. and Fanning, T. 1988 *Irish Medieval Tiles*. Dublin

Edwards, K.J., Hamond, F.W. and Simms, A. 1983 'The medieval settlement of Newcastle Lyons, Co. Dublin: an interdisciplinary approach', *Proceedings of the Royal Irish Academy* 83C, 351-76

Edwards, N. 1990 *The Archaeology of Early Medieval Ireland*. London

Empey, C.A.1982-3 'Medieval Knocktopher: a study in manorial settlement', *Old Kilkenny Review* 2, 329-42; 441-52

Empey, A. (ed) 1985 *A Worthy Foundation: the Cathedral Church of St Canice, Kilkenny 1285 1985*. Dublin

Esser, K.H. 1953 'Über den Kirchenbau des Hl. Bernhard von Clairvaux', *Archiv für Mittelrheinische Kirchengeschichte* 5, 195-22

Expugtatio Hibernica: The Conquest of Ireland, eds A.B. Scott and F.X. Martin. Dublin 1978

Fanning, T. 1973 'Excavations at Kells', *Old Kilkenny Review* 25, 61-64

Fanning, T. 1973-4 'Excavation of a ringfort at Pollardstown, Co. Kildare', *Journal of the Kildare Archaeological Society* 15, 251-61

Fanning, T. 1976 'Excavations at Clontuskert Priory, County Galway', *Proceedings of the Royal Irish Academy* 76C, 97-169

Faulkner, P.A. 1966 'Medieval undercrofts and townhouses', *Archaeological Journal* 123, 120-35

Flanagan, M.-T. 1993 'Anglo-Norman change and continuity: the castle of Telach Cail in Delbna', *Irish Historical Studies* 28, 385-9

Flanagan, M.-T. 1996 'Irish and Anglo-Norman warfare in twelfth-century Ireland', in T. Bartlett and K. Jeffries (eds) *A Military History of Ireland*. Cambridge, 52-75

Foley, C. 1989 'Excavation at a medieval settlement site in Jerpoint Church Townland, Co. Kilkenny', *Proceedings of the Royal Irish Academy* 89C, 71-126

Gahan, A. and McCutcheon, C. 1997 'Medieval Pottery', in Hurley, Scully and McCutcheon, 285-336

Gaimster, D. and Redknap, M. (eds) 1992 *Everyday and Exotic Pottery from Europe*. Oxford

Gardelles, J. 1972 *Les Châteaux du Moyen Age dans la France du Sud-ouest*. Paris

Gillespie, R. 1994 'Irish funeral monuments and social change 1500-1700: perceptions of death', in B.P. Kennedy and R. Gillespie (eds) *Ireland: Art into History. Dublin, 155-68*

Glasscock, R. 1968 'Kilmagoura', *Medieval Archaeology* 12, 196-7

Glasscock, R.E. 1970 'Moated sites and deserted boroughs and villages: two neglected aspects of Anglo-Norman settlement in Ireland', in N. Stephens and R.E. Glasscock (eds), *Irish Geographical Studies*. Belfast, 162-77

Glasscock, R.E. 1971 'The study of deserted medieval settlements in Ireland (to 1969)', in Beresford and Hurst (eds), 279-301

Gosling, P. 1991 'From Dún Delca to Dundalk: the topography and archaeology of a medieval frontier town, A.D. c1187-1700', *County Louth Archaeological Journal* 22, 225-353

Gowen, M. 1988 *Three Irish Gas Pipelines: New Archaeological Evidence in Munster*. Dublin

Graham, B.J. 1975 'Anglo-Norman settlement in Co. Meath', *Proceedings of the Royal Irish Academy* 75C, 223-48

Graham, B.J. 1980a 'The mottes of the Norman liberty of Meath', in Murtagh (ed), 39-56

Graham, B.J. 1980b *Medieval Irish Settlement: a Review*. Norwich

Graham, B.J. 1988a 'Medieval timber and earthwork fortifications in western Ireland', *Medieval Archaeology* 32, 110-29

Graham, B.J. 1988b 'Medieval settlement in Co. Roscommon', *Proceedings of the Royal Irish Academy* 88C, 19-38

Graham, B.J. 1993 'The High Middle Ages: c.1100-c.1350', in B.J. Graham and L.J. Proudfoot (eds) *An Historical Geography of Ireland*. London, 58-98

Greene, J.P. 1989 *Norton Priory: The Archaeology of a Medieval Religious House*. Cambridge

Grogan E. and Kilfeather A. 1997 *Archaeological Inventory of County Wicklow*. Dublin

Gwynn, A. 1992 *The Irish Church in the 11th and 12th Centuries*. Dublin

Gwynn, A. and Hadcock, N.D. 1970 *Medieval Religious Houses: Ireland*. London

Hadden, G. 1964 'Some earthworks in Co. Wexford', *Journal of the Cork Historical and Archaeological Society* 69, 118-22

Hall, D. 1988 'The late Saxon countryside: villages and their fields', in D Hooke (ed) *Anglo-Saxon Settlements*. Oxford, 99-122

Hall, D.N., Hennessey, M. and O'Keeffe, T. 1985 'Medieval agriculture and settlement in Oughterward and Castlewarden, Co. Kildare', *Irish Geography* 18, 16-25

Halpin, A. 1986 'Irish medieval swords c.1170-1600, *Proceedings of the Royal Irish Academy*, 86C, 183-230

Halpin, A. 1988 'Irish medieval bronze maceheads', in Mac Niocaill and Wallace (eds), 168-92

Halpin, A. 1997 'Archery material', in Hurley, Scully and McCutcheon, 538-554

Halpin, A. and Buckley, L. 1995 'Archaeological excavations at the Dominican priory, Drogheda, Co. Louth', *Proceedings of the Royal Irish Academy* 95C, 175-253

Hamlin, A. and Lynn, C.J. (eds) 1988 *Pieces of the Past*. Belfast

Harbison, P. 1976 'Native Irish arms and armour in medieval Gaelic literature, 1170 1600', *The Irish Sword* 12, 173-99, 270-84

Hennessy, M. 1996 'Manorial organisation in early thirteenth-century Tipperary', *Irish Geography* 29, 116-25

Henry, F. 1970 *Irish Art in the Romanesque Period AD 1020-1170*. London

Henry, F. and Marsh-Micheli, G.L. 1962 'A century of Irish illumination (1070-1170)', *Proceedings of the Royal Irish Academy* 62C, 101-64

Herity, M. 1988 'A survey of the royal site of Cruachain in Connacht IV. Ancient field systems at Rathcroghan and Carnfree', *Journal of the Royal Society of Antiquaries of Ireland* 118, 67-84

Herity, M. 1993 'Motes and mounds at royal sites in Ireland', *Journal of the Royal Society of Antiquaries of Ireland* 123, 127-51

Higham, R. and Barker, P. 1992 *Timber Castles*. London

Hogan, A. 1991 *Kilmallock Dominican Priory: an Architectural Perspective*. Kilmallock

Holm, P. 1986 'The slave trade to Dublin, tenth to twelfth centuries', *Peritia* 5, 317-45

Holland P. 1988 'The Anglo-Normans in Co. Galway: the process of colonisation', *Journal of the Galway Archaeological and Historical Society* 41, 73-89

Holland, P. 1996 'The Anglo-Normans and their castles in county Galway', in G. Moran and R. Gillespie (eds), *Galway: History and Society*. Dublin, 1-26

Hunt, J. 1974 *Irish Medieval Figure Sculpture, 1200-1600*. 2 vols. Dublin and London

Hurley, M.F. 1986 'Excavations in medieval Cork: St Peter's Market', *Journal of the Cork Historical and Archaeological Society* 91, 1-25

Hurley, M.F. 1987 'Kilferagh, Co. Kilkenny. Corn-drying kiln and settlement site', in Cleary, Hurley and Twohig (eds), 88-100

Hurley, M.F. 1997 *Excavations at the North Gate, Cork, 1994* . Cork

Hurley, M.F., Scully, O.M.B. and McCutcheon, S.W.J. 1997 *Late Viking Age and Medieval Waterford. Excavations 1986-1992.* Waterford

Hurley, M.F. and Sheehan, C.M. 1997 'Ovens and kilns', in Hurley, Scully and McCutcheon, 273-7

Hurley, M.F. and McCutcheon, S.W.J. 1997a 'St Peter's Church and graveyard', in Hurley, Scully and McCutcheon, 190-227

Hurley, M.F. and McCutcheon, S.W.J. 1997b 'Wooden artefacts', in Hurley, Scully and McCutcheon, 553-633

Hurst, J.G. 1988 'Medieval pottery imported into Ireland', in Mac Niocaill and Wallace (eds), 229-53

Johnson, D.N. 1998 'Lynch's Castle, Galway City: a reassessment', in C. Manning (ed), *Dublin and Beyond the Pale. Studies in Honour of Patrick Healy.* Bray, 221-252

Johnson, M. 1996 *An Archaeology of Capitalism.* Oxford

Jones, S. 1997 *The Archaeology of Ethnicity.* London

Jope, E.M. 1951 'Scottish influence in the north of Ireland: castles with Scottish features, 1580-1640', *Ulster Journal of Archaeology* 14, 32-47

Jordan, A.J. 1991 'Date, chronology and evolution of the county Wexford tower house', *Journal of the Wexford Historical Society* 13, 30-82

Jordan, W.C. 1996 *The Great Famine. Northern Europe in the early Fourteenth Century.* Princeton

Kerrigan, P. 1995 *Castles and Fortifications in Ireland 1485-1945.* Cork

King, D.J.C. and Alcock, L. 1969 'Ringworks of England and Wales', *Château Gaillard* 3, 90-127

King H. 1984 'Late medieval crosses in county Meath *c.*1470-1635', *Proceedings of the Royal Irish Academy* 84C, 79-116

Knight, J. 1987 'The road to Harlech: aspects of some early thirteenth-century Welsh castles', in J.R. Kenyon and R. Avent (eds), *Castles in Wales and the Marches.* Cardiff, 75-88

Lacy, B. 1988 'The development of Derry, 600-1600', in Mac Niocaill and Wallace (eds), 376-96

Langdon, J. 1988 'Agricultural equipment', in G. Astill and A. Grant (eds), 86-107

Le Patourel, H.E.J. 1978 'The excavation of moated sites', in Aberg (ed) 36-45

Le Patourel, H.E.J. 1992 'Ceramic horns', in Gaimster and Redknap (eds), 157-66

Le Patourel, H.E.J. and Roberts, B.K. 1978 'The significance of moated sites', in Aberg (ed), 46-55

Leask, H.G. 1936 'The collegiate church of St Nicholas, Galway', *Journal of the Galway Historical and Archaeological Society* 17, 1-23

Leask, H.G. 1937 'Irish castles, 1180-1310', *Archaeological Journal* 93, 143-99

Leask, H.G. 1944 'Ballymoon Castle, Co. Carlow', *Journal of the Royal Society of Antiquaries of Ireland* 74, 183-90

Leask, H.G. 1955-60 *Irish Churches and Monastic Buildings*. 3 vols. Dundalk

Leask, H.G. 1951 *Irish Castles and Castellated Houses*. Third edition. Dundalk

Leerssen, J. 1996 *Mere Irish and Fíor Ghael*. Cork

Leister, I. 1976 *Peasant Openfield Farming and its Territorial Organisation in Co Tipperary*. Marburg/Lahn

Lennon, C. 1981 *Richard Stanihurst the Dubliner*. Dublin

Lewis, C., Mitchell-Fox, P. and Dyer, C. 1997 *Village, Hamlet and Field. Changing Medieval Settlements in Central England*. Manchester

Long, H. 1994 'Three settlements of Gaelic Wicklow: Rathgall, Ballinacor, and Glendalough', in K. Hannigan and W. Nolan (eds) *Wicklow: History and Society*. Dublin, 237-65

Lorren, C. 1977 'La demeure seigneuriale de Rubercy', *Château Gaillard* 7, 185-92

Lydon J. 1967 'The problem of the frontier in medieval Ireland', *Topic* 13, 5-22

Lydon, J. 1981 'The mills at Ardee in 1304', *County Louth Archaeological Journal* 4, 259-63

Lydon, J. 1987a 'The expansion and consolidation of the colony, 1215-54', in Cosgrove (ed), 156-78

Lydon, J. 1987b 'The years of crisis, 1254-1315', in Cosgrove (ed), 179-204

Lydon, J. 1998 *The Making of Ireland*. London

Lynch, A. 1984 'Excavations of the medieval town defences at Charlotte's Quay, Limerick', *Proceedings of the Royal Irish Academy* 84C, 281-331

Lynn, C.J. 1975a 'The medieval ring-fort—an archaeological chimera', *Irish Archaeological Research Forum* 2, 29-36

Lynn, C.J. 1975b 'The dating of raths: an orthodox view', *Ulster Journal of Archaeology* 38, 45-7

Lynn, C.J. 1981-2 'The excavation of Rathmullan, a raised rath and motte in County Down', *Ulster Journal of Archaeology* 44-5, 65-171

Lynn, C.J. 1985 'Excavations on a mound at Gransha, Co. Down', *Ulster Journal of Archaeology* 48, 81-90

Lynn, C.J. 1986 'Some 13th-century castle sites in the west of Ireland: note on a preliminary reconnaissance' *Journal of the Galway Historical and Archaeological Society* 40, 90-113

Lyons, M. 1989 'Weather, famine, pestilence and plague in Ireland, 900-1500', in E. Crawford (ed), *Famine: the Irish Experience 900-1900: Subsistence Crises and Famines in Ireland*. Edinburgh, 31-74

MacCotter, P. and Nicholls, K.W. (eds) 1996 *The Pipe Roll of Cloyne (Rotulus Pipae Clonensis)*. Cloyne

MacNiocaill, G. 1964 *Na Buirgéisi, XII-XV Aois*. 2 vols. Dublin

Mac Niocaill, G. 1966 'The origins of the *betagh*', *Irish Jurist* 1, 292-98

MacNiocaill, G. 1985 'The colonial town in Irish documents', in Clarke and Simms (eds), 373-8

Maher, D. 1997 *Medieval Grave Slabs of County Tipperary, 1200 - 1600 A.D.* Oxford

Martin, F.X. 1987 'John, lord of Ireland, 1185-1216', in Cosgrove (ed), 127-55

McCarthy, M 1997 'The Faunal Remains', in Hurley, 154-8

McCarthy, M. and Brooks, C. 1988 *Medieval Pottery in Britain AD 900-1600*. Leicester

McCormack, F. 1997 'The animal bones', in Hurley, Scully and McCutcheon, 819-52

McErlean, T. 1983 'The Irish townland system of landscape organisation', in Reeves Smyth and Hamond (eds), 315-40

McMahon, M. 1988 'Archaeological excavations at the site of the Four Courts extension, Inns Quay, Dublin', *Proceedings of the Royal Irish Academy* 88C, 271-319

McNeill, T.E. 1980 *Anglo-Norman Ulster*. Edinburgh

McNeill, T.E. 1981 *Carrickfergus Castle*. Belfast

McNeill T.E. 1986 'Church building in the 14th century and the "Gaelic Revival"', *Journal of Irish Archaeology* 3, 61-4

McNeill, T.E. 1990 'Early castles in Leinster', *Journal of Irish Archaeology* 5, 57-64

McNeill, T.E. 1991 'Excavations at Dunsilly, Co. Antrim', *Ulster Journal of Archaeology* 54, 78-112

McNeill, T.E 1997 *Castles in Ireland. Feudal Power in a Gaelic World*. London

Meenan, R. 1992 'A survey of late medieval and early post-medieval Iberian pottery from Ireland', in Gaimster and Redknap (eds), 186-93

Meenan, R. 1994 'Post-medieval pottery', in Simpson, 54-77

Mills, J. 1891a 'Tenants and agriculture near Dublin in the fourteenth century', *Journal of the Royal Society of Antiquaries of Ireland* 21, 54-63

Mills, J. (ed) 1891b *The Account Roll of the Priory of the Holy Trinity, Dublin, 1337-46*. Dublin [reprinted with new introduction and essay by J. Lydon and A. Fletcher, Dublin 1996]

Mitchell, G.F. 1965 'Littleton Bog, Tipperary: an Irish agricultural record', *Journal of the Royal Society of Antiquaries of Ireland* 95, 121-32

Mooney, C. 1955-7 'Franciscan architecture in pre-Reformation Ireland', *Journal of the Royal Society of Antiquaries of Ireland* 85-87, 133-73; 125-69; 1-38, 103-24

Moore, M. 1987 *Archaeological Inventory of County Meath*. Dublin

Moore, M. 1996 *Archaeological Inventory of County Wexford*. Dublin

Müller-Wille, M. 1966 *Mittelalterliche Burghugel im Nordlichen Rheinland*. Köln

Murtagh, B. 1985-6 'St David's Castle: a fortified town house, Naas, Co. Kildare', *Journal of the Kildare Archaeological Society* 16, 470-78

Murtagh, B. 1988 'The Bridge castle, Thomastown, Co. Kilkenny', in Mac Niocaill and Wallace (eds), 536-56

Murtagh, B. 1989 'Hatch's Castle, Ardee, county Louth: a fortified town house of the Pale', *County Louth Archaeological Journal* 21, 36-48

Murtagh B. 1997 'The architecture of St Peter's Church', in Hurley, Scully and McCutcheon, 228-43

Murtagh, H. (ed) 1980 *Irish Midland Studies*. Athlone

Musgrave, E. 1997 'Family, household and production: the potters of Saintonge, France, 1500-1800', in C.G. Cumberpatch and P.W. Blinkhorn (eds), *Not so much a pot, more a way of life*. Oxford, 85-94

Ní Ghabhláin S. 1996 'The origins of medieval parishes in Gaelic Ireland: the evidence from Kilfenora', *Journal of the Royal Society of Antiquaries of Ireland* 126, 37-61

Nicholls, K.W. 1982 'Anglo-French Ireland and after', *Peritia* 1, 370-403

Nicholls, K.W. 1987 'Gaelic society and economy', in Cosgrove (ed), 397-438

O'Brien A.F. 1993 'Politics, economy and society: the development of Cork and the Irish south-coast region c.1170-c.1583', in P. O'Flanagan and C.G. Buttimer (eds), *Cork: History and Society*. Dublin, 83-154

O'Brien, C. and Sweetman P.D. 1997 *Archaeological Inventory of County Offaly*. Dublin

O'Callaghan, J. 1980-1 'Fortified houses of the sixteenth century in south Wexford', *Journal of the Old Wexford Society* 8, 1-51

O'Conor, K. 1992 'Irish earthwork castles', *Fortress* 12, 3-12

O'Conor, K. 1998 *The Archaeology of Medieval Rural Settlement in Ireland*. Dublin

Ó Corráin, D. 1972 *Ireland Before the Normans*. Dublin

Ó Corráin, D. 1978 'Nationality and kingship in pre-Norman Ireland', *Historical Studies* 11, 1-35

Ó Danachair, C. 1977-79 'Irish tower houses', *Bealoideas* 45-7, 158-63

O Donovan, P.F. 1995 *Archaeological Inventory of County Wexford*. Dublin

Ó Floinn, R. 1988 'Handmade medieval pottery — S.E.Ireland — Leinster Cooking Ware', in Mac Niocaill and Wallace (eds), 325-44

Ó Floinn, R. 1994 *Irish Shrines and Reliquaries of the Middle Ages*. Dublin

O'Keeffe, T. 1984 'An early Anglo-Norman castle at Ballyderown, county Cork', *Journal of the Royal Society of Antiquaries of Ireland* 114, 48-56

O'Keeffe, T. 1986 'Medieval architecture and the village of Newcastle Lyons', in P. O'Sullivan (ed), *Newcastle Lyons — a Parish of the Pale*. Dublin, 45-62

O'Keeffe, T. 1987 'Rathnageeragh and Ballyloo: a study of stone castles of probable 14th century date in county Carlow', *Journal of the Royal Society of Antiquaries of Ireland* 117, 28-49

O'Keeffe, T. 1990a 'The archaeology of Norman castles—part I: mottes and ringworks', *Archaeology Ireland* 4 (3), 15-17

O'Keeffe, T. 1990b 'The archaeology of Anglo-Norman castles in Ireland—part 2: stone castles', *Archaeology Ireland* 4 (4), 20-2

O'Keeffe, T. 1991 'Frontiers and fortifications in the Dublin region: the evolution of the Pale', in F.H.A. Aalen and K. Whelan (eds), *Dublin City and County: from Prehistory to Present*. Dublin, 57-77

O'Keeffe, T. 1994 'Lismore and Cashel: reflections on the beginnings of the Irish Romanesque', *Journal of the Royal Society of Antiquaries of Ireland* 124, 118-52

O'Keeffe, T. 1995 *The Town Walls of Medieval Waterford: History, Archaeology, and Restoration*. Unpublished report, Waterford Corporation

O'Keeffe, T. 1996a 'Rural settlement and cultural identity in Gaelic Ireland, 1000-1500', *Ruralia* 1, 142-53

O'Keeffe, T. 1996b 'The Romanesque portal of Clonfert cathedral and its iconography', in C. Bourke (ed), *From the Isles of the North*. Belfast, 261-9

O'Keeffe, T. 1997 *Barryscourt Castle and the Irish Tower-house*. Kinsale

O'Keeffe, T. 1998a 'The fortifications of western Ireland, AD 1100-1300, and their interpretation', *Journal of the Galway Historical and Archaeological Society* 50, 184-200

O'Keeffe, T. 1998b 'Aristocrats, immigrants and entrepreneurs: settlers and settlement initiatives in late thirteenth-century Ireland', *Ruralia* 2, 87-96

O'Keeffe, T. 1999a 'Townscape as text: the topography of social interaction in Fethard, Co. Tipperary, AD 1300-1700', *Irish Geography* 32, 9-25

O'Keeffe, T. 1999b *An Anglo-Norman Monastery: Bridgetown Priory and the Architecture of Augustinian Canons Regular in Ireland*. Kinsale

O'Keeffe, T. 2000a 'Romanesque as metaphor: architecture and reform in early twelfth century Ireland', in A.P. Smyth (ed) *Seanchas: Essays presented to Francis J. Byrne*. Dublin, 313-22

O'Keeffe, T. 2000b 'Architecture and regular life in Holy Trinity Cathedral, 1150-1350', in S. Kinsella (ed), *Augustinians at Christ Church: the Canons Regular of the Cathedral Priory of Holy Trinity, Dublin*. Dublin, 41-54

O'Keeffe, T. 2001a *The Gaelic Peoples and their Archaeological Identities AD 1000-1700.* Quiggin Pamphlet, Cambridge

O'Keeffe, T. 2001b 'Ballyloughan, Ballymoon and Clonmore: three castles of *c.*1300 in county Carlow', *Anglo-Norman Studies* 23, 169-99

O'Keeffe, T. *forthcoming* a Ireland's *Round Towers: Architecture, Ritual, and Symbolism in the Viking-Age.* Cambridge and Berkeley

O'Kelly, M.J. 1952 'Three promontory forts in Co. Cork', *Proceedings of the Royal Irish Academy* 55C, 25-59

O'Kelly, M.J. 1962 'Beal Boru, Co. Clare', *Journal of the Cork Historical and Archaeological Society* 67, 1-27

O'Neill, T. 1987 *Merchants and Mariners in Medieval Ireland.* Dublin

Ó Riain-Raedel, D. 1998 'A German visitor to Monaincha in 1591', *Tipperary Historical Journal*, 223-33

Ó Ríordáin, B 1971 'Excavations at High Street and Winetavern Street, Dublin', *Medieval Archaeology* 15, 73-85

Ó Ríordáin, S.P. 1940 'Excavations at Cush, Co.Limerick', *Proceedings of the Royal Irish Academy* 45 C, 83-181

Ó Ríordáin, S.P. and Hunt, J. 1942 'Medieval dwellings at Caherguillamore, County Limerick', *Journal of the Royal Society of Antiquaries of Ireland* 72, 37-63

O'Rourke, D. 1997 'Leather artefacts', in Hurley, Scully and McCutcheon, 703-735

O'Sullivan, M.D. 1962 *Italian Merchant Bankers in Ireland in the Thirteenth Century.* Dublin

O'Sullivan, A. 1995 'Medieval fishweirs on the Deel estuary', *Archaeology Ireland* 9 (32), 15-18

O'Sullivan, A. 1997 'Medieval fishtraps in Strangford Lough', *Archaeology Ireland* 11 (39), 36-8

O'Sullivan, A. 1998 *The Archaeology of Lake Settlement in Ireland.* Dublin

Ormond Deeds, ed E. Curtis, 6 vols. Dublin, 1932-43

Orpen, G.H. 1906 'Mote and bretasche building in Ireland', *English Historical Review* 21, 417-44

Orpen, G.H. 1907a 'Motes and Norman castles in Ireland', *English Historical Review* 22, 228-54, 440-67

Orpen G.H. 1907b 'Motes and Norman Castles in Ireland', *Journal of the Royal Society of Antiquaries of Ireland* 37, 123-52

Orpen, G.H. 1911-20 *Ireland Under the Normans*. 4 vols, Oxford

Otway-Ruthven, A.J. 1951 'The organization of Anglo-Irish agriculture in the middle ages', *Journal of the Royal Society of Antiquaries of Ireland* 81, 1-13

Otway-Ruthven, A.J. 1964 'Parochial development in the rural deanery of Skreen', *Journal of the Royal Society of Antiquaries of Ireland* 94, 111-22

Otway-Ruthven, A.J. 1964-8 'Enclosures in the medieval period', *Irish Geography* 5 (1964 8), 35-6

Otway-Ruthven, A.J. 1965 'The character of Norman settlement in Ireland', *Historical Studies* 5, 75-84

Patterson, N. 1994 *Cattle-lords and Clansmen. The Social Structure of Early Ireland*. Notre Dame, Indiana

Perros, H. 1997 'Anglo-Norman Settlement in Connacht in the thirteenth century', *Group for the Study of Irish Historic Settlement Newsletter* 7, 2-4

Pollock, A.J. and Waterman, D.M. 1963 'A medieval pottery kiln in Downpatrick', *Ulster Journal of Archaeology* 26, 79-104

Ponsford, M. 1991 'Dendrochronological dates from Dundas Wharf, Bristol, and the dating of Ham Green and other medieval pottery', in E. Lewis (ed), *Custom and Ceramics*. Wickham, 81-103

Pounds, N.J.G. 1990 *The Medieval Castle in England and Wales*. Cambridge

Rae, E.C. 1979 'The medieval fabric of the cathedral church of St Patrick in Dublin', *Journal of the Royal Society of Antiquaries of Ireland* 119, 29-73

Rae, E.C. 1987 'Architecture and sculpture, 1169-1603', in Cosgrove (ed), 737-79

Reeves-Smyth, T. 1999 *Irish Gardens and Gardening before Cromwell*. Kinsale

Reeves-Smyth, T. and F. Hamond (eds) 1983 *Landscape Archaeology in Ireland*. Oxford

Renn, D. 1968 *Norman Castles in Britain*. London

Renn D. 1994 'Burgheat and gonfanon: two sidelights from the Bayeux Tapestry', *Anglo Norman Studies* 16, 177-98

Reynolds, S. 1977 *An Introduction to the History of English Medieval Towns*. Oxford

Rimmer, J. 1969 *The Irish Harp—Cláirseach na hEireann*. Cork

Roberts, B.K. 1987 *The Making of the English Village*. London.

Roe, M.H. 1968 *Medieval Fonts of Meath*. Navan

Round J.H. 1902 'The castles of the Conquest', *Archaeologia* 58, 313-40

Ryan, M. 1973 'Native pottery in early historic Ireland', *Proceedings of the Royal Irish Academy* 73C, 619-45

Rynne, C. 1997 'The Patrick Street watermills—their technological context and a note on the reconstruction', in Walsh, 81-9

Rynne, C. 1998 *Technological Change in Anglo-Norman Munster*. Kinsale

Rynne, E. 1963 'Some destroyed sites at Shannon Airport, Co. Clare', *Proceedings of the Royal Irish Academy* 63C, 245-77

Saunders, A.1977 'Five castle excavations: reports of the Institute's project into the origins of the castles in England', *Archaeological Journal* 134, 1-156

Sharpe, R. 1992 'Churches and communities in early medieval Ireland: towards a pastoral model', in J. Blair and R. Sharpe (eds) *Pastoral Care before the Parish*. London, 81-109

Sheail, J. 1971 'County Gazetteers of Deserted Medieval Villages (known in 1968)', in Beresford and Hurst (eds), 182-212

Simington, R.C. (ed) 1931-61 *The Civil Survey A.D. 1654-1656*. 10 vols. Dublin

Simms, A. 1988 'The geography of Irish manors: the example of the Llanthony cells of Duleek and Colp in county Meath', in J. Bradley (ed), *Settlement and Society in Medieval Ireland*. Kilkenny, 291-326

Simms, A., Clarke, H.B. and Gillespie, R. 1986- *Irish Historic Towns Atlas*. Dublin

Simms, A. with Simms K. 1990 *Kells*, Irish Historic Towns Atlas Fascicle no. 4. Dublin

Simms, K. 1986 'Nomadry in medieval Ireland: the origin of the creaght or caoraigheacht', *Peritia* 5, 379-91

Simms, K. 1987 *From Kings to Warlords*. Woodbridge

Simpson, L. 1994 *Excavations at Isolde's Tower, Dublin*. Dublin

Simpson, L. 1995 *Excavations at Essex Street West, Dublin*. Dublin

Simpson, M.L. and Dickson, A. 1981 'Excavations in Carrickfergus, County Antrim, 1972-79', *Medieval Archaeology* 25, 78-89

Slater, T. 1988 'English medieval town planning', in D. Denecke and G. Shaw (eds), *Urban Historical Geography. Recent Progress in Britain and Germany*. Cambridge, 93-108

Sleeman, M. and Hurley, M.F. 1987 'Blackcastle, Co. Kildare', in Cleary, Hurley and Twohig (eds), 101-5

Stalley, R.A. 1971 *Architecture and sculpture in Ireland, 1150-1350*. Dublin

Stalley, R.A. 1973 *Christ Church Dublin. The Late Romanesque Building Campaign*. Ballycotton

Stalley, R.A. 1979, 'The medieval sculpture of Christ Church Cathedral, Dublin', *Archaeologia* 106, 107-22

Stalley, R.A. 1981 'Three Irish buildings with West Country origins', in N. Coldstream and P. Draper (eds), *Medieval Art and Architecture at Wells and Glastonbury*. London, 62-80

Stalley, R. 1984 'Irish Gothic and English fashion', in J. Lydon (ed), *The English in Medieval Ireland*. Dublin, 65-86

Stalley, R.A. 1987 *The Cistercian Monasteries of Ireland*. London and New Haven

Stalley, R.A. 1994 'A misunderstood Gothic masterpiece: the Cantwell effigy at Kilfane, Co. Kilkenny', in R.A. Stalley, *Ireland and Europe in the Middle Ages*, London, 220-33, 322 3 [originally published in 1987]

Stout, G. and Stout, M. 1997 'Early landscapes: from prehistory to plantation', in F.H.A. Aalen, K. Whelan and M. Stout (eds), *Atlas of the Irish Rural Landscape*. Cork, 31-63

Stout, M. 1997 *The Irish Ringfort*. Dublin

Sweetman, P.D. 1978 'Archaeological excavations at Trim Castle, County Meath', *Proceedings of the Royal Irish Academy* 78C, 127-98

Sweetman, P.D. 1981 'Excavations of a medieval moated site at Rigsdale, County Cork, 1977-8', *Proceedings of the Royal Irish Academy* 81C, 103-205

Sweetman, P.D. 1979 'Archaeological excavations at Ferns Castle, County Wexford', *Proceedings of the Royal Irish Academy* 79C, 217-45

Sweetman, P.D. 1984 'Excavations at Shop Street, Drogheda, County Louth,' *Proceedings of the Royal Irish Academy* 84C, 171-224

Sweetman, P.D. 1995 *Irish Castles and Fortified Houses*. Dublin

Sweetman, P.D. 1998 'Hall-houses', *Archaeology Ireland* 12 (41), 3-6

Thomas, A.C. 1971 *The Early Christian Archaeology of North Britain*. Oxford

Thomas, A. 1992 *The Walled Towns of Ireland*. 2 vols. Dublin

Topographia Hibernica: The History and Topography of Ireland, ed J.J. O'Meara. Dundalk 1982

Twohig, D.C. 1978 'Norman ringwork castles', *Bulletin of the Group for the Study of Irish Historic Settlement* 5, 7-9

Vince, A.G. 1988 'Early medieval Englih pottery in Viking Dublin', in Mac Niocaill and Wallace (eds), 254-70

Waldeier Bizzarro, T. 1992 *Romanesque Architectural Criticism*. Cambridge

Wallace, P.F. 1985a 'The archaeology of Viking Dublin', in Clarke and Simms (eds), 103-45

Wallace 1985b 'The archaeology of Anglo-Norman Dublin', in Clarke and Simms (eds), 1379-410

Wallace, P.F. 1992a 'The archaeological identity of the Hiberno-Norse town', *Journal of the Royal Society of Antiquaries of Ireland* 122, 35-66

Wallace, P.F. 1992b *The Viking Age Buildings of Dublin*. 2 vols. Dublin

Walsh, C. 1997 *Archaeological Excavations at Patrick, Nicholas and Winetavern Streets, Dublin*. Dingle

Walsh, M. 1965 'A watermill at Ballyine, Co. Limerick', *Journal of the Cork Historical and Archaeological Society* 70, 14-25

Waterman, D.M. 1954 'Excavations at Clough Castle, County Down', *Ulster Journal of Archaeology* 17, 103-63

Waterman, D.M. 1958 'Ballyfounder Rath', *Ulster Journal of Archaeology* 21, 39-61

Waterman, D.M. 1959 'Excavations at Lismahon, Co. Down', *Medieval Archaeology* 3, 139-76

Waterman, D.M. 1963 'Excavations at Duneight, County Down', *Ulster Journal of Archaeology* 26, 55-78

Waterman, D. 1968 'Rectangular keeps of the thirteenth century at Grenan (Kilkenny) and Glanworth (Cork)', *Journal of the Royal Society of Antiquaries of Ireland* 98, 67-73

Waterman, D.M. 1970 'Somersetshire and other foreign building stone in medieval Ireland, *c*.1175-1400', *Ulster Journal of Archaeology* 33, 63-75

Westropp, T.J. 1904 'On Irish motes and early Norman castles', *Journal of the Royal Society of Antiquaries of Ireland* 34, 313-45

Westropp, T.J. 1905 'Irish motes and alleged Norman castles: notes on some recent contributions to their study', *Journal of the Royal Society of Antiquaries of Ireland* 35, 402-6

Westropp, T.J. 1913 'Early Italian maps of Ireland from 1300 to 1600, with notes on foreign settlers and trade', *Proceedings of the Royal Irish Academy* 30C, 361-428

Westropp, T.J. 1918 'Lady Isabella's Fish Pond', Kilkee, Co. Clare', *Journal of the Royal Society of Antiquaries of Ireland* 48, 79-80

Williams, A. 1992 'A bell-house and a burh-geat: lordly residences in England before the Norman conquest', in C. Harper-Bill and R. Harvey (eds) *Medieval Knighthood* IV. Woodbridge, 221-40

Williams, B.B. and Robinson, P.S. 1983 'The excavation of Bronze Age cists and a medieval booley house at Glenmakeeran, county Antrim, and a discussion of booleying in north Antrim', *Ulster Journal of Archaeology* 46, 29-40

Wincott Heckett, E. 1990 'Report on textiles, Grand Parade II and Grand Parade I 1984', in M.F. Hurley, Excavations at Grand Parade, Cork II, *Journal of the Cork Historical and Archaeological Society* 95, 64-87

Wincott Heckett, E. 1997 'Textiles, cordage, basketry and raw fibre', in Hurley, Scully and McCutcheon, 743-60

Wilson, C. 1990 *The Gothic Cathedral*. London

Wood-Martin, W.G. 1886 *The Lake-Dwellings of Ireland*. Dublin

Yates, M.J. 1983 'Excavations at Carnaghliss', *Moated Sites Reearch Group* 10, 12

Index